DeVilliers and Taylor on
Point and Figure Charting

Victor DeVilliers
Owen Taylor

Introduced and edited by
Donald Mack

HARRIMAN HOUSE LTD
3A Penns Road
Petersfield
Hampshire
GU32 2EW

Tel: +44 (0) 1730 233870
Fax: +44 (0) 1730 233880
email: enquiries@harriman-house.com
web site: www.harriman-house.com

Devilliers and Taylor on Point and Figure Charting
first printed in the United States of America in 1933
Second edition 1934

First published in Great Britain 2000 by Pearson Professional Limited

This edition published by Harriman House Ltd
© Harriman House Ltd 2007

ISBN 1-905641-52-4
ISBN 13: 978-1-905641-52-9

British Library Cataloguing in Publication Data
A CIP catalogue record for this book can be obtained
from the British Library.

Printed and bound
by Lightning Source

DEVILLIERS AND TAYLOR ON
POINT AND
FIGURE CHARTING

ABOUT THE AUTHORS

Victor DeVilliers and Owen Taylor

We know so very little about the personal lives of each of these authors, but in surveying their other books and writings, a more informed picture emerges of their capabilities in their chosen field, stock and futures market analysis. From the quality and clearness of the writings in this and other of his works, it soon becomes apparent that Victor DeVilliers was not only very knowledgeable on the markets but he had the uncommon talent to put it into written words. (Most market authors are generally better traders and investors than writers.) On the other hand Owen Taylor was certainly extremely capable, being more the expert on the technical aspects of market analysis, something easily ascertainable from the Technical Analysis subjects that he presented in his own books and booklets.

It is to the credit of both authors that they recognized just how valuable to investors and traders the Point and Figure method could be and that they saw fit to produce this fascinating work on a subject that in its essence is just putting small "Xs" on graph paper. But how to put them to graph paper and how to read their meanings is what can separate the trading and investing boys from the trading and investing men. Surveying all of the writings that have been published over the years, we find there have been and are a number of good, very good and excellent books on the Point and Figure methodology and its star attributes. However, every once in a while someone comes along and writes what is easily the seminal work, the finest on its particular subject. Some 65 years later we can attest to the fact that Victor DeVilliers and Owen Taylor rule the roost on their chosen subject with the two volumes republished here, which taken together, have to be considered the ultimate – "The Bible of Point and Figure Charting."

ABOUT THE SERIES EDITOR

Donald Mack

If any phrase describes the editor of the *Traders' Masterclass Series*, which is dedicated solely to bringing back to traders and investors everywhere many of the great and rare Technical Analysis classics from the past, that phrase would be "a perpetual student of the market." Students in high school or college eventually graduate. Not so students of speculative markets. The study and the work is never finished, especially when there is an enduring interest in Technical Analysis. The editor's interest grew by leaps and bounds when in the late 1970s and the 1980s he established in Los Angeles the only bookstore in the USA that dealt exclusively in stock and commodity books; those that were in print at the time and those that were out of print. Current books were generally unchallenging and of various degrees of quality. Many out-of-print books were also of varying degrees of quality, but so many fascinating rare works from the 1920s to the 1950s, of great creativity and marvellous technical analytics and application came his way, that a lifelong appreciation of their quality grew.

Almost needless to say, more attention was focussed on the old books than on the new, for he found those old books that made up the great classics were superior to the new in so many ways. While he was operating the bookstore, there was a natural inflow and outflow of many thousands of books and from those thousands of books a personal library and collection numbering a good 5,500 plus individual titles was put together. A little of the knowledge contained in these great market classics rubbed off on the editor (actually more than a little) and he trusts that it will also rub off on the many market students of today and tomorrow as they also come in contact with the superb Technical Analysis classics that will come their way through this Series.

CONTENTS

VOLUME 2
ADVANCED THEORY AND PRACTICE OF THE POINT AND FIGURE METHOD

EDITOR'S INTRODUCTION

If we honestly weigh up the two combined volumes that make up this Course and closely examine their merits in their particular area of specialization – Point and Figure (P&F) charting and analysis – the verdict, in this writer's opinion, has to be that these works comprise the finest writings ever produced on P&F. He therefore has not the slightest problem in making the comparison that this work is to P&F analysis as Richard Schabacker's unmatched masterpiece *Technical Analysis and Stock Market Profits: A Course in Forecasting** is to the area of Technical Analysis (TA) – its undisputed "Bible." To their credit, Messrs DeVilliers and Taylor have written that which we can genuinely call "the Bible of Point and Figure Charting and Analysis;" they can also be seen to have given flesh and sinew to a subject that at the time and ever since has superbly seen their mission fulfilled here.

However, just like the Schabacker Course, it should be noted that these two P&F volumes (intriguing as they are) on this very popular analytical method have unfortunately remained practically unknown to traders and investors in the US and the world for far too many years. To be accurate though, this is not quite so, for Mr DeVilliers, on his own some years later, wrote a treatise on the same subject and used the same title as this earlier work. What he wrote has occasionally been reprinted to meet the need for more material on this under-covered methodology, material which is always being sought and which there is relatively little available to meet the demand. However, as a fair evaluation, I would describe this later DeVilliers book as an abridged version in which he incorporated some material from the original two volumes that he had co-authored. But in making any comparisons, it will soon be seen that this later book comes out as a shortened and a pale imitation of his earlier collaboration with Owen Taylor, giving strength to the impression that Taylor was the guiding *technical* light in the partnership and DeVilliers the *writing* light.

Anyone seeking a copy of this meticulous DeVilliers and Taylor work will generally be out of luck. It has only very rarely showed itself the past several

---

* This 1932 classic masterwork recently republished in 1997 by Financial Times Pitman Publishing is available from booksellers the world over and an absolute 'must' for market students.

decades since the original 1934 publication date for reasons that equally apply to just about all the books that now make up, or will make up, this Traders' Master-class Series of market classics. This can all be put down to one very major culprit – the ravages of Time. That the goddess of Time chooses who she shall be a literary friend to and who she shall not is an enigma that can be welcomed by those who are so favored, and lamented by the greater number whose writings fall by the wayside and remain lost to succeeding generations. Thus it has been more often than not, in our chosen field of stock and commodity market liter-ature, that the Time goddess sadly has turned out to be more the stern enemy of so much of this literature and friendlier to only a relatively select few.

In many ways that was the fate of the original editions of the re-published works you are reading from right now, and except for a very rare surfacing, they just have not been seen by very many for several decades. However, once in a while and in mysterious ways there comes the Great Spirit, to those who are open to it, and with it help from those higher spiritual entities (for the want of a more accurate or better description) that choose to eventually save that which they choose to save. As will soon be seen in what follows, this can be put down to some unknown guardian angel(s) that almost solely had to have been respon-sible for a very fortuitous intervention that saved, and made possible to pass on this masterpiece on P&F charting and analysis (among several others). Involved here is a story that goes back to the early 1980s when I was operating my unusual bookstore in Los Angeles that uniquely specialized in stock and commodity books. At the bookstore, while I dealt in those market books that were currently in print at the time which I would describe as mostly "ho-hum," there were other books that intrigued me much, much more that I really sought – the rare older books and the great market classics that by then were long out of print, very scarce, and very hard to find.

One of my customers (so fortunate for us all that he was) at the time was living in Seattle and inquired of me as to whether I would be interested in purchasing some out of print books that he had on hand and was no longer interested in. Well, between postal contacts (no e-mail then) and a visit to Seattle we managed to exchange the necessary funds for books and books for funds, resulting in their addition to my bookshop on my return to Los Angeles. In the course of all that interchange, the details of how those books (and what an absolutely fabulous collection they were) came to eventually be in Seattle was told to me.

It seems that my book-selling customer was living in New York City some years earlier and was interested in starting, or carrying on, an investment advisory business. To do this he needed appropriate offices and the ideal location for those offices was the nearby Wall Street area. Finally locating suitable premises at the well known 150 Broadway Building and in preparing to move in, he had met with the landlord's agent in his new-to-be offices to make the final arrangements. While there the agent pointed to a large pile of papers and books in the center of the room and remarked to our friend "Say, you're in the stock market business aren't you?" "Yes I am," was the reply. "Well, so were the people who had their offices here before you. They left this material which you see piled on the floor here and I'm waiting for the waste collectors to pick it up to clear the way for you to move in. If it's of any interest, give me a few bucks and you can have it." Then slightly more than a few bucks changed hands, and as the reader will see, so was saved for posterity the finest lot of exceedingly rare books and courses that ever came my way, or probably anybody else's too.

All I can say is "What material it was!" In that collection of papers, books, etc. designed to be destroyed was one of the most noted *ever* of market books (again among others), one that in itself is one of the all-time greatest of classic technical writings. So well known and famous is this one book that many reading this Introduction will with just a few descriptive words recognize it instantly. Importantly it has to be seen that while it was a book, in this case it wasn't a book – it was the manuscript of a book – original bound typewritten papers accompanied by the author's hand-drawn illustrations and handwritten notes. And who was this author and what was the title of this book that he himself eventually published (only 1,000 copies ever saw the light of day with that publishing)? Well, the date of that publication was 1946, the year following the end of World War II. From my personal knowledge, I for one certainly wouldn't describe that year, in general, as being an especially notable one for published books devoted to our favored field of technical analytics.

However, the 1946 date alone should awaken the memories of a number of devotees to that author's writings, recognizing it, in turn, as the extremely noteworthy year that this work made its so very prestigious contribution to market analysis. That 1946 date so memorably marks the time that we can all look back on as the really notable exposition of a field of market analysis that has been pivotal in opening up one of the most followed technical approaches today. And that "we" refers to thousands and thousands (probably millions now) who in the fifty-plus years that have passed are exceedingly grateful for, and have to and do stand in awe of this monumental work. The book's title – *Nature's Law: The Secret of the Universe* – the opus magnus of its now well known author and conceptualizer Ralph Nelson Elliott, the creator of the Elliott Wave Principle.

How this unique manuscript, the supreme exposition on the Elliott Wave, found its way to the 150 Broadway offices of the people who were also the publishers of this monumental work on the P&F Method by DeVilliers and Taylor, in all probability, will remain consigned to the arcane knowledge of the market gods. Why it happened to be there most probably we will never know, but fortunately for us it was and very fortunately also for us it was saved. As a side note to the manuscript's whereabouts today, it was eventually brought by myself to the attention of, and acquired by, the one person today who is undoubtedly the leading exponent of the tenets of the Elliott Wave Principle as originally propounded by R. N. Elliott. Normally being the ultimate market book collector that I was, I would not have let so valuable an original literary masterpiece go, but as it was it was really more fitting that it belonged in someone else's hands other than mine. For this reason I contacted Robert "Bob" Prechter in Gainesville, Georgia. Knowing Bob to be the dedicated and leading collector of original Elliott material that he is, the *Nature's Law* manuscript certainly went to where it deserved to be.

Additionally in that pile destined for destruction were six or seven each of the original two volumes of this re-published work that you, the reader, are presently reading from, the only such original printings ever to come my way. When dealing in market books as I was doing at the time, understandably the heart leaps up when what amounts to the ultimate comes your way – the rare, the very rare, and the exceedingly very rare market classics that always seem to make their appearances in most unexpected ways. That's how it was when these two original P&F gems, which together make up this "Bible of Point & Figure Charting and Analysis," wound up in my market bookstore. And in a larger sense, it was a result of this legacy from this fortunate series of events that has made the possibility of this re-published edition a reality, and that great numbers of stock and commodity market P&F afficionados will now for many years be able to study, appreciate, and put to use the superb P&F knowledge incorporated in this exposition. It is potentially sad that such great material, if it hadn't been saved the way it was, could very easily have gone for good, rarely, if ever, to appear on the scene again.

Just to wrap up this tale of good fortune of the saving of a large number of extremely rare market works, there were many more in that 150 Broadway pile. One of the most outstanding of market classics also to be saved was a complete and totally unknown Course written by Harold Gartley in 1933 which preceded his later 1935 Course *Profits in the Stock Market*, a work itself unfortunately not known except to a limited number of TA afficionados. So worthy is this Course, in this writer's strong opinion, that it easily belongs to the highest level of *all* the technical writings that in total have been published over the past 70 years. He has no hesitation in easily ranking it as the *second* finest work *ever* on TA, *just* being surpassed by the previously mentioned *Technical Analysis and Stock Market Profits* by Richard W. Schabacker which I rank as the finest book ever on this major subject. However, not to be outdone, there has to have been some unseen working of Divine intervention and design that this really unknown 1933 Gartley Course, written two years before *Profits in the Stock Market*, was destined to be rescued as it was. Fate must want it joined to the other great TA classics in our Masterclass Series that have been re-published the past few years. It certainly deserves to be in that honored company and the chances are good that once again it will see the light of day to enlighten investors and traders the world over.

In DeVilliers and Taylor's own Introduction to Volume 1, I believe the reader might be taken aback a little and left wondering when they see the reference to a third volume. Their Introduction shows that the present combined Volume 1 and Volume 2 are really a part of what is a three-volume set. There's a story here, and in keeping with my aim in all introductions that I write for each of the great market classics that I choose for re-publication, I try more to personalize each work with the strongest connections that I can (not always easy) to the original great market mind(s) who originally produced it. I feel it is vital that I especially do this because of the unique nature of these superb speculative writings, and for the reason that in most market books the reporting on the authors generally leaves bland personalities at best. Market books can be notorious on this score when we come to the 'who' of who wrote them, why did they feel they had to write what they wrote, and what have they written that really separates them (if it is the case) from the more standardized dross found in so many other market books.

Returning to the pile of papers and written works that lay on the floor of that room at 150 Broadway, there was also to come my way two original copies of this exceeding rare P&F Volume 3 which, as I write this in 1999, I wish so very much were now in my personal possession, but such is not the case. One of the two Volume 3s I kept for my personal collection, later to meet a sad demise; the other I sold to someone who was very much into P&F charting and who just had to have it. I thought I knew who this was, but on checking with them I now know that my recollection was faulty. So if by some chance the person who was the recipient reads this, please contact me at the e-mail address at the end of this Introduction – I sure would like to have a copy of it again. Or should anyone else have a copy of this rare work, or any other fine classic that they feel should be preserved for the ages to come so that future market students may be able to see the great classic market writings that we have had a chance to study, please contact me. It would be a shame if those to follow were to be deprived of a great deal of the greatest of the great.

What is evident from the authors' own Introduction in Volume 1 is that they replaced the Introduction originally printed in 1934 with their Introduction that had to have been written in 1941 or 1942. That, in turn, now calls for some conjecture. On an earlier page where I wrote "About the Authors," it may be recalled that I mention that I felt that Victor DeVilliers was much the better writer of the two, and Owen Taylor was really much the better technical analyst. This division of contributed specialist effort is not only deduced from the material in this book, but also proven to myself from having read the books and booklets they both individually produced in the years preceding this P&F work and in the years afterwards. If I am right, then they themselves probably came to a similar conclusion when weighing up the merits of working together on this subject which was certainly crying out for the superior coverage of its methodology and analytical aspects that they gave it and which we meet as we get into the contents of this masterwork.

Going on from the Authors' Introduction, and as the pages are turned to get into the main P&F chapters that follow, the first thing that will immediately grab the reader's attention will be the two odd looking pages that will be found preceding the text of the book's body. What is to be seen is something unique, very unique, and something that I cannot recall ever seeing in any market book on any analytic methodology, let alone any P&F book. So be prepared for the displays of "Mechanical Principles" we are all about to meet. For it is there we come upon "The Lever ... The Fulcrum ... the Catapult," our introduction to the principles of Physics. Later in the text we are also destined to meet "The ideal Fulcrum ... The Broad Fulcrum ... The Recoil Fulcrum ... The True Catapult ... The False Catapult ... The Semi-Catapult ... The True Semi-Catapult ... The False Semi-Catapult."

With the coverage given by the authors in 1934 to all these creative mechanical principles, there is a great truth illustrated here that this writer never tires of making. He makes this point in the light of so much misguided thinking that abounds with so many of the millions of (professional and individual) traders and investors that make up the investment game around the entire world. This truth is an old "shibboleth" that keeps popping up all over the investing scene, especially from those that are relatively new to investment and investing. Over and over again so many find it extremely hard to accept that something written

80, 70, 60, 50, 40 years ago on pulling profits out of any speculative market can have much going in its favor. This all comes down to commonly accepted thinking that with all the wonderful computer power at hand and with all the marvelous mathematical market brainpower (PhD's to the left of us and PhD's to the right of us), we have or will have all the answers. So now it is out. How lucky we are to be for in the near future we with our computers are almost guaranteed to soon be millionaires(?).

So what possibly can a bunch of computerless market minds writing years ago have to contribute to us today? Well, the answer, in a nutshell, is that the mainstay PhD rocket-scientist mathematicians that are so revered in Wall Street and the City of London financial circles (shall we ignore the fiascoes of their participation in Long Term Capital Management and the many other hedge funds?) just do not have much of a chance in the contest. Perhaps, just perhaps, as exemplified by the horrific results derived from the grand operations of LTCM, the point will come across that mathematical power applied to investors' and traders' analysis in speculative marketplaces is a waste of time. It always has been, and barring a miracle of the ages, always will be beyond the application of mathematics to analyze people and their actions, which are at the end of the day what constitutes speculative markets – anything else is fluff. And fluff mathematics (which is what it is in coming to terms with people and their predictive actions), no matter how much they are held in the esteem of the investment powers-to-be as the way to miraculously come up with great investment results, just won't do it.

So that really beggars the question "just what will do it?" The answer to this question has always been around ever since the first markets came into being centuries ago, and the same answer will be with us in centuries to come – work hard, study even harder, and learn and learn and learn. Then apply it all through individual application in the ways that suit each individual's leanings. Looking at the stark reality of speculative investment, just suppose everybody had the answer to 100 percent sure profits on every transaction they do. Who would sell if they knew it was a 100 percent time to buy, and who would buy if they knew it was a 100 percent time to sell? It just couldn't happen, and it never will either.

There is no way going through any human mental gymnastics whatsoever to predict what the future holds and what may or may not come to fruition. We cannot nor will we ever beat what we call the "Spirit of the Market" which has and always will continue to confound human designs to beat it. What we can do is recognize that speculative markets are down to individual decision-making, even in the largest of investment organizations, and each decision-maker has to go with all the tools, the methods, and the analyzing and trading skills that they the individual can muster.

With every buy or sell decision coming down to some method, some approach, or some seemingly rational, or even irrational, thinking process, there has to be the *actual* act of buying or selling or it all remains in the realm of fantasy. Sticking with the more rational approaches, we have to start with the two ultimate major schools of investment analysis and thought – Fundamental Analysis and Technical Analysis. As this writer is a fervent, totally mad, and dedicated technical analyst, we'll start by throwing out all considerations of Fundamental Analysis (mainly involved with the study, evaluation, and projection of a company's accounts) and its practitioners, fundamental analysts. It has to be appreciated that even though he is solidly in the Technical Analysis camp, he still is very fair-minded and applauds the contribution they render to the field of investment analysis as the noble fundamental analysts that they are. That certainly is being extremely fair to their side, even though he wouldn't let his daughter (should he have such) marry one of the scoundrels.

Like any great school of natural analytical thought, there has to be some solid foundation underpinning Technical Analysis's *raison d'être*, that upon which it will stand, that from which it is all launched and that which it all purports to be. The basic starting point for TA will be found to center around three main charting methods that represent the foundation of each analytical technique. The oldest method is the one that we in English refer to as Japanese Candlesticks, and which today has many adherents inside and outside its country of origin. Almost comparable in form to Candlesticks, if not quite in analytical interpretations, but with much more emphasis on the passage of Time (more than with Candle- sticks), we have Line and Bar Charting which originated this century in the USA.

But the charting methodology that is near and dear to many of us at times is Point and Figure Charting whose origination is generally credited to have taken place in the nineteenth century. By some sources it has even been credited to the venerable Charles H. Dow, one of the founders of the Dow-Jones Company and the first editor of *The Wall Street Journal*. However, it is this writer's belief that P&F charting was used by market traders earlier than Dow's possible creation of this form of charting, for it probably was a bit before Dow's rise to eminence when the old glass-domed ticker machines were churning out the trades as they occurred on the different exchange floors. Situated as these machines were in brokers' offices all around the country, from the start brokers and customers reading the tape and trading on the printed figures must have needed a fuller picture at hand of the action that had taken place and was currently happening.

The answer had to be that records would be necessary to follow price movements over months, weeks, days, and intraday also. Who it was that initially devised the P&F method of charting will have to remain totally unknown to us, but there can be no getting away from their memorial – the P&F charts that have and continue to proliferate around the investment world.

Today we draw P&F charts using entries composed of all "Xs", or alternatively "Xs" and "Os" in the manner as explained in the following pages by Messrs DeVilliers and Taylor. Our market forebears in the last century used the exact same P&F methodology, but their notation nomenclature was slightly different and now would be a good time to lay it out for any reader who may not be aware of what those of yesteryear referred to as "Point" and as "Figure." Back then it was normal to record a price change whenever a stock price hit or went through the next full number following the last current figure. As an example we could in linear form write that a stock traded in the following order starting with a price of 45: 45-46-47-48-49-50-49-48-47-46-47-48-49-50-51-52-53-54-53-52-51-50-51-50-49-48-47-48-49-48-47-46-45-46-45-46-45-44-43-42-41-40-39-40-41-42-43-44-45-46-47-48-49-50-51 and on and on. Where the word "Figure" came into usage was that that was exactly how the preceding figures were charted, as follows:

54			54							
53			53	53						
52			52	52						
51			51	51	51					51
50	50		50	50	50					50
49	49	49	49		49	49				49
48	48	48	48		48	48	48			48
47	47	47	47		47		47			47
46	46	46					46	46	46	46
45	45						45	45	45	45
44									44	44
43									43	43
42									42	42
41									41	41
40									40	40
39									39	
38										
37										

So if we were back in the nineteenth century, this is how we would be laying out our P&F charts; but some time later (probably in the twentieth century) writing the actual figures as above was felt to be a bit cumbersome and the entry method was changed. The change was to keep the price scale on the left and use "Xs" to indicate an upward movement of prices and "Os" when prices move in a downward direction. Later on it was found that just using "Xs" alone would suffice and that change of direction was clearly evident as one got used to reading the chart.

So there we have the whole basis of charting P&F graphs. And on top of everything it is easy to actually graph. Even though practically every analytical software program around today will produce P&F charts to the exact specifications of the user, with their ease of insert, the suggestion from this quarter is that those charts that are the most important should be graphed by hand. This writer can do no better than to quote one of our esteemed Masterclass Series book buyer's comments which appeared in an article in the November 1999 issue of the renowned *Technical Analysis of Stocks & Commodities* magazine. Interviewed by the Editor, John Sweeney, was Hamilton Lewis whose company manages some $95,000,000 and who gives credit to P&F graphs and techniques as being the major tool in his analytical approach.

Notably Hamilton drew attention to the fact that, though he could use a computer to keep his P&F charts up to date, he still updates them by hand. When questioned why he has chosen to forego the ease and the quickness of the computer, his answer went right to the heart and soul and key of all Technical Analysis. "If you do it yourself you get a keen understanding of where the market is." So here in a nutshell is what technical analysts have to strive for whether one uses P&F charts, Line-and-Bar charts, or Candlesticks – and in the P&F material that is now upon us in the following pages, one of these masterly ways is so beautifully explored.

DONALD MACK
Series Editor
E-mail: Dmack144@aol.com

THE POINT AND FIGURE METHOD OF ANTICIPATING STOCK PRICE MOVEMENTS

BASIC PRINCIPLES

VOLUME 1

by

Victor DeVilliers

and

Owen Taylor

OTHER WORKS BY THESE AUTHORS

VICTOR DEVILLIERS

Financial Independence at Fifty

How to Buy Low and Sell High

Detecting the Buying and Selling Levels

The Point and Figure Method of Anticipating Stock Price Movements –
with Owen Taylor

Advanced Theory and Practice of the Point and Figure Method – with Owen Taylor

OWEN TAYLOR

Vital Guideposts to Successful Trading and Investing

Charts – How to Make and Read Them

Short Selling – For Trader, Investor and Business Man

Stop Orders – How to Use Them For Profit

Low Priced Stocks – When and How to Buy Them

Puts and Calls – How to Profit From Them

Key to Stock Price Movements – Logic of Stock Market Trends –
with Edwin L. Ayres

The Point and Figure Method of Anticipating Stock Price Movements – with Victor
DeVilliers

Advanced Theory and Practice of the Point and Figure Method – with Victor
DeVilliers

PREFACE TO FIRST EDITION

Experiences of the recent bear market which had its termination in July 1932 caused many former investors and traders to turn to the literature of economics and market technique in order to get a better understanding of the principles underlying stock price movements. Many have come to realize the futility of depending upon tips, rumors, and gossip to guide them in their market commitments. Countless others have come to the conclusion that statistics and fundamentals serve only to aid the manipulators, banking sponsors and insiders to unload their stock on the unwary.

All will agree that a correct analysis of the technical position of stocks and the market in general is the only key to consistent profit from speculative and trading commitments.

Until the publication of the original edition of this work, it was the privilege of the few who made fortunes from speculation to have the advantage of this, the most logical and pragmatical of all methods used for the purpose of plotting the price course of stocks and commodities. This Method has been the keystone and bulwark of the plans of America's most successful speculators and commentators, from Charles Henry Dow, the father of the art of anticipating stock price movements, down to and including those who have profited most during 1929 and subsequently.

We offer you the principles of this tried and proven Method because we feel that a broad dissemination of this information will do much to prevent the excesses of bull market peaks and also help avoid the unreasonable deflation of values, as well as the vicious cycles of forced selling and the resultant suffering of depression lows which so surely must follow.

We desire to express our appreciation to Mr. J. Martiney of the publisher's technical staff for the many helpful suggestions given and his care in the preparation of the charts used in this work.

We gratefully acknowledge our indebtedness to Charles Henry Dow, William Peter Hamilton, James R. Keene and others whose works and achievements have been an inspiration and a guide.

Victor DeVilliers
Owen Taylor
New York City
January 1934

INTRODUCTION TO FIRST EDITION

The Point and Figure Method had its beginning sixty years ago and subsequently has been used by some of the eminently successful operators in their important stock market campaigns. With the passing of the years, the Method has been refined, improved and adapted to changed market conditions. *The underlying principles of the Method, however – based on the immutable Law of Supply and Demand –* are *unchanging and are constantly effective.*

The theory and practice of the Method is fully treated in

Vol. 1 *The Point and Figure Method of Anticipating Stock Price Movements* (written in 1933 – revised in 1934)

Vol. 2 *Advanced Theory and Practice of the Point and Figure Method* (written in 1933 – revised in 1934)

Vol. 3 *The Time Tested Technique of the Point and Figure Method* (written in 1939 – augmented in 1940 and 1941).

The first two of these three texts were written from the viewpoint of the individual stock trader at a time when pool operators gave strong impetus to market movements. Such operation injected a manipulative or artificial element into the supply and demand relationships in the market. But Supply and Demand – whether artificial or genuine, manipulative or otherwise, and whatever their causes – are the forces that create price change. The Point and Figure Method measures these forces and enables one to arrive at sound and reliable conclusions as to subsequent price action.

This Method, a generation ago, was used largely to create profits through market operation. Today it is used by some of the largest and highest ranking fund managers whose objectives are capital and income conservation and growth. The Method also is used by commodity processors for guidance in the purchasing and hedging of their extensive inventory requirements.

In placing these texts in your hands we are conscious of their literary and technical limitations. If some principles are treated dogmatically it is for the purpose of fixing them firmly in your mind. If some of the many principles appear to overlap or seemingly conflict with others, we ask you to disregard it at the start and simply master each principle as it is expounded. Weighing and coordinating these principles is the vital factor in Point and Figure analysis. Development of skill in this technique will be accomplished and hastened by practice on your part.

Instances of extraordinary success in investment account management and in commodity market operation, through Point and Figure means exclusively, are constantly coming to our attention. Such success is attributed to the skillful use of the principles set forth in these modest texts. We mention this as an inspiration to you and to emphasize that this work is of far reaching value and importance.

Stock Market Publications Inc.

The Point and Figure Method
of
Anticipating Stock Price Movements
is the

ONLY METHOD

BASED ON

Logical and Scientific
MECHANICAL PRINCIPLES

such as

THE LEVER. . .
THE FULCRUM. .
THE CATAPULT. .

These MECHANICAL PRINCIPLES are all
involved in Stock Price Movements

PROFITS ARE AVAILABLE FOR
THOSE WHO WILL APPLY THEM

Fig B

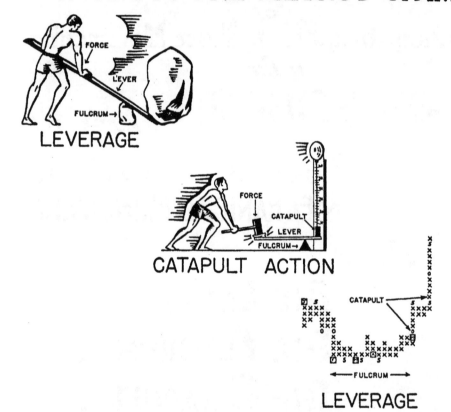

SCIENTIFIC MECHANICS
of POINT and FIGURE METHOD CHARTS

LEVERAGE and CATAPULT ACTION
CREATE · PROFITS · FOR YOU

1

THE PRINCIPLES OF THE POINT AND FIGURE METHOD

■ Logic is the basis of this Method

■ Irrelevant fluctuations eliminated

■ How the Method got its name

■ Graphs are logical and scientific

■ Introductory summary of important principles

■ Needed accessories are few

■ Plotting a stock price movement

■ One point charts the basis of the Method

■ Accessories and working tools

Fifteen years before the turn of the last century, Charles H. Dow, student, scientist and philosopher, a brilliant economist and a well respected financial writer, began to observe and study the phenomena of Stock Price Movements. He was the founder of the *Wall Street Journal*. His writings, though not prolific, are the beginnings of all price movement comment, his observations the foundation underlying all technical methods, and his studies and graphic records the seeds from which the Point and Figure Method grew.

The work of Dow was ably carried on by his protege and successor, William Peter Hamilton, who edited the *Wall Street Journal* until his death in 1929. The writings of Hamilton form the principal source from which Dow's Theory of Stock Price Movements has become available for study.

At or around the beginning of the present century, when the expansion era was in full swing, a group of speculators recognized in Dow's research* a clear illustration of price movements portrayed through the use of figures which showed a repetition of pattern as it unfolded its tracings on Dow's graphic records. The patterns thus formed were oft-times repeated, and established a precedent and guide to future price movements. Here, then, was the beginning of a truly scientific and logical method of anticipating stock price movements.

Fifty years of background, millions of dollars of profits taken out of the stock market, and thousands of hours of study and development, are historical events which commend this time tried Method to you.

In explaining the basic principles of the Point and Figure Method, we will show that the full point and full figure fluctuations in variable equities, be they commodities or stocks, are the vital statistics which hold the key to technical position and the future price path.

Professionals and others who have been successful in their judgment and anticipation of market action, have reached their conclusions by aid of recorded data of one kind or another. In practically every field of endeavor, whether it be in the arts or sciences, in the industrial world, or in the stock and commodity markets, full and detailed records of past and current essential data must be kept. It is of little consequence whether these records are maintained as tabulated figures or by means of logs or charts, which are merely graphic representations and plottings of those essential records.

---

* See pages 36 and 153, *The Stock Market Barometer*, by W. P. Hamilton.

Charts of stock price movements are vital. There is an ancient Chinese axiom dating from the Confucian era which states, "A picture is better than a thousand words." It is self-evident that a picture conveys a clearer and more detailed message than a mass of words or columns of tabulated figures. Since instant comparison and maximum condensation are vital to the art of anticipating stock price movements, we endorse the practice of keeping and maintaining up-to-date charts. Graphic representations of the fluctuations of stock prices are vitally important to a critical analysis of technical position and are the keystone of the Point and Figure Method.

LOGIC IS THE BASIS OF THIS METHOD

Few will dispute the fact that the old fashioned custom of relying solely upon published statistics of sales and earnings for market commitments, must now be relegated to the past. All will agree that by the time these statistics become available for public consumption, others, principally the insiders, the sponsors and the manipulators, have already profited amply therefrom and are ready to unload their commitments as the news becomes public property. We must, therefore, find a method which will show us when the insiders are buying and also indicate when they are commencing to sell. Given the ability to recognize their acts on our charts, it follows logically that we will be able to buy when the insiders buy and sell out when they sell.

The patterns portrayed on our charts and application of the principles of the Point and Figure Method will show us when buying is overcoming selling and vice versa. If you are ready to agree that the present movement of stock prices, as recorded on the ticker tape, is the best and surest indication of the probable direction of the future price trend, then this Method can be used to show the way.

It should be needless for us to state that some intensive study and a thorough understanding of the principles are necessary before you can hope to capitalize on that knowledge. Once a solid foundation is laid, your judgment will develop in a logical manner, and you will quickly begin to recognize many profitable opportunities. You will be more certain of yourself, and the courage of your convictions will materially increase your capital.

IRRELEVANT FLUCTUATIONS ELIMINATED

The market fluctuates in countless fractional transactions which, in the final analysis, have little or no influence on future price paths. One of the basic principles of the Point and Figure Method is to eliminate the irrelevant and regard only the important movements upon which our deductions are based. Only full point changes are considered, and fractional variations are totally disregarded.

HOW THE METHOD GOT ITS NAME

The Point and Figure Method derives its name from the fact that we record by *figures* all full *point* changes. This plan or system of plotting and recording the movements of the market in general, and of selected individual stocks, is a basic principle of this particular Method. In this one characteristic, it is totally different from any other plan, method, or system of anticipating stock price movements.

GRAPHS ARE LOGICAL AND SCIENTIFIC

A casual glance at the illustrations in this work will show a new kind of chart which, in contrast to all others, has a scientific basis to recommend its use. The Point and Figure graphic records are made up of a series of symbols composed of X's, fives and zeros. The special design of graph paper which we suggest for use with this Method shows the relationship of these symbols to each other and to the past and probable future price movement. Familiarize yourself with the form and style of these important aids, namely, the charts upon which we rely for our conclusions. Point and Figure charts condense the price fluctuations in such a manner that you will soon learn to recognize accumulation, mark-up, and distribution and thus be able to make your commitments more profitable.

INTRODUCTORY SUMMARY OF
IMPORTANT PRINCIPLES

The Method will be fully explained in every detail as we proceed. Each step will be carefully developed and clarified before we proceed with the next. All will be illustrated with examples from recent market action, showing the application of the principles. So that you may have a bird's-eye view of the scope of the work, we list a summary of the important principles underlying the Point and Figure Method.

1. The Method develops the ability to recognize the technical position of individual stocks and of the market in general.
2. The Method is consistent and logical, definite and positive, eliminating, as far as possible, guesswork and emotional influences.
3. The data is recorded in such a manner as to create and force the development

of true geometrical and symmetrical patterns easily discernible and classified, and which repeat themselves in the progression of the price path.

4. The patterns thus formed create precedents by which subsequent price movements are easily judged.

5. The Method disregards fractions resulting from minor and irrelevant fluctuations. It also ignores volume. The Method is simple and complete in itself.

6. The Method dispenses with news, fundamentals, statistics, and the reasons for price movements. It concerns itself primarily with cause and effect.

NEEDED ACCESSORIES ARE FEW

The data which we record in order to create the basis for the application of this Method is, primarily, all one point changes of the price movement as it fluctuates. This principle is the same whether we apply it to stock price movements, market indices, or commodities. As a matter of fact, the Point and Figure Method of anticipating price movements may be applied to any form of equity for which a free and open market exists, and in which there are price fluctuations.

When full point variations of the price movement are known, they are recorded by figures. Our records are unlike the conventional vertical line or bar charts in that they are created through the use of symbols. The symbol "x" is used to record the digits 1, 2, 3, 4, 6, 7, 8, and 9. The figure "5" is used to indicate figures ending with the digit five. The symbol "0" is used to indicate figures in multiples of tens. At this point, it would be well for you to examine the illustrations used in this book in order that you may have a better understanding of this elementary principle used in making our charts.

The full figure one point changes are recognized by the price fluctuations when they reach each new full one point change. The change thus noted is recorded, whether it be the next higher or the next lower figure, and the change must be recorded each and every time it shows on the tape. At this point, let us emphasize the fact that herein lies the vast superiority of this Method over all others. When we record all full figure changes, we are better able to detect accumulation, distribution, and the characteristics peculiar to the particular stock or commodity under observation. Note, here, that we disregard all movements of seven-eighths points or less, when fluctuations are in eighths. In cases where fluctuations are in tenths or dollars, we must determine whether we will plot the full one-dollar changes or whether the changes in tenths would better serve our purpose.

PLOTTING A STOCK PRICE MOVEMENT

After we obtain the full figure changes, we proceed to make our graphic record from that data. We require for that purpose, graph or charting paper ruled for quick and easy use. Ideal paper for this purpose is "Ideal Charting Sheet Number 5001." This paper is ruled with vertical and horizontal columns, arranged with shadowed symbols "0" and "5," and with the horizontal columns for these important digits accentuated.

The vertical columns on our charts are used to limit the plottings of the price movement as long as it continues in one direction without a reversal. As soon as a reversal occurs, and we find the needed square already occupied, we move to the next right-hand vertical column. This vital principle must be fixed firmly in your mind, as it is the only one that may give you difficulty later on when you proceed to make your own charts.

The Point and Figure Method relies on price changes only, and the graph paper is designed to properly record those changes. The day-to-day time factor and daily volume are ignored. The columns of squares are scientifically designed so as to permit the plotting of true trendlines and to force the development of true geometrical and symmetrical patterns which facilitate accurate comparisons and dependable diagnosis.

In the case of a stock selling at $20 per share, we would record the zero in the square on the 20 line. The next record would be made when the stock sells at flat price 21, or at flat price 19. Should it go down to 19⅞, or up to 20⅞, no change would be made.

ONE POINT CHARTS THE BASIS OF THE METHOD

When a series of full figure one point changes of a price movement have been recorded, they create a scientific basis from which to draw conclusions. Because of the fact that similar causes usually create similar effects, our conclusions have a dependable basis not available through the use of any other method.

In addition to the one point charts, one may easily prepare from them either three or five point charts or both. These are helpful for gauging the technical position of any and all issues, volatile or otherwise, and for revealing the broader intermediate moves of stocks and the market.

ACCESSORIES AND WORKING TOOLS

In addition to graph paper, one needs a record of the actual full figure changes garnered from the most accurate source, the ticker tape.*

When using this especially designed paper and the daily service which is available, it is a relatively simple matter to keep current the needed changes on one hundred stocks and the important popular averages or indices, in about thirty minutes each day. Form this habit, as it will afford you an opportunity to analyze the patterns as they unfold themselves on your charts and thus take advantage of the implications which develop, first in one issue and then in another. The little effort expended in keeping these charts up to date will soon pay you handsomely, for you will be training yourself in stock market technique in a way not afforded by any other method.

---

* Full Figure Daily Data published by Stock Market Publications, New York, N. Y.

2

THE WEIGHT OF AUTHORITY
BEHIND THIS METHOD

- Refined to coordinate with present day markets
- Mystery and complications have been clarified
- Expensive financial and economic reports unnecessary
- Certain factors taken for granted
- Analytical technique easy to master
- Losses limited while profits accrue
- Method weighs forces of buying and selling

The Point and Figure Method has grown from a crude beginning which started more than fifty years ago. Charles H. Dow, the founder of the art of anticipating stock price movements, created much which led to the development of the technique of this Method. Dow, in his research, was interested primarily in recognizing the main, broad, long term trend which results from the movement of major capital into or out of common stock equities. This main trend was rightly termed the "Capital Movement Trend" by Mr. Edwin L. Ayres in his book *Key to Stock Price Movements*.* The secondary corrections to the main trend, though of interest to Dow, were not the goal of his efforts. He considered the secondary movements highly misleading and concluded that the shorter day-to-day swings were unimportant.

However, we must bear in mind that since Dow's work was completed, the stock market and America's financial structures have undergone revolutionary changes. Common stock equities of American corporations have attracted a world-wide speculative following, unprecedented in the history of finance and of speculation.

In Dow's era, a move of 20 to 30 points in the Industrial or Rail Index consummated in a period of a few years was considered a complete bull cycle. Under present day conditions, we note, on occasion, moves of 10 to 20 points in either or both indexes completed in a few weeks. Three, nine or sixteen million share days, such as were recently witnessed, were undreamed of at the time when ten or a dozen stocks were the active trading mediums, and volume was limited to a few hundred thousand shares a day. One can, therefore, understand why Dow passed lightly over the minor and secondary movements and sought only to ascertain the main trend. These minor and secondary movements have now become all important. Their study, analysis and the understanding of how to use them form the basis of the most successful method of stock price anticipation.

It has been intimated that this Method was first successfully used by James R. Keene during the merger of the United States Steel Corporation in 1901. Mr. Keene was employed by the sponsors of the Steel Corporation to distribute to the public the original stock of the corporation, which its real founder, Andrew Carnegie, refused to take in payment for his equity and profits resulting from the merger.

Mr. Keene, originally a Western mining promoter, was a skilled tape reader, a shrewd observer, and a successful market operator. His ability has never been surpassed and rarely, if ever, equaled. It has been stated by his close associates

---

* *Key to Stock Price Movements – Logic of Stock Market Trends*, Stock Market Publications, New York, N.Y.

that the Point and Figure Method was known to and used by him during all of his successful campaigns.

REFINED TO COORDINATE WITH PRESENT DAY MARKETS

Like all knowledge, the Method has developed with the passing of years and has been refined, improved, and coordinated with the ever changing conditions of stock market action. The scientific basis of the fundamental principles underlying the Method alone accounts for its survival while most other methods have been relegated to the past. You may confidently depend upon the Point and Figure Method knowing, first, that it rests upon a sound scientific basis and, secondly, that it is vastly superior to any other plan for anticipating stock price movements. In the past as well as at present, it has been and is relied upon by many of Wall Street's most successful interests.

The data which should be kept will be described in utmost detail. Bear in mind that there is a great weight of authority behind this data, and we ask of you to respect its implications. We have found by the trial and error method those refinements needed to fit the basic principles to present day markets. It was ascertained that a careful checking and rechecking of the conclusions arrived at by means of this Method is of vital importance and cannot be over emphasized.

MYSTERY AND COMPLICATIONS HAVE BEEN CLARIFIED

The Point and Figure Method, as here presented, is devoid of mystery and complications and has proven itself of incalculable aid to your authors. We begin by reducing the vast accumulation of transactions comprising market action to the important and relevant moves, which are plotted on charts. From these graphs showing the present market action, we are able to judge the probable future direction and extent of a stock's movement.

The Point and Figure Method permits stock market trading to be considered a serious business with a scientific, substantial, and definite background, based upon actual facts rather than guesswork.

Like all other businesses, it demands the making and preserving of certain simple and vital records. It demands that you study those records carefully and permit your judgment to be based upon solid facts. None will deny the old copy book maxim "Practice makes perfect." The Point and Figure Method actually compels practice and extensive study which soon becomes a habit as well as a fascinating hobby.

EXPENSIVE FINANCIAL AND ECONOMIC REPORTS UNNECESSARY

This Method dispenses entirely with the expense and labor involved in the purchase and maintenance of bulky reports, statistics, balance sheets, earnings statements, and other cumbersome paraphernalia hitherto associated with trading and investing. The substitution of the simple records required by this Method is, in itself, an important consideration and a welcome relief.

CERTAIN FACTORS TAKEN FOR GRANTED

The following facts are taken for granted by the Point and Figure Method:

(a) That the correct valuation of a stock, at any given time, is the price paid for it at the time of the consummated sale. This is because the forces underlying the law of supply and demand and the consensus of opinion of the buyers and sellers have determined the value at the time the sale is made.

(b) That the last published price of a stock reflects all that is known by the general public at the time when established, as a result of a sale and purchase which consummates a transaction.

(c) That the insiders, who are presumed to know more about any particular stock than the public, cannot completely conceal their future intentions with regard thereto.

(d) That the plans of the insiders will be revealed in due time by the technical action of the stock itself.

The Point and Figure Method is not a system for "beating the stock market." It is the result of the rationalization of logical principles successfully used by important market interests.

ANALYTICAL TECHNIQUE EASY TO MASTER

Assuming that the student will keep the required records, there remains only the need of an understanding of the technique of reading and interpreting them. In the pages to follow, we illustrate for you in detail and with clarity the technique of interpreting the patterns which develop on your Point and Figure Charts.

While proficiency may not come at first, yet, in a short time, through study, practice, and observation, the habit of correct thinking in terms of the Point and Figure Method will become apparent, and the resulting sound judgment will soon replace uncertainty and confusion.

It is confidently expected that, as a result of this study, observation, and practice, the reader will learn to properly appraise the price movements, analyze the technical condition, and deduce therefrom plausible conclusions, the correctness of which will soon exceed the errors you are apt to make. With proficiency attained, your market operations cannot help but result in profit.

LOSSES LIMITED WHILE PROFITS ACCRUE

Success in trading and investing, whether by method or by chance, comes not as a result of being perfect, but in consequence of completing a sufficient number of successful transactions netting substantial profits to offset the few errors which may show limited losses.

In order to limit losses and to check possible errors, we employ the simple technical aid known as "stop orders." It is unnecessary for us to go into detail here, as the theory and application of stop orders are fully described in many other works.*

In no other enterprise or business is it possible to protect profits or check losses with the same ease and facility as is possible in the stock or commodity markets, through the simple expedient of stop orders. We strongly endorse the use of stop orders except where "averaging" or "pyramiding" is resorted to. Many admonitions have been given against averaging and pyramiding, yet this Method not only tolerates, but, at times, presents ideal points at which both may be resorted to, for the reason that each commitment is independent and is made on its own merits. This will be fully explained in a later chapter.

A pyramid is created when the profits accrued on a position are used to buy additional commitments. This practice usually develops into an inverted pyramid when it is resorted to in connection with credit – borrowed funds – used to finance a margin account. An inverted pyramid is exceedingly dangerous because the load gets top-heavy, as the human weakness to make huge and quick profits invites an over-extended commitment, which, as a general rule, is wiped out on the first technical reaction.

We average a position by buying additional quantities of stock as it sells lower in the price range. This Method indicates ideal points at which to make additional commitments for the purpose of averaging one's cost.

METHOD WEIGHS FORCES OF BUYING AND SELLING

The Point and Figure Method actually measures the forces of supply and demand, and records the support and resistances at all points. It permits of a wide range of visualization through its lucid, graphic records which allows quick and ready comparison of one stock with others and with the market in general, as reflected by a good index and, most important of all, with its previous technical action. These records, if properly compiled from reliable sources, will indicate the true trend of the market and of stocks, and will point out the best trading and investment opportunities.

The Method indicates when and what to buy. It also cautions when to get out, first, through clear signals to act, then, through definite indications for the logical placement of stop orders. It teaches you to adopt a professional approach to your market transactions. Professionals may be considered as the insiders, pools, independent operators, stock sponsors, bankers, and others usually referred to as "they" by many market commentators.

---

* *Stop Orders – How to Use Them for Profit*, by Owen Taylor.

3

ADVANTAGES OF THIS METHOD OVER OTHERS

■ Speed and ease of recording data
■ The Method ignores volume
■ Price changes versus volume
■ Supply versus demand
■ Volume easily manipulated
■ Facility of this method
■ The utter simplicity of the records
■ Manipulation readily detected
■ Use all full figure changes in making charts
■ Method is superior to inside information
■ Isolation develops best results
■ Our charts reveal plans of the majority
■ How the move begins
■ Stock market trading is a business
■ Inside information unnecessary
■ One point charts show all

There are certain definite and inherent advantages of the Point and Figure Method not possessed by any other method. These advantages are: (a) the elimination of non-essentials, (b) the ease of condensation, and (c) the speed by which results may be achieved. These superior qualities are again stressed in order to point out that the simplicity of this Method does not curtail its accuracy and dependability. A simple machine with a few well constructed parts will operate far more efficiently than a complicated mechanism with ponderous accessories. So it is with the Point and Figure Method.

SPEED AND EASE OF RECORDING DATA

The Method provides, amongst other things, clarity and simplicity in the keeping of its graphic records. This results in the creation of logical and clean-cut patterns on the graphs and higher speed in the plotting of the necessary data. It will enable you to maintain the records of more stocks, and be a source of checking and correlating all of the facts, with a view of arriving at a correct interpretation of market activity and profiting therefrom.

THE METHOD IGNORES VOLUME

The Point and Figure Method entirely dispenses with the recording of the volume of sales. Many have felt this to be a distinct deficiency under the belief that volume is a dominant factor. We are unwilling to concede that volume is the vital influence which, in the final analysis, governs the price movement. It is conceded, however, that volume is an influence when used as an aid in other methods. In our opinion, the Point and Figure Method has proven itself so much more reliable, that we are satisfied from our research and experience to conclude that *the number of price changes and the manner in which they combine themselves have a more scientific foundation than the influence of volume in the anticipation of price movements.*

PRICE CHANGES VERSUS VOLUME

Let us analyze the effect of the influence of volume as against the effect of price change only. What is the aim of all methods which seek to anticipate stock price movements? Do we seek to know how many shares are exchanged? Or, do we desire to determine whether stocks are passing from weak holders into strong hands and vice versa? All will agree that it is the answer to the latter question which will permit us to profit most from our knowledge. Taking for granted the known fact, namely, that each transaction printed on the tape is at the same time a purchase by one and a sale by another, it is of little consequence to know the exact number of these transactions. What we desire to ascertain is where in the price scale they occur and their relationship to each other.

Let us approach the problem in a logical manner by taking note of the definitely known elements, in order to determine whether price changes or volume have most influence.

In a speculative market, where the laws of supply and demand are operative, we must have fluctuations in prices. These fluctuations are due mostly to differences of opinion which cause what is technically known as the bid and asked spread. Experience has taught us that *a great number of fluctuations in a congestion area usually indicates either accumulation or distribution.* When stock is offered for sale at the market, we must take the nearest bid price; and when one is anxious to purchase a stock and offers to take it at the market, he must pay the nearest asked price. The price changes of a stock, as it moves from one price to another, are caused by the difference of opinions of those who are buying and selling. These fluctuations have proven themselves more informative for our purpose than has volume.

SUPPLY VERSUS DEMAND

Furthermore, let us consider the effect of supply and demand on any product or commodity, be it stock, equities, or horseshoes. When demand is greater than supply, prices move upward. Should supply be greater than demand, then prices are forced downward. When demand has absorbed all the supply at any given price, it will begin to absorb the supply available at the next higher price at which offerings are available. As the demand increases, prices correspondingly increase. Prices recede as a result of absence of demand or an oversupply.

These factors show that price, as such, holds the key to supply volume as well as to demand volume. These fluctuations or price changes, when plotted by means of the principles outlined for you in this book, will more accurately indicate the technical condition, the relationship of supply to demand, than any other known method which can be used for the purpose.

VOLUME EASILY MANIPULATED

Volume, as well as price fluctuation, can be artificially manipulated. Manipulations of volume at any given price level are deceptive and cannot reveal the difference between true and artificial demand. As contrasted with that principle, consider how easy it is to detect artificial support resorted to for the purpose of distribution when many changes in the price of a stock show that it cannot absorb the supply at the upper registered level, or that demand is insufficient to reach to the next level of supply. This principle becomes more clearly apparent as you compare these conditions in one particular stock with the market and other stocks. Volume indications have a tendency to vary greatly with the changes in the floating supply of stocks as well as changes due to the open short interest in the market. We, therefore, conclude that price changes of themselves, with their relationship to each other and to the market and other stocks for comparison, are vastly superior than is volume, used with any other combination. Herein, then, lies the vital and vast superiority of the use of price changes and the Point and Figure Method.

FACILITY OF THIS METHOD

This Method permits and facilitates the easy recording of the essential data, and a simple and logical method of analysis. The direction of the trend, the extent of the move, and a reasonable approximation of the culmination thereof, are all easily determinable. Through the aid of the one, three, and five point charts, one may be reasonably certain of the shorter immediate swings and the more profitable intermediate trend moves, as well as the main broad swings of the bull and bear market cycles – the Capital Movement Trend.

We can visualize at a glance, through the aids afforded by this Method, namely, the one, three, and five point charts, the broad zones of accumulation and distribution in the main swings, as well as the closer areas of supply and demand of the narrower and more speculative intermediate trend moves. Our data shows, at a glance, the moves by important areas, by months, by days, by the all important dividend periods, by seasonal influences, and by main business cycle influences. It also shows the results of speculative influences, as well as the effects of long range investment buying and selling.

THE UTTER SIMPLICITY OF THE RECORDS

Examine now Chart Figure 3.1. This is an illustration of a hypothetical move from a start and low of 50, to a high of 55, and a close at 54. Here we illustrate a one day move which by other methods would not permit of technical analysis, yet by the Point and Figure Method, we are given two possible price paths, each of which would connote a different technical condition.

Fig 3.1   One point charts

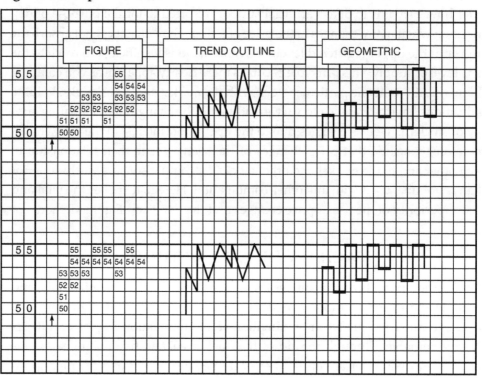

Note the upper half of the illustration, which we diagnose as bearish. Study carefully the three separate and distinct methods by which data may be recorded when using this Method. The first plan is recording *by figures*. Trace the move, 50, 51, 50, 51, 52, 51, 52, 53, 52, 53, 52, 51, 52, 53, 54, 55, 54, 53, 52, 53, to 54, the close. The pattern just to the right of the figure chart is called a *trend outline chart* and illustrated the same move. On the extreme right you may observe the *geometrical chart* of the same move. Note now that all of this action may be recorded by one day's market fluctuations in a fairly active issue in normal markets. This illustration is bearish because it indicates stock in supply around the 52, and 53, levels with a temporary push through to 55, near the close.

Now regard the lower half of our illustration Figure 3.1. Trace the move, 50, 51, 52, 53, 52, 53, 54, 55, 54, 53, 54, 55, 54, 55, 54, 53, 54, 55, 54. This move is diagnosed as bullish because it indicates scarcity of offerings below 55, and its ability to hold the advance above 53.

The analysis above is made on the actual movement of the issue as shown. If the immediate previous action was plotted and available for comparison, our diagnosis might change.

MANIPULATION READILY DETECTED

Records of fluctuations, upon careful analysis, reveal the manipulation. You have seen in the foregoing paragraph how the action which takes place during any market day is broken up into its important fluctuations, namely, its component parts, in order that we may be able to detect what the manipulators, pool operators, and insiders may be doing with the issue. No method as yet devised will show manipulation as clearly and as surely as a diagram made according to the principles of the Point and Figure Method.

Stock sponsors and operators vary their plans of campaign. Some prefer to depress a stock and make it look very weak, even though it is their aim to mark it up to substantially higher prices. Others, whose tactics are bolder and more open, do not hesitate to bid up the price of a stock very rapidly, taking all blocks offered on the way up, and thus creating a spectacular move. The latter method is daring but very effective, because spectacular moves attract wide public appeal through the aid of board room traders and others who watch tape action, as well as comments in the newspapers which usually follow spectacular moves as they develop on the tape.

When operators resort to such spectacular manipulation, lively tape action excites gossip in board rooms and thus attracts a great following for the issue. No matter what procedure is selected by the insiders in any stock, our Point and Figure charts will reveal the areas in which they are accumulating stock and will, with equal accuracy, show zones of distribution.

USE ALL FULL FIGURE CHANGES IN MAKING CHARTS

Build up your Point and Figure data carefully, using for your purpose either the transactions recorded directly from the tape or the full figure daily changes supplied by the publishers of this book. When you plot all of the full figure fluctuations, you have a true representation of what is taking place in the issue. While Point and Figure charts may be compiled from the financial page quotations of your local newspaper, records thus compiled are not nearly as dependable for forecasting purposes as are those with *all* of the full figure fluctuations.

The charts built up from authentic data consisting of the actual full figure changes, will always develop patterns in the progression of a move which soon become easy to recognize and classify. A careful study of past performances recorded in the same manner will reveal to the student several important factors which have vital forecasting significance – in that they show the proper points at which to make commitments.

THE POINT AND FIGURE METHOD

These patterns are created as a result of better buying than selling when the move is in the upward direction, and, likewise, when the move is down, they reflect the reverse – better selling than buying. Since a similar cause is always followed by a like effect, these patterns, as they develop, are generally followed by the same type of subsequent action. As we cannot build a house without some kind of foundation, so a stock cannot advance materially unless accumulation has first taken place. Since accumulation will always register on our charts, it becomes but a matter of careful observation and analysis to be able to recognize a move as it is developing and before it really gets started. In addition, we are able to know the exact point at which the risk may be limited while the profit possibilities are preserved to their fullest possible extent.

These characteristic patterns on our Point and Figure Charts always develop, no matter what the condition of the market may be. It is immaterial whether it be a slow day with a half million shares as the average, or a fast session, with five million shares as the average; our Point and Figure charts will reveal, with accuracy, the technical condition of the price movement as plotted and observed.

METHOD IS SUPERIOR TO INSIDE INFORMATION

Since it is the purpose of all market analysis to determine the balance between the forces of supply and demand, we seek a means of accurately measuring those forces. Whether demand be on the part of the well-informed insiders, stock sponsors, manipulators, or the consensus of opinion; whether it be one or more of the foregoing groups, or whether it result from sufficient outside public participation, it will bring about the same results on our Point and Figure charts. By means of the use of the Point and Figure Method, anyone who will devote sufficient time to the mastery of its principles can place himself in possession of the knowledge that will put him on an equal footing with the influential forces, whether they be insiders or outsiders. No basis for a movement in any stock can be completed without leaving definite indications in its price path together with their logical implications as the action of the stock traces its movements clearly on our Point and Figure Charts.

ISOLATION DEVELOPS BEST RESULTS

As a matter of fact, those who apply the principles of this Method and handle their transactions independently are in a better position than members of a syndicate or a pool operation, for reasons later explained. Prices advance or decline because of the operation of the forces of demand and supply. While it is true that major interests, large scale operators, syndicates, and pools can temporarily accelerate or retard a movement, we must, nevertheless, keep in mind that no human force or group can very long obstruct the real trend of the market as it moves, because of influences of general economic cycles.

In the last analysis, all speculative operations, whether undertaken for trading profits or for long term investment capital appreciation, must be in harmony with the main trend of the capital movement cycle, or they will result in grief and loss to those who undertake them. Those who operate with one to five hundred share lots of a stock are in vastly better position than are the large groups who must necessarily employ thousands and perhaps hundreds of thousands of shares in their operation. The small operator can reverse his position quickly, while the large scale operator cannot quickly turn about, by reason of the very size and extent of his commitment and the inability of the market to absorb so vast an amount of stock into the floating supply without breaking the movement wide open and causing a major reversal.

Thus, you see that the use of the principles of this Method is more reliable than inside information. We have actual knowledge of the most potent and vital influence, namely, the actual price changes, which must be considered as the verdict of the market resulting from the consensus of all opinions which influence the issue or commodity in which we are operating.

Adhere to the principle of isolation. Turn a deaf ear to all gossip, rumor, inside tips, and other information. Your Point and Figure Charts are more reliable than any other source of information available.

OUR CHARTS REVEAL PLANS OF THE MAJORITY

Our charts reveal, in a condensed form, all that is known to the insiders and unknown to others, about the movement of a stock up to the very last moment. What more can anyone wish to know?

Authentic and reliable inside information must not, and cannot be disclosed. Disclosure may wreck costly plans. When such information is disclosed, it is no longer inside information, and then it is not worth knowing, for it immediately becomes common property and usually develops to be the most costly type of information in Wall Street. It generally leaves you long of stock while the insiders have sold their stock and are out of the market. Remember, the news and information you get is only what the insiders and sponsors wish you to know, and then only after they have profited therefrom.

HOW THE MOVE BEGINS

In recent years, the market has more quickly responded to combined public sentiment. Millions of investors and speculators comprise that public. On occasions, their demands have taken the market completely out of the hands of the insiders. Their inactivity has, at times, upset many well laid plans of some of the best banking and financial brains in the country. When these millions begin to act or show tentative signs of activity, the alert major interests – the sponsors, bankers, pool operators, and insiders – endeavor to anticipate their demands. The insiders and operators can only anticipate and start the move by quickly completing their positions and temporarily taking stock out of the floating supply. This operation is often completed in secrecy during inactive markets, when all offerings are soon absorbed without indications of demand appearing on the tape. Then follows the demand or the beginning of the demand of the outside public. After this buying has commenced, sponsors continue to accelerate the advance in harmony with the trend, buying and selling on balance, so that the value of their position, completed at the lower level, increases, as prices are forced higher.

As an illustration, a syndicate operation may own, let us say, 10,000 shares of a certain issue at an average price of $10 per share. As the price begins to advance, the manager of the syndicate buys and sells on balance, yet always holds at least the amount originally accumulated, until the market price of the stock is far above the average cost of his position. At the predetermined higher price level, he begins to sell more than he buys and only buys a sufficient quantity to hold the price of the stock at approximately the level at which he wishes to distribute his inventory, accumulated substantially lower down. *These operations are always apparent from the patterns formed by the price changes and portrayed on our Point and Figure Charts.* When you possess this information, remember, you, too, may be considered one of the insiders.

Students who take this Method seriously and apply themselves to a better understanding of it are in a more advantageous position than the insiders, since, at the first signs of danger, their smaller positions can be quickly liquidated, enabling them to stand aside while the large scale interests are struggling to complete their campaign.

STOCK MARKET TRADING IS A BUSINESS

Again, we wish to emphasize this important fact – stock market trading or investing is a serious business and requires careful study and application. No other business offers similar opportunities for gain as often or as quickly as does the stock market. No other business permits one to limit loss or to insure ultimate success as do your transactions in the market, when you thoroughly understand market technique. Remember, your stock market transactions may be closed out quickly or you may reverse your position or protect it by placing strategic stop loss orders.

In business, it is the major interests who dominate, and the larger the unit, the more efficient can be its management; yet that is not applicable to the stock market. Here, a very large commitment may prevent quick action when speed is essential.

It is well to remember when you hear of inside information that is unsupported by positive confirmation from your Point and Figure Charts that many insiders have, in the past, made serious errors. Testimony before governmental committees has revealed only a few of the grave mistakes made by many well grounded in the fields of finance, economics, and banking. Inside opinion, inside judgment or so-called inside information, may on occasion be very good, but if your transaction is not properly timed, you may be wiped out, notwithstanding the good intentions of your informant.

INSIDE INFORMATION UNNECESSARY

It is best, at all times, to rely upon logical judgment, the result of conclusions arrived at through a careful analysis of actual facts. It is far more dependable than guesswork, tips, rumors, or so-called inside information. Your full figure changes, your knowledge of their implications, the direction of the trend, and your faith in your own self, is all you need when you employ the principles of the Point and Figure Method.

Inasmuch as market knowledge, by and large, is not an exact science, errors of interpretation cause errors of judgment, and hence faulty conclusions may occur on occasions. The most positive indications may be reversed almost momentarily. Therefore, if in the beginning you err occasionally, do not be discouraged. Profit from your mistakes, note the error carefully and resolve never to commit it again. Bear in mind, as you proceed, that coming events are usually anticipated or discounted by major interests and the insiders. When, in the face of bad news on a particular issue, formations indicative of accumulation develop, despite such adverse news, it is wiser for you to follow the insiders than to pay attention to the news, which may have been deliberately released in order to cause the uninformed to dispose of their stocks at a low level.

ONE POINT CHARTS SHOW ALL

The one point figure changes, as they register on your charts, reflect all of the buying and selling. When such price changes have completed the pattern, the picture thus formed is the best sort of inside information, since it may be indicative of an impending up move or down move, as the case may be. When your three point charts confirm the conclusions reached by a study of your one point charts, you will then have corroborative proof, and your judgment is thereupon confirmed. Should the implications of your one point charts be confirmed by the three point and also by the five point charts of the same stock, then you may consider your knowledge absolute and definite, and you must act accordingly.

Be ever alert and study at all times. Remember, the patterns which are traced on your charts result from the action of individuals. Your chart discloses the balance of all influences. It tells you what is taking place and when to prepare for the move as well as how to take advantage of that information.

4

THE VITAL POINTS

- Vital point I – recording full figure changes
- Vital point II – only full figure changes
- Vital point III – suitable graph paper
- Vital point IV – use of horizontal and vertical columns
- Vital point V – trend reversals
- Vital point VI – only one symbol to a square
- Vital point VII – move over diagonally
- Vital point VIII – skip no squares
- Vital point IX – formation of congestion area
- Vital point X – the full fulcrum
- Vital point XI – first buying point
- Vital point XII – the catapult
- Vital point XIII – secondary buying point
- Vital point XIV – the semi-catapult
- Vital point XV – third buying point
- Vital point XVI – watch for distribution
- Vital point XVII – trend lines
- Vital point XVIII – forecasting the extent of the move

The one point price fluctuations are the starting base of this reliable and time tried Method of anticipating stock price movements. For the purpose of clarifying the basic principles, we reiterate and codify these principles so as to avoid any possibility of doubt or question.

The Vital Points underlying the Point and Figure Method are as follows:

I   *Record all full figure fluctuations* registered on the tape.

II   Plot these changes on suitable graph paper through the use of symbols representing the full figure changes.

III   Make no record of a transaction unless a *flat full figure* change has actually been registered.

IV   Use horizontal columns for specific price levels and vertical columns for price movements continuing in the same direction.

V   When a reversal of the price movement develops, move over to the first right-hand column and plot the subsequent changes of prices.

VI   A square already occupied by a symbol cannot again be used to accommodate another.

VII   A move to the next right-hand vertical column must be in a diagonal direction, either one square higher or one square lower than the last recorded full figure.

VIII   No square may be skipped; the pattern traced must be a continuous joining of squares.

IX   Be alert to recognize and observe the formations known as congestion areas.

X   Analyze congestion areas in order to properly take advantage of a developing full fulcrum.

XI   Make commitment near base of a full fulcrum with a stop just below lowest point of support.

XII   Watch for the development of the full catapult point.

XIII   Make commitment at the catapult point with a stop close below.

XIV   Watch for the development of the semi-catapult.

XV   Make commitment at the semi-catapult point with a stop close below.

XVI   After an extended advance, be on the alert for first signs of distribution.

XVII   Learn the technique of the use of trend lines.

XVIII   Study and master the principle of the Count to gauge the extent of future moves.

VITAL POINT I – RECORDING FULL FIGURE CHANGES

We have set forth as Vital Point I the fact that we must record *all full figure fluctuations* which have registered on the tape. Many persons, after a casual study of the Point and Figure Method, may reach the conclusion that Point and Figure Charts prepared from newspaper data, that is the opening, the high, the low, and the close which are published daily in financial sections of newspapers, are sufficient from which to gather the full figure changes necessary to prepare our one point charts. However, this is not the case. One is not able to obtain *all* of the full figure changes from newspaper quotations. All full figure changes are necessary because only by recording *all* of them are we able to develop the proper congestion areas, which, in turn, show full fulcrums and subsequent catapult and semi-catapult formations.

There is little advantage to the study and use of this Method unless you make records of *all* full figure fluctuations. Furthermore, it is absolutely essential to record all of the full figure changes if we are to depend upon the count method for the purpose of anticipating the extent and probable culminating point of the next move. The technical terms used herein are more fully explained in subsequent chapters of this work.

While it may be truthfully stated that some of the low priced stocks do not fluctuate a full point during the day, and, therefore, the needed data could be obtained from the newspaper, it must be emphasized that even though we be interested in a low priced stock which does not fluctuate actively during a trading day, we must plot the movement of the active stocks in order to get the pulse of the market and thus be able to judge the trend and turning points. Even in low priced stocks, it is difficult to get an accurate analysis of all full figure changes unless one has access to the tape so as to know whether the high or low was first established and their exact relationship to the close.

VITAL POINT II – ONLY FULL FIGURE CHANGES

No transaction is recorded on our charts unless it be a flat, full figure change to the flat full figure above or below the last recorded price. A stock may fluctuate seven-eighths points above its last recorded figure, and seven-eighths points below, giving it a total fluctuating band of one and seven-eighths points, before we enter a new change on our graphic records.

VITAL POINT III – SUITABLE GRAPH PAPER

Graphs or charts, whichever you choose to call them, are absolutely essential to this Method. These condensed pictorial representations of the course of the price movement with its oscillations, its advances and declines, are absolutely essential to a scientific study of stock price movements. Charts may be made on any kind of paper which is suitably ruled for the purpose. We especially recommend Ideal Charting Sheets for Point and Figure Charts, because they have been carefully designed in order to facilitate the preparation of the charts and permit instantaneous analysis after the records have been completed.

VITAL POINT IV – USE OF HORIZONTAL AND VERTICAL COLUMNS

The recommended graph paper for use with this Method is laid out in columns of squares vertically and horizontally arranged similar to a checker board. The lines dividing the vertical divisions are all of uniform thickness. These vertical columns are used for containing the price movement as they continue in the same direction. The horizontal columns of squares are used to represent specific price levels. The lines dividing the horizontal columns vary in their thickness, for we accentuate the columns for the "5's" and heavily accentuate the columns for the "10's." The plan for accentuating the "5" and "10" squares is very helpful for swift recording and quick analysis. In addition, this especially designed paper has silhouetted figures representing the "0's" and "5's," which facilitate quick placement of these particular price levels on the page.

VITAL POINT V – TREND REVERSALS

Vertical columns are used to include the price movements in one direction, up or down, until a reversal develops. When a reversal does develop and we require a symbol to be placed in a square that is already occupied, it is necessary for us to move over to the next immediate adjoining right-hand column. After the first figure is recorded in a new column, we may proceed either upward or downward from that point, but not both. We must be especially careful to note that in every case we must have more than one symbol in a vertical column.

VITAL POINT VI – ONLY ONE SYMBOL TO A SQUARE

Since no square can be used twice, it is essential that upon reversal of the trend of the stock price movement we move over to the next right-hand column. Each

Fig 4.1 XYZ: one point chart

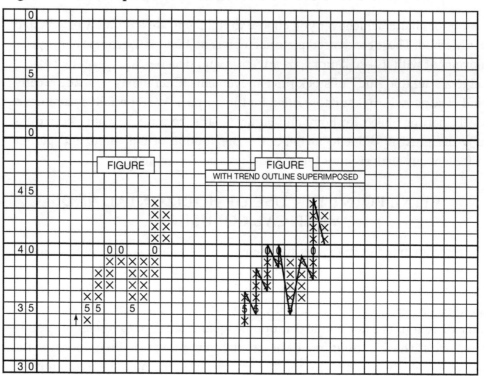

reversal in trend which calls for an "x" to be placed in a square already occupied requires that we move over to the next right-hand column. In cases where a reversal requires only a one point change, after which the trend is again established in the previous direction, it is not necessary to move over to the next column, for the change in trend would require a plotting in a square above or below the first one used in the new column. This square, above or below, being empty, we proceed to plot our next symbols. Thus, you will see that in no case can we have only one "x" in a vertical column.

To cite an example, let us analyze the move in XYZ, Figure 4.1. We start plotting the action of this stock at full figure 34, and indicate an upward move to full figure 36. After 36, a reversal to 35 is required, but since the 35 square is already occupied, we move over diagonally, (never horizontally) to the next right hand vertical column. Now the up move is again established and we continue in the same column plotting our symbols above the 5, first figure recorded in the new vertical column group.

A similar situation develops on the reaction from 38, back to 37, from the second column in use to the third column. Another like example occurs on the one point reaction from the first full figure 40, down to the second 39. Now we come to a difference which develops after the stock rallies from 39, to 40. A sharp subsequent reaction develops and carries back down to 35. Here you see how in one instance a one point change moves over to the first right-hand column, while another one point change continues in the same column with subsequent changes again moving over to the next right-hand column.

This is one of the most important principles to be carefully observed in preparing your Point and Figure Charts. Study it carefully and know it thoroughly before you proceed with the work. Unless you thoroughly understand the principles of making these important one point records, you cannot hope to correctly analyze formations which are developed. You cannot hope to arrive at proper and reliable conclusions if you base analysis and deductions on incorrectly prepared data.

VITAL POINT VII – MOVE OVER DIAGONALLY

This point needs very little further explanation, for it is carefully indicated for you on illustrations throughout the book and fully detailed in our previous paragraph.

VITAL POINT VIII – SKIP NO SQUARES

In the progression of symbols across our graph paper, no square may be skipped. The pattern traced must be a continuous joining of squares of those above, below or adjacent to the diagonal corners. It is only through the proper development of the price path patterns that the important zones of accumulation and distribution will become recognizable. Moreover, trend lines cannot be accurately plotted unless the patterns are likewise accurate and symmetrical.

VITAL POINT IX – FORMATION OF CONGESTION AREA

The most important pattern that will develop on your charts is that which is known as the congestion area. It represents what is technically known as a trading range and shows the struggle between the forces of supply and demand, either at the bottom of the move where accumulation is being completed or at the top of the move where distribution is taking place. At intervening points on the rallies and declines, congestion areas of minor significance form as a result of temporary consolidation. You will soon learn to recognize the importance of the several different types of congestion areas which are formed on your charts.

VITAL POINT X – THE FULL FULCRUM

The most important congestion area to form on your charts will be the full fulcrum. A full fulcrum congestion area develops after an extended down move when the forces of demand overcome the forces of supply and a base is formed, followed by two or more attempts to rally. The first indication of strength occurs after accumulation begins at the bottom, when a sharp upmove develops and subsequently fails with a recession to the previous support point or to a point slightly above the previous support level. Here, after a little backing and filling, the stock develops technical strength and a new rally carries it higher than the last previous high point, at which point, a full catapult develops.

VITAL POINT XI – FIRST BUYING POINT

When you are sure that a full fulcrum is in the process of formation, it is wise to make a commitment as near to the base of the congestion area as is possible, with a stop placed just below the lowest point of support. This is the best place to establish your long position, for here you have the opportunity of gaining the greatest number of points advance with the least possible risk, limited through the employment of a "stop order."

VITAL POINT XII – THE CATAPULT

The second important place to establish your long position "on stop" is the full catapult point. The law of probability strongly points to the fact that you will quickly see profits after establishing your position at this point. The true full catapult which develops after a full fulcrum has been completed, normally shows from 3 to 6 points profit before a technical correction registers a paper loss on your position. The "stop" used to protect this long position should be placed one point below half way between the low of the base in the fulcrum and the full catapult point.

VITAL POINT XIII – SECONDARY BUYING POINT

Never fail to take advantage of every full catapult as it develops on your chart. Occasionally you may err and suffer temporary paper loss, but in the vast majority of cases, the full catapult point always develops quick profits for a position established there, especially at the inception of an intermediate or main uptrend following a protracted period of declining prices.

VITAL POINT XIV – THE SEMI-CATAPULT

The semi-catapult is somewhat similar to the full catapult with the exception that it develops during the advance. After a stock moves off the base known as a full fulcrum and an extended move is in progress, it hesitates and forms temporary congestion areas on the way up. These small congestion areas, usually resulting from minor technical reactions during the advance, create semi-catapult positions as soon as the strength in the stock registers a new high price over the high previously established before the technical reaction.

VITAL POINT XV – THIRD BUYING POINT

Make a long commitment at the semi-catapult point each time it develops. Protect this position with a "stop order" placed just below the lowest point established on the technical reaction preceding the semi-catapult figure. You may occasionally lose one or more of these positions and suffer the loss of a point or two between the semi-catapult price and your stop order. However, your losses will be limited while your chances for profits are far in excess of the probability of loss. Profits will accrue to this position in more than six out of ten times established, which profits should be far in excess of losses, especially if the "stop order" suggestion is followed.

VITAL POINT XVI – WATCH FOR DISTRIBUTION

After an extended advance, be on the alert for the first signs of distribution. A trading range or congestion area which is built up after a sharp advance in price will be the point for you to watch for first signs of distribution. Use a "stop order" if you are in doubt; or sell on strength soon after you have recognized the beginning of distribution. Technical aids for determining signs of distribution will be found in Volume 2 entitled *Advanced Theory and Practice of the Point and Figure Method*.

VITAL POINT XVII – TREND LINES

Trend lines are helpful technical aids to use in conjunction with your Point and Figure Chart. The technique of the use of trend lines is fully described in the advanced book prepared for students who have already mastered the principles outlined in this book.

VITAL POINT XVIII – FORECASTING THE EXTENT OF THE MOVE

The "count" principle of gauging the extent of future movements can be applied by those who have thoroughly mastered the elementary technique of the Point and Figure Method. Through the use of certain well established scientific principles, your Point and Figure Charts will show the probable culmination point of the next move. The system of the "count" is highly technical in its character and fully described in the Advanced Theory of this Method.

5

APPROVED METHOD OF ASSEMBLING AND MAINTAINING PROPER DATA

- The ticker tape
- Source of all data
- Daily full figure fluctuations available
- Method ideal for those at distant points
- Application of the data
- How to prepare and collate the needed data
- Proper graph paper helpful
- Arrange charts orderly
- How to select the issues to record
- Clarifying the use of the symbols
- Moving to next vertical column
- Use of symbol "0"
- One cardinal principle
- Gaps are not recorded
- How the gap occurs
- Plotting the gap
- The one point chart
- The three point and five point charts
- Condensing the one point moves
- Other helpful aids
- The method substitutes for tape reading
- Trend outline and geometrical charts
- The proper issues to chart
- Commodity price movements

We have made clear to you the fact that this time tried Method depends for its accuracy upon a radical and entirely different principle. Price changes, that is the fluctuations in the price of a stock, are more important as the basis upon which to judge its technical condition than are either volume or price range. Price range is the zone between the high and the low which the stock registers each day.

A carefully compiled transcription of these price changes will point the way to more consistent and greater profits, with less guesswork and more confidence in your market commitments.

Before we begin to make the chart, it is most important that we obtain the exact price changes in the order in which they occur, and that we be certain of the source of our data. It is vital and most important to the proper application of this Method that we obtain *all* of the price changes and plot them *all*. The most vital signals given by this Method are those occurring in the trading ranges, the congestion areas, either at the termination of moves at bottoms and tops, or in the consolidation areas, during the advance or decline.

A trading range is the zone in which a stock backs and fills, i.e. fluctuates above the level of support where sufficient buying is encountered to absorb all offerings and the resistance level above where the demand is unable to absorb the supply. A trading range is sometimes called a "line movement" especially when it is used to describe this action on the part of a market index. In the latter case it shows the base, that level at which sufficient capital is available and desirous of being exchanged for stock, and the resistance level above where the holders of stock desire to exchange their equities for cash.

It, therefore, becomes evident and is of vital importance that all fluctuations be obtained from reliable sources and that they be carefully recorded in the order in which they occur.

THE TICKER TAPE

Many years ago, Stock Exchange authorities recognized the importance of creating and preserving actual records of all transactions as they occur on the floor of the Stock Exchange. It was then that the ticker tape, as we know it today, was conceived. In the beginning, the records were crude, but as the market broadened in the number of corporate issues traded and this country grew in wealth and importance, the ticker became more highly developed, so that now it is capable of high speed, and the price fluctuations are printed almost as quickly as they occur. It is only on rare occasions that the new, high speed ticker lags, a few minutes at most, behind the actual transactions.

SOURCE OF ALL DATA

The ticker tape is the official Stock Exchange record of all transactions, and it automatically becomes the source of all data for this or any other method of anticipating stock price movements. Whether you are guided by vertical line bar charts, by moving averages, by statistical information, business conditions, or by the actual technical condition of the stock itself, the source of all information as to the price, the range, the daily closing, daily, weekly, monthly, or yearly, high and low prices, or actual price fluctuations, the ticker tape is the original source of all information. All errors which occur in the recording of the transactions effected on the floor of the New York Stock Exchange are quickly corrected on the tape, sometimes within a minute or two after the error occurs. The ticker tape, therefore, is considered the very best source from which to get the price fluctuations so vitally necessary to the use of the Point and Figure Method.

DAILY FULL FIGURE FLUCTUATIONS AVAILABLE

It is not necessary for you to be in your broker's office in order to procure all of the full figure fluctuations. The publishers of this book provide that service, and it is published daily. In order to insure the accuracy of the information, they have a trained and skilled staff of men who read closely all transactions on the ticker tape.

Each morning, the previous day's changes are carefully checked against data supplied by the Stock Exchange blue sheet and the three most reliable daily financial publications. Errors, if any occur, are carefully noted by the service on the succeeding day in a special errata column.

In the less volatile issues it is possible to approximate the full figure changes from the stock market quotations as published in your daily newspaper. Price fluctuations compiled from newspaper openings, highs, lows, and closes, are not nearly as dependable as the information garnered directly from the tape. In one case, you are assured of all full figure fluctuations, while in the other, a great number of full point changes may be missed. This is vital and important because as you proceed with your work, you will soon realize that complete campaigns of accumulation and distribution can be effectuated in one, two or three market days. As a general rule, Point and Figure Charts compiled from newspaper quotations will rarely show a complete fulcrum, catapult or semi-catapult formation. These formations will develop when you plot *all* of the full figure fluctuations.

Just as a house cannot be built unless a foundation or base is first laid, so a stock cannot rally to any degree, as a general rule, without first creating a congestion area or base from which to advance. Therefore, you must realize that in order to have fullest advantage from your knowledge of the Point and Figure Method it is absolutely essential that you record all of the full figure fluctuations.

METHOD IDEAL FOR THOSE AT DISTANT POINTS

For students and observers at distant points, this Method offers a splendid opportunity for observation and study. Even though your "Full Figure Daily Data" may be three or four days late in arriving, your charts will always tell the story in ample time for you to have fullest advantage of moves as they develop.

If you are a great distance from New York City and cannot get the accurate full figure changes, we suggest the following procedure. Obtain from your brokerage office, customers man or daily newspaper, your tentative full figure fluctuations, and enter them on your charts by making pencil dots in the squares representing the temporary and estimated changes. A day or two later when you receive your accurate full figure changes, carry forward your chart in ink. Thus, you will have the opportunity of being right up to the minute on the few stocks in which you may have a commitment, and when authentic figures arrive, you are assured of having the correct changes for inking in your graphic records for future reference and study.

APPLICATION OF THE DATA

After you are certain that you are obtaining all of the authentic full figure fluctuations, it is well for you to form the habit of recording the changes each day. It is best to maintain charts of at least fifty, and if possible, one hundred active stocks, as well as of the following averages, namely, the Dow Jones Industrials, the Dow Jones Rails, the Dow Jones Utilities and the New York Herald Tribune Index of 100 Stocks.

A one half point chart compiled from figures representing the half hourly running line of the Dow Jones Industrial Averages is also very informative of the nearby minor swings. Elsewhere in the book, we supply full detailed explanations of this half point, half hourly running line index.

For the sake of emphasis and clarity and in order to give the student a proper start, we describe, hereunder, the different types of charts which may be built up from the basic data, namely, the one point figure changes.

HOW TO PREPARE AND COLLATE THE NEEDED DATA

It is of vital importance that you keep all the needed data in a uniform, neat, and compact arrangement. The authors have devoted serious thought to this problem and the publishers have designed a series of special charting papers which are ideal for the purpose.

PROPER GRAPH PAPER HELPFUL

We recommend and use, exclusively, "Ideal" charting sheets #5001, printed on white paper, for our one point charts; #5003, printed on buff paper, for our three point charts; and #5005, printed on blue tinted paper for our five point charts. No. 5001.5, our half point paper, is especially recommended for fractional Point and Figure Charts. Nos. 5001, 5003, and 5005, are printed on good quality rag stock, 8½ × 11, and are perforated for the conventional three-ring binder. These sheets are convenient to inspect, easy to remove, and ideal for the purpose of study and comparison. The ruling, especially designed, presents a simple arrangement for the digit, cyphers and full figure fives.

The sheet is so laid out that it may be read at a glance with the minimum probability of error. The price level is quickly realized, so that in going through your binders of charts, your attention can be concentrated on a study of technical conditions rather than on irrelevant details.

All of the charts reproduced in this book were drafted on these special "Ideal" charting sheets. The sheets are printed in a special color of ink which permits you to make your charts in pencil or in ink. When using pencil, the special color of the background graph lines permits the pattern to stand out in contrast to that background, even though you use a hard #3 pencil, which permits the plotting to be made without smudging, as is sometimes the case when a softer pencil is used.

As you progress with your work, you will soon be able to keep a graphic record of the movements of 100 stocks and five averages within the one half hour period.

ARRANGE CHARTS ORDERLY

The charts kept in your loose leaf binder should be segregated into one, three, and five point groups. Since the sheets are printed on different colored paper stock, one may easily differentiate them and quickly select the desired chart. The arrangements within the binder may be altered in accordance with your personal preference. We have found it more convenient to group the charts in alphabetical order according to the name of the stock. In this way, comparisons and daily changes are made quickly and easily.

One need not feel that the pressure of other affairs will prevent one from mastering this Method. Primary records, the one and three point charts, can be kept and maintained by any clerk or stenographer. Any intelligent assistant, after a little preliminary study of the principles of this Method, can keep all the needed data and pass on the finished work for study and analysis.

HOW TO SELECT THE ISSUES TO RECORD

In selecting your group of stocks, it is well to include a minimum of fifty of the most actively traded issues. Whether or not you intend to trade in any or all of these stocks is of no consequence. In addition to the individual issues which it is important for you to keep, it is wise to record the movements of at least three or four of the important popular averages. We suggest the Dow Jones 30 Industrials, the Dow Jones 20 Rails, the Dow Jones 20 Utilities and the New York Herald Tribune Averages. The Dow Jones Averages are shown and quoted wherever American stocks are traded in. The Herald Tribune Average is a weighted index of 100 stocks and a better, truer, and more ideal cross section of the market as a whole. It is less volatile and more dependable due to the fact that it is not easily manipulated.

In addition to the four indexes suggested above, your authors keep and observe a one half point chart of the Dow Jones 30 Industrials, calculated on a half hourly interval. The running line half point half hourly index is a very helpful aid in determining the short swing trends and their terminations.

While at first glance it may appear that the necessary data herein before outlined will cause an insurmountable amount of work, nevertheless, we want to call your attention to the important fact that the greatest losses in the stock market were occasioned by hasty judgment, want of incentives, and lack of knowledge of actual market action.

Investment and trading is a serious matter. If you desire to succeed and take profits from the stock market, you must expect to work and study. The work is interesting, the necessary materials inexpensive, and the compensation far in excess of the value of the effort and time consumed.

If you want to have the greatest benefit from your knowledge of this time tried Method, we urge you, once more, to keep and maintain the one point moves in

100 stocks and five averages and the three point moves for the same group. Five point charts, which were mentioned before, are not absolutely essential. They are helpful and can be used for the important indices in order to aid in judging the main trend, and as condensation charts for the more volatile issues.

CLARIFYING THE USE OF THE SYMBOLS

Recording these price movements, as we have already explained, is done through the use of three simple symbols, "x," "5," and "0." The symbol "x," stands for any full figure which does not include a five or a cypher. Therefore, the symbol "x" may stand for the digits one to four, six to nine, eleven to fourteen, sixteen to nineteen, and so forth and so on. The symbol "5" represents all the multiples of five, such as five, fifteen, twenty-five, thirty-five, etc. Note here, that the figure "5" is used only where the figure ends in five and not when it ends in zero. The symbol "0" is used to represent all multiples of ten in the progression of the price movement, 10, 20, 30, 40, 50, 60, 70, etc.

Examine, now, one or more of the charts included in this book in order to get a better and clearer understanding of the use of these symbols. Charts show in clear and simple manner how to use the "x," the "5," and the "0," in their proper places in the price progression and the pattern formation which it creates.

Examine Figure 4.1, headed "XYZ: one point chart." Note how we have illustrated the use of all three of the symbols. The first and lowest "x" represents the full figure 34. The first figure, "5," immediately above the first "x," represents the full figure 35 and indicates a progression in an upward direction from 34, to 35, as the stock moves upward. The "x" above the first single figure "5" stands for 36. This shows a move of two points from full figure 34, to full figure 36, or a move to 36⅞, which would be the fullest extent of an upward move represented by an "x" in the 36 square. The second full figure "5," indicated in the next right-hand column, again represents the price progression and a reversal of the former trend.

MOVING TO NEXT VERTICAL COLUMN

Note, here, one of the most important principles in plotting the price movements by the Point and Figure Method. When the trend direction of a stock changes and the required square is already occupied by a symbol, it is necessary to move over to the next adjacent right-hand column. This is very important and one of the principal stumbling blocks which may give you trouble if you do not thoroughly understand it. The chart of "XYZ" at this point indicates a move in a downward direction, from the previous 36 full figure or 36 and a fraction, to the full figure 35 or 34 and fractions above the flat full figure 34.

After plotting the symbol in the 35 square, the trend again changes, and the price movement progresses in an upward direction. The next full figure required is a 36. Since the 36 square is open, we may plot this by recording our "x" just above the "35" most recently recorded. The move then continues in an upward direction registering 37 and 38, before a reversal takes place. Thereafter, we are required to indicate a downward move to 37 or fractionally lower, and since the 37 square in the column is already occupied, we are required to move over to the first right-hand column. Again the trend changes. Now we require a 38 indication, and the symbol "x" is placed in the square just above the 37 most recently recorded.

USE OF SYMBOL "0"

The move continues upward, 39, and full figure 40, is registered. Here we have the first opportunity of using the symbol zero. "0," then, is placed in the square above the 39, on the 40 horizontal line. Thereafter, a down move to full figure 39 is recorded and we find it necessary to move over to the next right-hand column, because the 39 square is already occupied. The stock then rallies to 40, and we plot the 40 above the 39 already recorded. A sharp down move follows, and the stock registers full figure 35, before a change in trend takes place. This requires symbols to be placed in the 39, 38, 37, 36, and 35 squares. Since the 39 square is already occupied, we move over one vertical column to the right and indicate the down move to full figure 35. The stock then rallies to 39, requiring symbols in the 36, 37, 38, and 39 squares in the next adjacent right-hand column. Now a one point reversal is recorded, requiring us to move over to the next adjacent vertical right-hand column where we plot an "x" in the 38 square. The stock then rallies sharply, making full figure 44, and we proceed with our recording, placing an "x" in the 39, "0" in the 40 square, "x" in 41, 42, 43, and 44 squares. Now a reversal takes place, and the stock sells off making the full figure 41. Again we are required to move over to the next right-hand column in order that we may record our "x" in the square for 44, and we carry to 43, 42, and 41, terminating the move as indicated.

In order to make it clear for you, we have designated the direction of the move by showing a black line superimposed over our symbols on this illustration. Note that we have used the symbol "x" to indicate the prices 34, 36, 37, 38, 39, 41, 42, 43, and 44. The symbol "5" indicates the price 35, and the symbol "0" indicates the price 40, in recording the full figure changes.

When we commence to plot the movement of a stock with the full figure 34, no change is made until either full figure 35 or full figure 33 is registered on the tape. Thus, should the stock go down from 34 to 33⅛, no change on our records would be made. Similarly, a move upward to 34⅞ would be disregarded. You see, therefore, that a stock may fluctuate 1⅞ points without requiring any change on our Point and Figure data.

ONE CARDINAL PRINCIPLE

Fractional fluctuations are disregarded unless a new flat full figure is completed. We urge you to trace carefully, again, the move in XYZ by one point fluctuations as illustrated in Figure 4.1. Note the fact that fractional fluctuations are completely disregarded. A move which fails to record a new flat full figure is considered of no importance and, therefore, not taken cognizance of.

GAPS ARE NOT RECORDED

Since vertical line bar charts have come into wider vogue, several technicians have laid down certain principles based upon the phenomena known as gaps. Gaps on a bar chart are created as a result of a thin market and occur (1) when the high of a day is lower than the low of the preceding day, and (2) when the low of a day is higher than the high of the succeeding day. Thus, you see, one gap is created by strength which leaves an opening between the low of the new day and the high of the previous day, and the other by weakness, which leaves a gap between the low of the preceding day and the high point made after the weakness developed.

In vertical line technique, commentators have noted that gaps created by a thin or unusual market are, as a rule and in the majority of instances, closed over sooner or later by subsequent market action. The principle of gaps and their subsequent closings is not to be relied upon in all instances. While it is customary for gaps to close shortly after they are left by market action, it is not a fixed rule, and cannot be thoroughly relied upon. Gaps exist in many issues, both above and below present market action. In rare cases, some take years before subsequent action will close the gap.

The Point and Figure Method completely disregards the gap phenomenon and its theory. Since we are interested in price fluctuations and the recorded trail of the price path, the mere fact that no transaction takes place at any particular point in that path is of little consequence and is not taken into consideration.

HOW THE GAP OCCURS

Let us illustrate and show you an actual example of how the Point and Figure Method provides for gaps in the price track of a price movement. Let us assume, for instance, in XYZ, that full figure 38, recorded at the bottom of the fifth rally when the stock moves down from full figure 39 to full figure 38, represents the closing at a particular day, and that overnight some bullish news is released unexpectedly and a sudden demand is created for the stock of the XYZ company. A news item such as "XYZ dividend rate raised from $2 to $4" might create such a situation.

Let us suppose that some trader wishes to buy one thousand shares quickly believing that subsequent market action will show good profit for a new position established at this point. He places an order with his broker to buy 1,000 shares of XYZ, "at the market." The quotation on XYZ, is: "38½ bid, offered at 40."

The block of shares offered at 40 is only 200, and, therefore, the broker must take 200 at 40, 100 at 40¼, 100 at 40¾, 300 at 41, 100 at 41⅛, and 200 at 41¾. This transaction on the tape would appear as follows:

```
XYZ
2s40–40¼–40¾–3s41–41⅛–2s41¾
```

With the previous close having been registered at 38, these transactions shown on the tape would require the following changes in our graph:

PLOTTING THE GAP

Following the 38 in the vertical column and above, an "x," would be plotted in 39, even though no transaction appeared between the previous 38 and the opening 40. The next symbol recorded would be the zero in the 40 square, and then the "x" in the 41 square, representing transactions up to and including the 200 shares sold at 41¾.

Subsequent action of XYZ for the rest of the day included a continuation of the strength up to 44⅝, followed by a reaction to 41.0 where the stock closed. That action on the tape would be illustrated by a continuation of plotting "x's" in the vertical column up to and including the "x" representing the figure 44, and then the reversal of the trend showing the "x" in 43 moving over to the next right-hand column, then 42, and finally 41, where the stock closed.

Thus, you see, in order to develop the proper technique for creating reliable patterns on our Point and Figure Charts, we disregard the theory of gaps since it has no influence on our conclusions.

THE ONE POINT CHART

Since all conclusions and subsequent records are compiled from your one point charts, it is the best policy to keep them with greatest care. One point charts should be made in the simplest manner possible and by means of the "x," "5," and "0", symbols hereinbefore described.

While any square ruled paper may be used for this purpose, it is better to use the specially designed paper which is available for this purpose and which will permit the accurate plotting of trend lines and the quick recognition of the 5 and 10 levels, as well as the full fulcrum, the catapult, and semi-catapult as they develop.

In order to get a better and clearer conception of market action, it is advisable also to compile a substantial quota of charts and keep them up to date, since a comparison of the patterns formed on the individual charts will enable you better to judge the important trends and the vital turning points. No matter what your plans may be, whether you trade for the shorter swings or invest for the longer pull, you will require these one point charts. No reliable analysis of technical condition can be made without them.

It is from the one point charts that we are able to recognize zones of accumulation, the beginning of the mark-up, the vital points at which to place long positions, the critical points at which stop orders should be placed, and, finally, indications of distribution.

THE THREE POINT AND FIVE POINT CHARTS

In addition to these one point charts, we will require, as a check on our work, three point charts of the same stocks and averages which we have plotted by one point moves. Three point charts are a resume of the action and are compiled solely from the moves indicated on your one point records. These three point charts enable you to keep a clear picture of the intermediate swings of most stocks. They give a true basis for analysis of the more volatile issues.

CONDENSING THE ONE POINT MOVES

Three point charts eliminate minor technical fluctuations and show the broader congestion areas. In making your three point chart, you must always remember that your one point records must show a move of not less than three points in the opposite direction before it is recorded on your three point condensation chart.

For example: We start with the figure 40. Your one point chart must show a move to the figure 43, before any record whatsoever is made on your three point chart. This move from 40, to 43, would be plotted on your three point chart in the same manner as it is plotted on your one point chart. From 43, before we could plot a reversal on the three point chart, your stock must register a reaction to 40, or lower. However, should it react to 42, or 41, no change would be made on the three point chart. Now, in minor technical reactions to 42, or 41, followed by a subsequent rally, which would go above the previous 43, the move would be plotted by one point moves in the same column on your three point chart as the price advances above 43. Let us say, for example, that the stock rallies to 47, without a full three point reversal from 43. The added figures on your three point chart would be 44, 45, 46, and 47. Thus, you see that your three point chart will show a straight run from 40, to 47, with no other indications recorded. Temporary declines of less than three points are ignored on this chart, and continued subsequent advances above the previous high prices, should they occur, are carried forward by one point registrations in the same column. Three point charts are plotted only of trend reversals which are three or more points in extent. In all other respects, your three point charts are made in the same manner as are your one point charts.

The five point charts condense the price changes to moves of five points or more but not less. They are helpful in connection with the indices when prices fluctuate broadly and when they register in the higher price ranges, such as was witnessed in 1929. Five point charts are also very helpful in that they simplify the interpretation of the wider moving highly volatile stocks. Issues which advance or decline thirty to fifty points in a single intermediate market cycle must be plotted by five point moves, since these charts give the most dependable and satisfactory presentation of the technical condition of the issue. Five point charts are also helpful for the determination of the main and long term trends. They condense the time factor and show long term accumulation and distribution, thus indicating the trend or movement of capital as it comes into variable equities – common stocks – near the bottom of a bear market, and as it moves out of variable equities into bonds or other forms of wealth, at or near the top of a bull market. Five point charts are not necessary for all stocks and need only be kept of the highly volatile issues and the market indices.

The technique of preparing five point charts is exactly the same as that of preparing three point charts with the exception that it requires a reversal in trend direction of five or more points before that reversal is plotted. Continuations of direction of trend are plotted by one point moves until a full five point reversal is recorded on your one point chart.

OTHER HELPFUL AIDS

The three types of charts enumerated above may be considered the foundation and scientific keystone upon which this Method is based. In addition, it is sometimes advantageous to make half point charts of complete half point movements in low priced stocks which do not fluctuate sufficiently by full one point moves to give a satisfactory record on one point charts. Furthermore, half point charts are helpful in plotting the Dow Jones Industrial Index on an hourly, as well as on a half hourly basis.

THE METHOD SUBSTITUTES FOR TAPE READING

The half point charts are very helpful for many purposes. They permit the exponents of this Method to entirely eliminate from their operations the need for watching the tape. Under present day market conditions, half point charts of individual stocks, as well as half hourly changes, of the Dow Jones Industrial Index comprise a better and far more reliable basis for judgment than can be had from tape reading. Half point and quarter point charts are more sensitive and give an understandable basis for a detailed record which is vastly superior to the memory of any human being.

A running line of the Dow Jones Industrial Index, compiled on a half hourly basis, is very helpful as an aid in determining the narrow swings of the market. The running line index will be fully explained elsewhere in this work. In plotting commodities, it is sometimes helpful to compile your charts on the basis of quarter point moves or half point moves, as the occasion requires. In some instances, when the commodity prices fluctuate in money values as expressed in units and tens, our primary data charts can be made of each tenth penny fluctuation. Since we ignore fractions when making our one point primary charts, we would ignore fractions between the full figure and the half figure in making half point charts. Quarter point charts would be made by ignoring all one-eighth point moves.

We urge you, when making your Point and Figure Charts, to be sure to get all of the fluctuations.

TREND OUTLINE AND GEOMETRICAL CHARTS

Students and observers who are beginning to recognize the importance of a sound knowledge of stock market technique will find the trend outline and geometrical charts exceedingly helpful. Though not absolutely essential in the application of this Method, they are easy to read and very helpful. Geometrical charts are especially helpful since they show the trading range congestion areas and manipulation. They are also of great assistance to those who wish to use "stop orders," for the reason that a clear picture of the trading range limitations is always indicated.

Trend outline charts are made by merely joining the tops and bottoms, the extremes of the moves, with a diagonal line. They are illustrated in Figures 4.1 and 5.1. These charts differ from vertical line charts and are sometimes used by vertical line technicians as a condensation of the conventional vertical line charts. They enable one to eliminate the time factor and show the important swings of prices – the trend of speculation.

The geometrical chart is made by plotting the extremes of moves with horizontal lines and joining these horizontal lines by vertical lines, thus creating a geometrical pattern. (See Figure 5.2.)

Both geometrical and trend outline charts may be superimposed upon your one, three and five point charts by plotting the trend outline or the geometrical

Fig 5.1   XYZ: one point trend outline

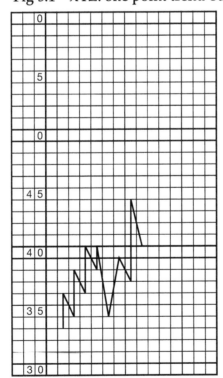

Fig 5.2   XYZ: one point geometric

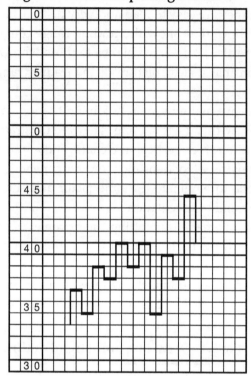

pattern over your symbols either in ink, or in crayon of different color from that which you use for the purpose of recording your basic data.

THE PROPER ISSUES TO CHART

When preparing a set of charts, it is natural and wise to plot the foremost market leaders. From time to time, market leadership will change. Therefore, as one group or one issue loses its popular investment or speculative following, it will be necessary to start charts on the new leaders. The following issues are suggested, at this time, as a good grouping, and, if carefully compiled and analyzed day by day, will guide the student and observer to a proper and prompt recognition of the vital turning points in the market:

Air Reduction
Allied Chemical
American Can
American Smelting
American Sugar Refining

American Telephone
American Tobacco "B"
Atchison
Auburn Automobile
Case Threshing Machine
Celanese
Consolidated Gas
Dome Mines
DuPont
General Motors
International Harvester
National Biscuit
New York Central
Sears Roebuck
Standard Oil of N.J.
Union Pacific
U.S. Industrial Alcohol
U.S. Steel
Western Union
Woolworth

No two technicians would select or agree upon the same list of leaders; therefore, we leave it to your individual selection to plot and record those issues which suit you best. However, keep a broad group so that the influence of their united action, both from the investment and speculative angles, will guide you in the recognition of important zones of accumulation, the trend of the market, as well as the zones of distribution.

COMMODITY PRICE MOVEMENTS

In a subsequent volume, the authors of this book will show in full detail, application of the Point and Figure Method to the analysis of commodity price movements. The Point and Figure Method has been used successfully as an aid in anticipating the future price movements of wheat, cotton, corn, grain, silver, and any other basic commodity dealt in on any Exchange where a free and open market exists and price change fluctuations are carefully and accurately recorded.

As the work applying to commodities is more highly technical and more advanced, this subject cannot be discussed now. Those desiring to use the Point and Figure Method for the purpose of anticipating commodity price movements should and must master thoroughly all of the principles explained in this work as well as in the book *Advanced Theory and Practice of The Point and Figure Method*.

6

THE SCIENTIFIC FUNDAMENTALS

- The fulcrum
- Leverage
- Watch for a fulcrum
- The ideal full fulcrum
- Down trend a prerequisite to fulcrum formation
- Supply equals demand
- Advantage of figure charts
- The buying points
- The broad fulcrum
- The recoil fulcrum
- The catapult
- The true catapult
- The false catapult
- The semi-catapult
- Use "stops" to protect position

We have stated that three scientific principles of mechanics known as the *fulcrum*, *catapult*, and *semi-catapult* are important to this Method and form the keystones upon which it is based.

THE FULCRUM*

In the science of mechanics, the fulcrum is defined as "the support on which a lever turns and the means by which influence is exerted." Leverage is defined as "the mechanical power gained by using a lever." A lever in mechanics is any rigid bar capable of turning about a fixed point and having counteracting forces applied at two other points.

Since the purpose of all observation and study of stock price movements is the determination of the important points from which the rallies and declines have their inception, the pattern known as the fulcrum must be carefully regarded when it develops on your Point and Figure Chart.

The fulcrum may develop as a base or as a ceiling near the top of the move where it will form in reverse. It invariably forms at the extremes of an intermediate cycle.

LEVERAGE

As in mechanics, where the principle of leverage is operative through the fulcrum point, so on your Point and Figure Charts, leverage is created when a congestion area forms a fulcrum after an extended move in the price of a stock. As the course of the price path builds up patterns on your Point and Figure Chart, you will begin to notice three types of fulcrums which occur and recur at the vital turning points in the price movement. These patterns repeat themselves very often and with such regularity that you will soon reach the conclusion that no advance or decline of proportions worthwhile anticipating can occur unless the inception of the move arises from one of these three types of fulcrums which we will later describe in detail.

WATCH FOR A FULCRUM

After a base has formed and it develops to be a fulcrum, the leverage there exerted creates a rally of such force and extent that the stock soon reaches the

---

* See Frontispiece, Figure A.

catapult point from which it quickly develops a further sharp upward movement. Therefore, it becomes one of the cardinal principles of this Method to be on the alert and heed carefully the development of a fulcrum formation on your chart. Three types of fulcrums will develop: (a) *the ideal fulcrum*, (b) *the broad fulcrum*, (c) *the recoil fulcrum*.

THE IDEAL FULL FULCRUM

The ideal full fulcrum always develops at the bottom of secondary culminations and at the top of major swings in new high territory (see Figures 6.1 and 6.2). It may be considered as the head and shoulder formation at the top and the reverse head and shoulder formation at the bottom. It develops as a result of forces, which, when they occur, always create two ideal positions for students of this Method to observe carefully and make long commitments from which quick and substantial profits soon accrue.

Fig 6.1   The ideal fulcrum

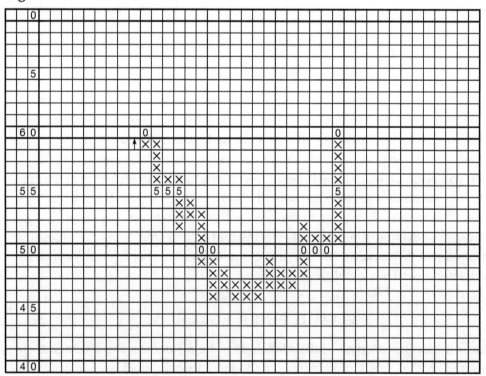

Fig 6.2   The ideal fulcrum

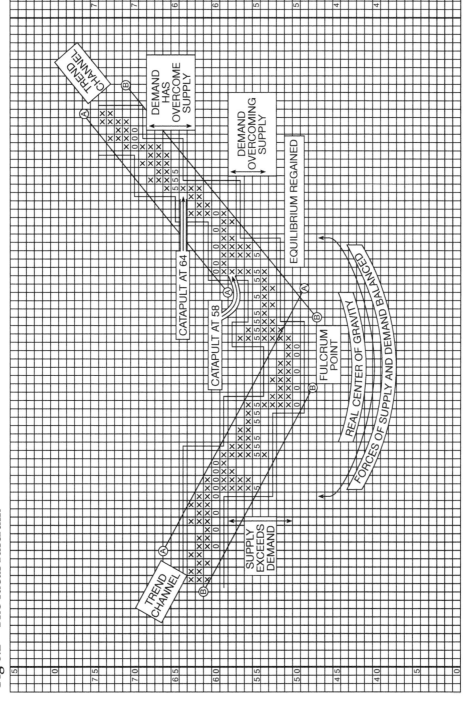

DOWN TREND A PREREQUISITE TO FULCRUM FORMATION

The ideal full fulcrum develops after a down trend has been halted and the price path builds up a pattern which moves over in the trend channel from the lower trend line to the upper trend line as a result of a series of rallies and declines. This action builds up a congestion area with a flat base. From this series of minor rallies and declines, two to five points in extent, which halt within a limited range developing a flat base, a sharp quick rally occurs that may result either from short covering or actual buying which creates the sharp run-up because of the absence of offerings overhead. This sharp advance is then usually followed by a temporary corrective decline which is arrested at a point above the low level established before the first run-up. Subsequent to the second series of rallies and declines, another sharp advance develops which must exceed the high point of the previous rally. The second high point, which is a full figure above the previous rally top, then becomes a *catapult point*.

Once the stock has developed sufficient strength to hurdle the catapult point, it usually and speedily develops a substantial advance to higher levels, and the reverse occurs when this formation appears near the top of an extended advance.

SUPPLY EQUALS DEMAND

The full fulcrum develops at the point where the center of gravity shows the balancing of the forces of supply and demand.

A down trend channel formed prior to the fulcrum point indicates that the supply of stock exceeds the demand. At the fulcrum point, the forces begin to balance. After the first rally where the reaction holds above the previous base level, equilibrium is regained and a new up trend channel is in process of being established. Here, demand begins to overcome supply, and a catapult point eventually develops. At the catapult point, demand has overcome supply, and the advance to substantially higher levels begins.

ADVANTAGE OF FIGURE CHARTS

Complete fulcrums may develop in the market action of one or two days or possibly may take several weeks. On many occasions, Point and Figure Charts will show this ideal formation developing while conventional vertical line charts show nothing more than a temporary halt in the down trend. And, in reverse, at the top of a move such conventional vertical line charts would show merely a failure to penetrate the previous top, while your Point and Figure Charts would show a complete fulcrum formation in reverse.

THE BUYING POINTS

Two important buying points are indicated as the fulcrum develops on your chart. One is in the base, with a stop order placed to limit loss from one to three points below, and the second is at the catapult point with a stop placed below the 50 per cent correction level, which must be considered a normal reaction.

THE BROAD FULCRUM

The broad fulcrum (see Figure 6.3), which will develop on your charts, requires close observance and careful analysis. It develops as a result of two or more rallies after the base has been formed and will occur after a full catapult has developed but failed to carry through. Broad fulcrums may indicate one of two conditions: either the lack of aggressive sponsorship, i.e. the absence of aggressive buying, or

Fig 6.3 The broad fulcrum

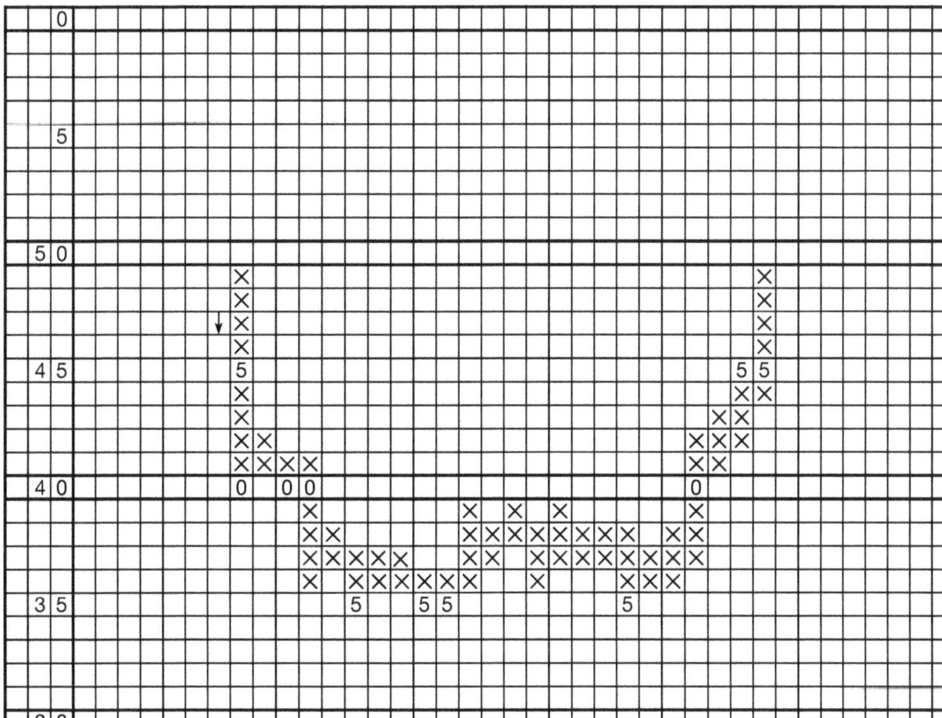

the close balance between the forces of supply and demand. It is well to protect closely a position which has been established in a fulcrum that later develops to be a broad fulcrum. Seek the first opportunity to close out the position by the "stop-order"[1] method after the stock has advanced above your cost price.

THE RECOIL FULCRUM

The recoil fulcrum (see Figure 6.4) develops subsequent to a sharp and direct down move after a base forms with ascending bottoms instead of flat bottoms. This type of base usually develops a symmetrical triangle with the vertex occurring just below the catapult point. You will observe that in the recoil fulcrum a catapult position usually occurs a point or two over the vertex of the triangle. Note, then, that this formation develops as a result of a sharp decline followed by sharply descending tops and sharply ascending bottoms.

Fig 6.4   The recoil fulcrum

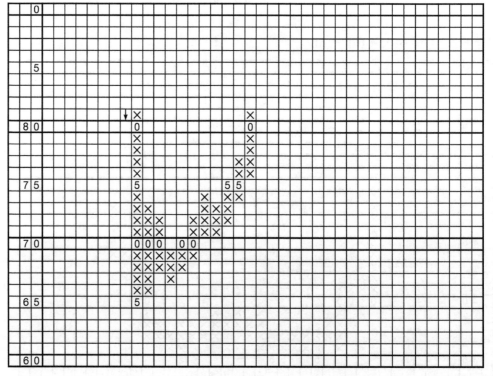

---

[1] See *Stop Orders* by Owen Taylor.

THE CATAPULT[2]

The next important principle in the Point and Figure Method is the catapult which develops after the formation known as the full fulcrum.

The encyclopedia describes a catapult as "an ancient military engine used for hurling missiles." The word "catapult" is also defined: "to rush suddenly."

A catapult point on your Point and Figure Chart is that price from which a sharp rally should develop. A catapult develops directly as the full fulcrum is completed and is that point just above the previous rally top created before the completion of the full fulcrum. Catapults are of two types: (a) the true catapult, (b) the false catapult.

THE TRUE CATAPULT

The true catapult (see Figure 6.5) invariably develops profits without registering a reaction which would cause loss to a commitment established at that point. A minor, temporary, technical reaction from the catapult point or one or more points above the catapult position is a normal occurrence, and tolerable allowance should be made for it when establishing your position at the catapult point.

THE FALSE CATAPULT

Occasionally, during a period of indecision and uncertainty, near the bottom of a secondary correction or near the top of a major move in a bull market, a new high level above previous highs will be established, and either a false catapult (see Figure 6.6) or semi-catapult develops. When a false catapult develops, we must be on the alert, for a stock which creates false catapults is in the act of changing its technical position. The failure of a catapult to develop profits immediately is an indication that the congestion area immediately preceding, which you may have diagnosed to be a full ideal fulcrum, is developing into a zone of distribution and must be carefully watched lest the previous base level be violated.

In the great majority of instances, your false catapult position will permit you to close out your commitment without loss. A stock which has created a false catapult will, in many instances, come back close to that point so that you can sell out your position with but a fractional loss. This position may be protected with a "stop" below the congestion area or a "stop" just below the 50 percent reaction point after the catapult has been developed. In either case, subsequent strength

---

[2] See Frontispiece, Figure B.

Fig 6.5   The true catapult

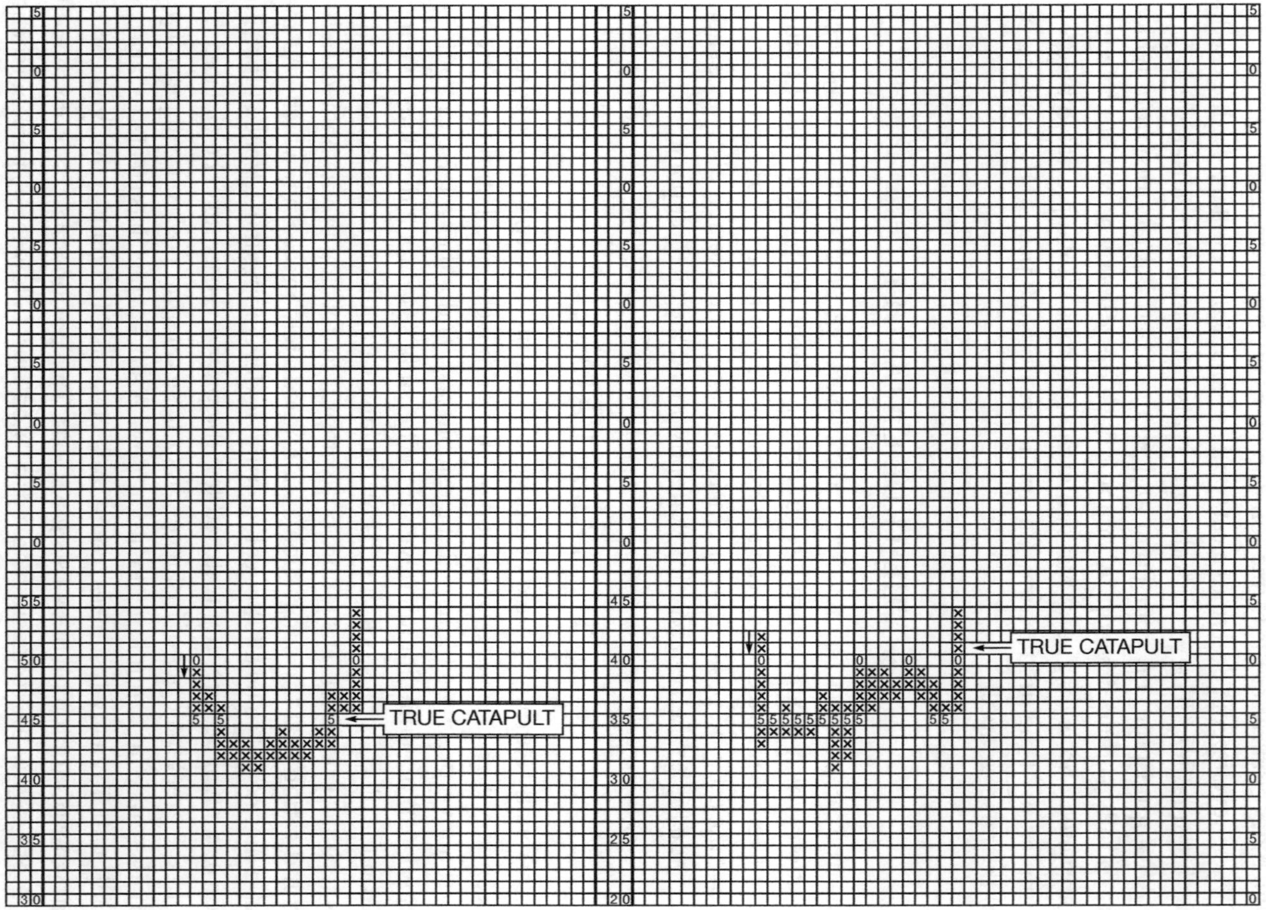

Fig 6.6   The false catapult

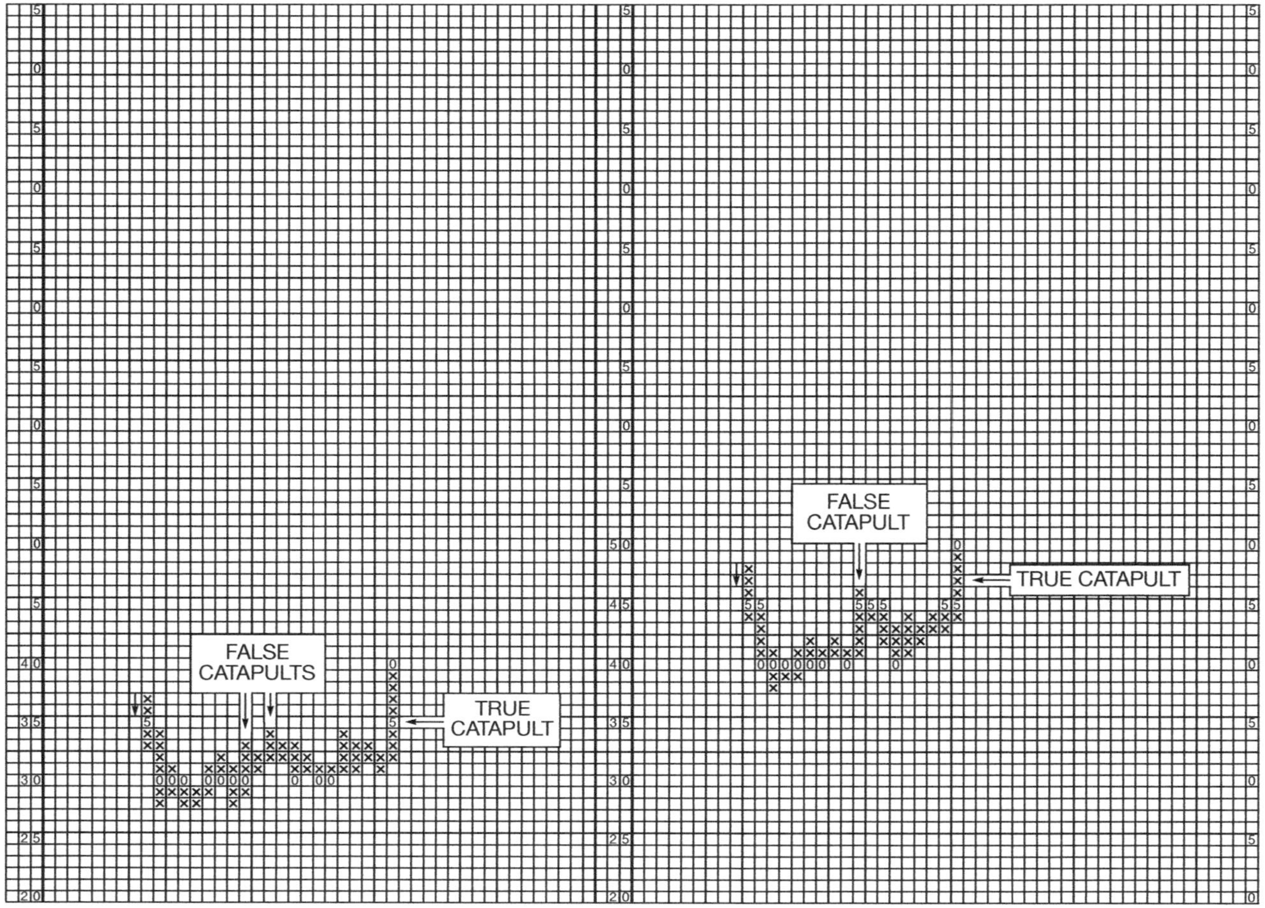

should be used to move up your "stop-order" so that the failure of the position to develop into a true catapult will not cause you serious loss.

THE SEMI-CATAPULT

In addition to the two important points for establishing commitments, namely: (1) in the base of the full fulcrum, (2) at the full catapult point; there develops a third which is known as a *semi-catapult* position (see Figures 6.7 and 6.8).

The semi-catapult position develops *during an advance* in stock as a result of a minor, narrow and limited trading range congestion area usually built up on your Point and Figure charts and from which a stock has a minor technical correction. A semi-catapult point, in this instance, develops after a technical setback when the stock rallies and creates a new high above the immediate preceding congestion area top. There are both *true* and *false* semi-catapults which develop in the price progression (see Figures 6.7 and 6.8).

USE "STOPS" TO PROTECT POSITION

The semi-catapult position is the third important point at which to place your commitment. It usually develops profits quickly for you. The proper place for "stop-order" protection on this commitment would be below the low made during the technical correction. After strength develops, the "stop" thus placed below the technical reaction level should be advanced to an "at the flat" position, thereby insuring the commitment against loss.

Fig 6.7   The true semi-catapult

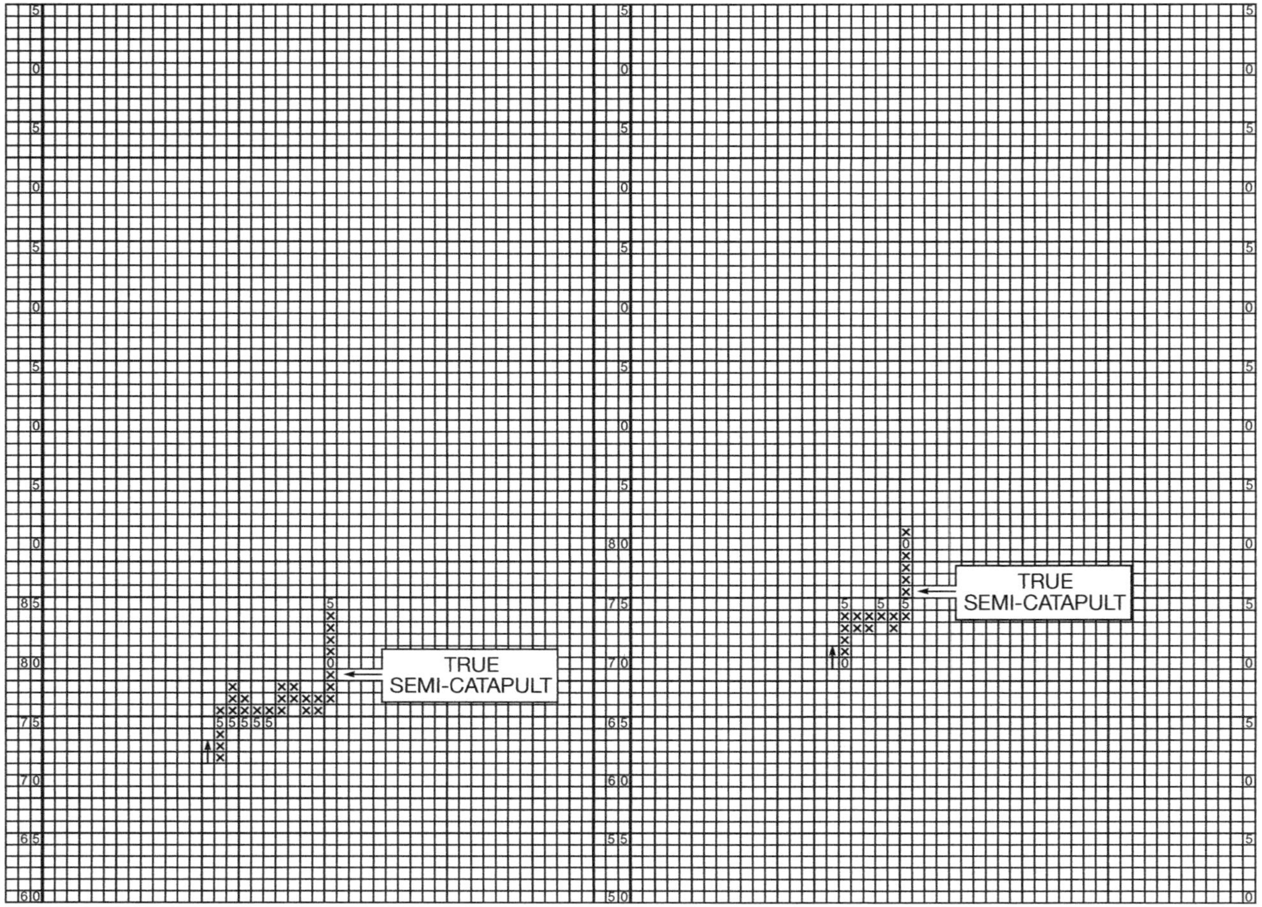

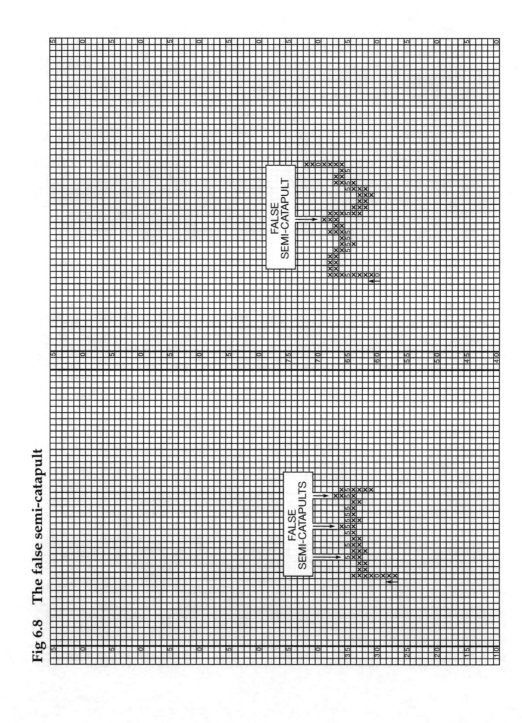

Fig 6.8 The false semi-catapult

7

THE PRINCIPLES OF CHARTING

For the purpose of giving you a clear understanding of the plan by which the charts are made according to the Point and Figure Method, and illustrating the coordination of the one with the three point or the one with the three and five point charts, we show an hypothetical move in the common stock of the XYZ corporation.

THE ONE POINT CHART

Figure 7.1 is a one point chart illustrating a theoretical move of the common stock of the XYZ corporation. The first full figure change shown on that chart is the symbol "5" recorded at the top of the first vertical column. This indicates that the stock sold at 25 or between 25 and 25⅞, both inclusive, on the first day in January.

In order to indicate that this was the first full figure in the month of January, instead of using the symbol "5," we substitute therefore the symbol "J." "J" indicates that this transaction is the first full figure transaction to be recorded in the month of January.

From the level of 25, the stock sells down to 21, or fractionally lower, but not below 20⅛ before it rallies. This calls for symbols in the squares representing 24, 23, 22, and 21. From the low on this reaction, the stock rallies and makes 24, or fractionally higher, but not above 24⅞, before a reversal is recorded. Therefore, to plot the rally, we put the symbol "x" in the squares for 22, 23 and 24.

MOVE TO NEXT COLUMN

Note, here, that the rally requires moving over to the next right-hand column, because the square 22, in which we were to place the symbol "x" was already occupied, and we move over to the second vertical column. We proceed to plot 22, 23 and 24, and then a one point reversal calls for a symbol in the 23 square, which, being already occupied, requires us to move once more to the next right-hand column. Moving up, we place a symbol "x" in the 24 square, and the symbol "5" in the 25 square. Then weakness develops which is stopped at 20, or above the flat figure 19. This requires symbols to be placed in the 24, 23, 22, 21, and 20 squares. In the 20 square, we place the symbol "0" as indicated on the chart. From 20, a rally develops to 23 and a fraction, requiring symbols in the 21, 22, and 23 squares. Thereafter, further pressure develops and a reaction during the latter part of the month carries XYZ down to 15. We place symbols in the 22

Fig 7.1   XYZ: one point chart

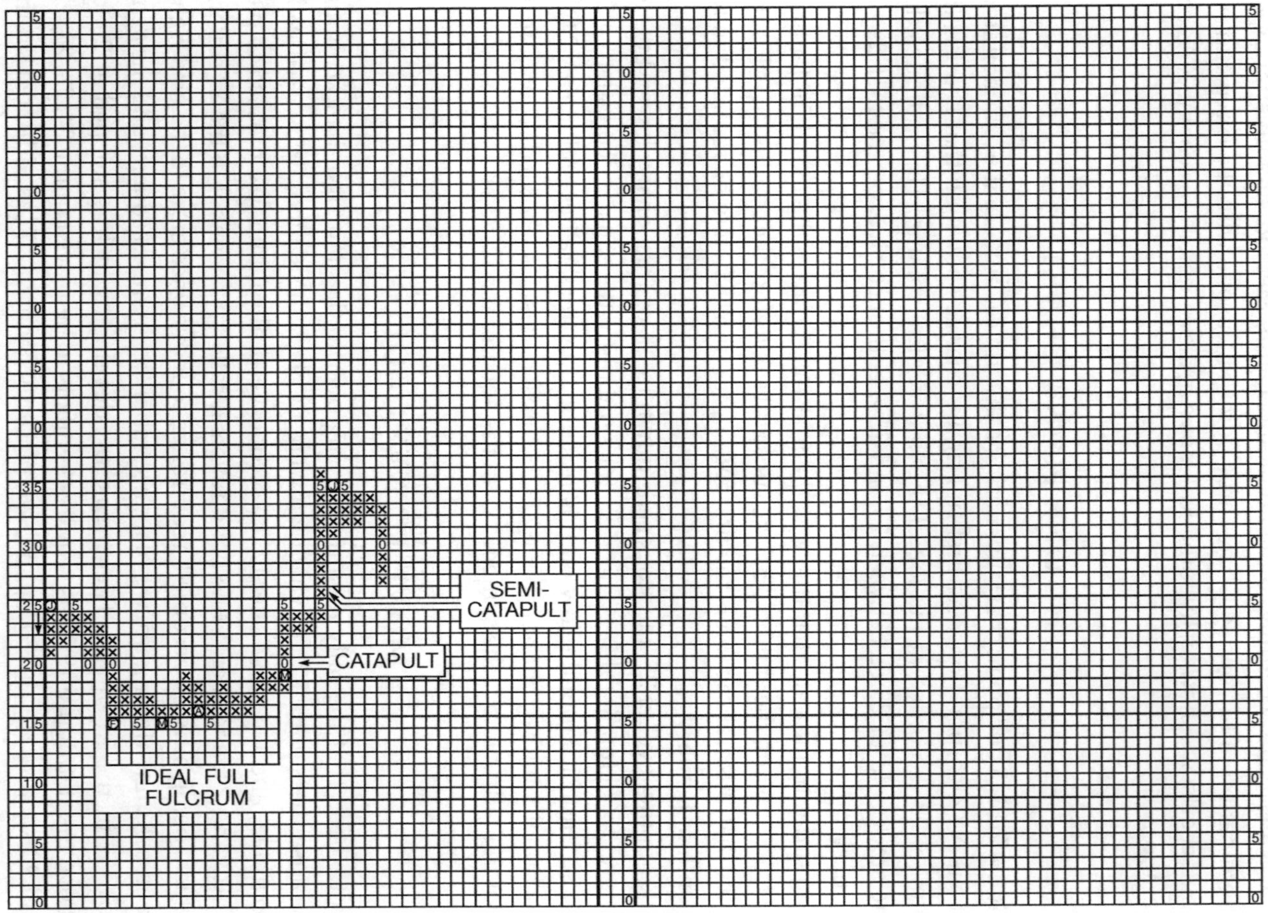

and 21 squares, a zero in the 20 square, "x's" in the 19, 18, 17 and 16 squares, and since the full figure 15, is registered on the first day of February, we use the symbol "F" to show that the full figure 15, was the first full figure registered in the month of February. A rally then develops to 18, which is plotted as indicated; a reaction to 15, plotted as shown; another rally to 17; a reaction to 15, which is the first full figure change registered in the month of March; a rally to 16; a reaction to 15; and then a sharp short covering rally to 19.

SIGNS OF A FULCRUM

Here we have the first indication that a fulcrum is forming since the congestion area has moved the pattern over to the upper trend channel line. A short covering rally carrying the stock to 19, meets the requirements of our ideal fulcrum formation. After the rally, a sell-off carries the stock back down to 16, rally to 17, reaction to 15, rally to 18, reaction to 16, rally to 17, reaction to 16, rally to 19, reaction to 18, rally to 19, reaction to 18, and then a rally establishing a full catapult position at 20, which promptly carries through to 25. Here develops a minor technical reaction to 23, a rally to 24, reaction to 23 and another rally establishing another full catapult position at 26. The stock now rallies sharply from the full catapult at 26, until it makes a high of 36, for the move. Then there is a reaction to 31, a rally to 35, reaction to 32, a rally to 34, and then a reaction to 27. These moves are clearly illustrated on the one point chart, Figure 7.1, which we ask you to study carefully.

TECHNICAL AIDS

In addition to the symbols, "x," "5," and "0," we use the first letter of each month to show the first whole figure recorded in that month. Dividend payments and ex-dividend dates are registered by plotting a circle to encompass the first full figure registered on or after the ex-dividend date. When the stock sells in a zero square, on or after the ex-dividend date, instead of using a circle to encompass the square, which might complicate matters, we use a dash in the center of the zero symbol used to indicate the multiples of tens on our charts. In addition to indicating dividend payments with the circle and dash, we make a memorandum at the foot of the column to show the amount of the dividend paid, and the date the stock sells ex-dividend. This principle of indicating dividend payments and dates is not illustrated on our theoretical charts, but it will be found on other charts contained in this book.

Examine carefully this one point chart of XYZ which we used to illustrate the move and which we have traced with you. Note the fulcrum formation as well as the full catapult position indicated by arrows.

We shall proceed to show you how a three point condensation chart is compiled from the one point record just completed.

THE THREE POINT CHART

Take the three point chart of XYZ, Figure 7.2, and compare it with the one point chart, Figure 7.1. Let us trace the move. The three point chart starts with the first full figure 25, records the reaction as noted on the one point chart down to 21, as well as the rally to 24. The three point chart disregards the reaction to 23, but

Fig 7.2   XYZ: three point chart

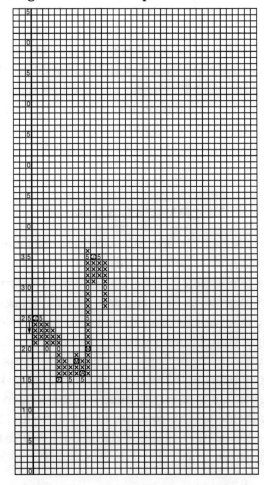

when the rally from 23, to 25, registers 25, the three point chart properly shows the move by adding a 5, above the 24 square already recorded.

The next move which is transferred to the three point chart is the reaction down to 20, followed by the rally to 23, and then the reaction down to 15, because each of these moves is three points or more. Since the rally to 18, is three or more full points, we show it on our three point chart and plot the move 16, 17, 18. This is followed by a decline to 15, again, which is also plotted. Then comes a series of minor rallies and declines less than three points in extent which are ignored by our three point technique.

The next move of importance which is plotted on the three point chart is the rally which terminates at the figure 19. Notice that we plot 16, 17, 18, and 19. The reaction from 19, to 16, is also plotted on the three point chart, but the subsequent rally to 17 is disregarded. Where the reaction from 17, to 15, occurs, the fact that the 15, is lower than the 16, plotted on the three point chart causes us to add the 5, below the last 16 recorded. The rally from 15, to 18, being three or more points in extent, is plotted and we add the squares 16, 17, and 18. There follows, then, a decline to 16, a rally to 17, another decline to 16, all of which are disregarded until the subsequent rally to 19. This requires that we put an "x" above the previously recorded 18, and our three point chart now shows a rally from 15, up to 19. The minor rallies and declines of one point from 19, to 18, and up to 19, down to 18, up to 19, again are all disregarded. However, the move from 18, up to 25, is plotted on the three point chart, but the reaction on the one point from 25, down to 23, rally to 24, the next reaction to 23, all are disregarded, and the next move which carries through the catapult point to 36, is plotted.

The decline to 31, is recorded, likewise the rally to 35, also the decline to 32, but the rally to 34, being less than three points, is ignored. The decline which follows carries down to 27, requiring on our three point chart the added figures of the last decline calling for symbols in the 31, 30, 29, 28, and 27 squares.

DETERMINING THREE POINT MOVES

Thus you have learned that in compiling a three point chart from the moves already recorded on your one point chart, we plot on the three point chart only rallies or declines which are of three or more full points in extent. In order to determine which are the moves to use, we consider the last recorded figure as zero, and count one, two, three. If the move carries to the third square or further, we record it. If it is less than three full figures away from the previous point recorded, it is ignored. Notice, also, a move which carries beyond the previous recorded point in the same direction is carried forward when a further move of one point or more past the previous high or low price is registered on the one point chart.

The principle involved is as follows:

> Record all moves of three or more points in extent. Disregard reactions or reversals of less than three points. Continue the previous recorded direction by one point plottings as soon as the price exceeds the previous low or high.

Three point charts, in addition to their function of general condensation, form the basis for analysis of the more volatile, highly speculative, medium and high priced issues, and for the broader swings of the market. Three point charts also show the worthwhile intermediate trend swings, because they eliminate all minor technical corrections.

THE USE OF FIVE POINT CHARTS

Five point charts are used to indicate broad zones of accumulation and distribution in the main trend when plotting the market indices, and are used as basic condensation charts for the more volatile issues which move 10, 20, or 30 points in a single speculative cycle. Five point charts condense the time factor and show long term accumulation and distribution, and are invaluable guides to the Capital Movement Trends.

Turn, now, to Figure 7.3, five point chart of "XYZ." Notice, here, that we plot from the *one point data* only those moves which are of 5 or more points extent. A stock must rally or decline to the fifth from the last recorded square before our five point chart records a reversal. Nevertheless, a continuation of the move in the already plotted direction is recorded by one point additions until a full five point reversal occurs. In making five point charts, we determine whether or not the move is plotted by starting to count zero at the last recorded square, then, if the move is to or beyond the fifth square, it is plotted.

Compare your five point chart of XYZ, Figure 7.3, with your one point chart, Figure 7.1, and note how this Method provided a highly efficient condensation of the time factor.

Fig 7.3 XYZ: five point chart

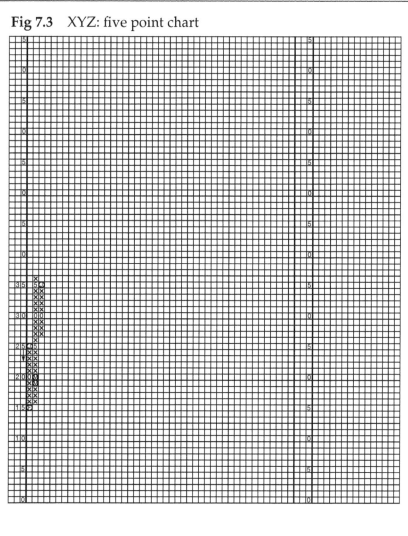

8

ANALYZING TECHNICAL POSITION

■ The price path characteristics
■ Patterns of the leaders duplicated in the secondary issues
■ Solid formations give confidence
■ Watch for changes in activity
■ Strong and weak technical position
■ Weak technical position
■ Gauging the length and culmination of the moves
■ The count
■ Coordinating your studies

After you have gained a comprehensive understanding of the Method and the technique of making the charts, the next step is to study the formations as they develop, and then to classify and analyze them. It is important to know whether a stock is under accumulation in a strong technical position, under distribution in a weak technical position, or merely in an indeterminate neutral position.

THE PRICE PATH CHARACTERISTICS

In studying the movements of stocks, it is well to have in mind the old saying, "Stocks must fluctuate." Price paths on your one point charts will develop patterns that reflect the peculiar characteristics of each stock. You will begin to observe that a given advance in a certain issue is usually followed by a definite type of technical correction. You will be amazed to observe the harmonious rhythm with which certain types of issues advance or decline, and which generally repeat themselves in the price progression path. While some stocks move harmoniously, other issues are very erratic with sharp advances followed by equally sharp declines, and thus complete their technical correction.

PATTERNS OF THE LEADERS DUPLICATED IN THE SECONDARY ISSUES

You will note, again and again, that the key issue in any group develops its characteristic pattern, which is usually duplicated by the secondary issues in the same group. A catapult developing in the leader of the group one day will more than likely be followed by a similar formation in the secondary issues soon thereafter. Study carefully the number of points advance and the correction area which follows. Learn whether the correction area is a reaction of 50 or more per cent of the advance or a congestion area in which the stock fluctuates back and forth while it is consolidating the move. The first correction which is greater in proportion to the last advance than the previous corrections which occurred during the advance is the first sign of distribution. Watch carefully for the first more than normal reaction.

SOLID FORMATIONS GIVE CONFIDENCE

During an advance, we prefer to see fairly solid congestion areas after each markup. This indicates each stage of the advance to be well consolidated before the next up move develops. When the progression of the move proceeds with only normal and minor technical reactions, it is an indication that the technical condition of the stock continues strong. If the formations are irregular and confusing, with no uniformity of pattern, we suggest caution. It is an indication of conflict and uncertainty. Such formations, during a major advance, give rise to hollow spaces similar to air chambers beneath the congestion points. These occur as the technical corrections over-extend themselves and create intervening blank spaces in the form of arched ellipses, semi-circles or irregular hollow patterns. Such formations are usually advance warnings of stubborn resistance to the advance and indicate supply meeting demand at the higher levels, with a strong possibility of a change of trend forthcoming. This indication developing on the three point chart is particularly indicative of the imminence of a reversal in trend.

WATCH FOR CHANGES IN ACTIVITY

You will observe from your charts that stocks fluctuate narrowly during periods of major accumulation. Soon thereafter, activity, sharp advances and equally sharp technical declines follow. This is usually a sign of the beginning of an extended move. Watch carefully for it. When a stock alters its most recent fluctuating habits, it is wise to be on the alert, for it is a sign of either accumulation or distribution.

STRONG AND WEAK TECHNICAL POSITION

The technical position of a stock or the market, as represented by an index, is strong when demand exceeds supply. This condition develops after a period of accumulation which has followed a major decline. A strong technical condition also exists after a mark up followed by a congestion area which develops to be consolidation.

When stock is purchased and taken out of the floating supply, technical condition is very strong. As a stock develops a strong technical position, the one point charts should show an extended line of work in the congestion area, either with a well formed, fairly solid, flat base, or a series of bases like a descending stairway, the bottom base containing the greatest number of squares along the support line. This type of base occurs very often. An exceedingly strong base develops after a sharp decline when each successive rally and decline builds up a triangle with its vertex to the right. When this formation develops to be accumulation, an extremely strong technical position exists.

WEAK TECHNICAL POSITION

A weak technical position develops after a series of extended advances which are uncorrected by congestion areas of consolidation. As the move progresses, the advances are not as vigorous as the early ones, and soon the ascending move begins to give way to a series of confused and halting patterns created by the churning motion near the top, which you will recognize as distribution. This formation occurs when supply begins to overcome demand.

At this point, it is important to check against your three point charts in order to observe the consolidated moves and to judge whether or not a real ceiling, which is apt to precede a drastic reversal, has been formed. Should this formation near the top of an extended move begin to develop reactions which leave air pockets, arched ellipses and other hollow areas beneath the congestion zone, it is an ominous sign and time to close out the position or to protect it by close stops.

GAUGING THE LENGTH AND CULMINATION OF THE MOVES

For the more advanced students and technicians, the Point and Figure Method affords a purely mechanical means of judging the length and culmination of future moves. This system, although not absolutely accurate, is extremely helpful in judging the proper moment to close out a position. It is truly mechanical and involves little judgment to make it operative.

THE COUNT

This system, an individual characteristic of the Point and Figure Method, is popularly known as "the count" to students and technicians. Because of the fact that it is somewhat involved and requires a lengthy explanation with multitudinous concrete examples and considerable study before it can be understood, it is omitted from this volume and will be found in the more advanced work entitled *The Advanced Theory and Practice of the Point and Figure Method*, by the same authors.

COORDINATING YOUR STUDIES

We have stated that it is vitally important to record the action of the market by plotting the important and popular indices, as well as the half hourly, half point movements of the popular Dow Jones Industrial Index. The conclusions which you will make resulting from the study of the charts of these indices should be used to influence the opinion arrived at from the study of individual issues. It is well to remember that you buy and sell individual stocks; therefore, it is most important for you to make your commitments based upon your analysis of the individual issues, substantiating your judgment through the influences of the averages. *Always remember that we buy and sell stocks and not index numbers.*

You have now completed a full and detailed course on the elementary principles upon which the Point and Figure Method is based. In order that you may get a clearer understanding of how to apply your knowledge of the Method, we will proceed to take you through a complete intermediate trend cycle move of several issues as illustrated in Chapters 9 and 10. In Chapter 11 you will learn how to plot and analyze the half point, half hourly running index lines of the Dow Jones Industrial Averages. In Chapter 12, by aid of the Point and Figure Method five point chart on which are plotted the moves of the New York Times index, we will show you how a knowledge and application of this Method would have avoided drastic losses which many suffered in 1929, when the last bear market had its inception. Lastly, we will take you through the campaign of Atlas Tack, illustrating to you the application of the knowledge you have acquired, and showing how such knowledge and application would have permitted you to buy and sell with the insiders and share in the sensational moves which were completed by the insiders in that campaign.

9

ANTICIPATING THE ACTION
OF U.S. STEEL

■ The full ideal fulcrum

■ The catapult position

■ The semi-catapult position

■ Consolidating the gains

■ The final mark up

■ The end of the move – a reverse fulcrum

■ The short positions

■ Geometrical charts

■ The trend outline charts

■ The three point figure charts

■ The five point charts

■ Summary

Examine chart Figure 9.1, which shows the one point moves of U.S. Steel during the primary trend cycle of 1933.

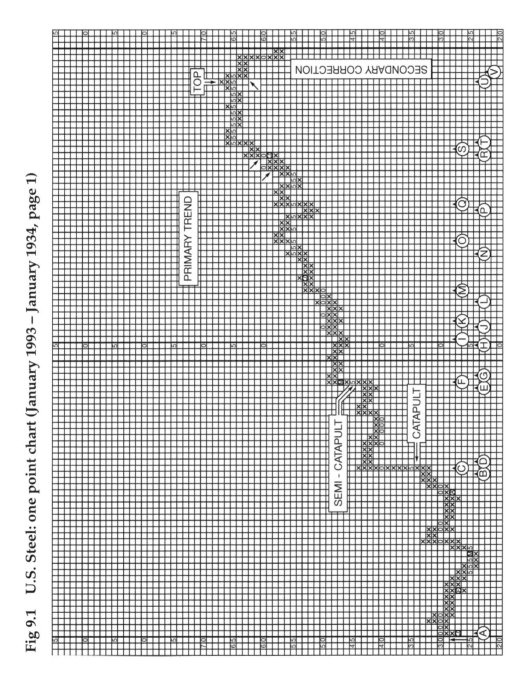

Fig 9.1   U.S. Steel: one point chart (January 1993 – January 1934, page 1)

THE FULL IDEAL FULCRUM

Figure 9.1, shows all one point moves in U.S. Steel from the first day of January 1933, up to near the close of the month of June of the same year. Charts like this are compiled from the Full Figure Daily Data supplied by the publishers or from the one point moves which you may obtain from actual tape action. In the previous chapters we have shown the correct procedure for the plotting of one point moves. Examine this chart Figure 9.1. Notice the congestion area between the column marked "A" and the one marked "B." You will recognize this to be an ideal full fulcrum, which meets almost exactly the requirements as laid down in the definition for this type of formation. The first column indicates an up move starting with the first day in January, after which the action proceeds with its backing and filling until the low point was reached, and which was established before the fourth of March, when President Roosevelt was inaugurated. The rally to full figure 33 was created after the bank holiday, when the market opened up sharply and exceptional strength developed. The subsequent correction which carried down to full figure 27, was completed later in March. In April the stock began to develop new strength and a sharp up trend was recorded with ascending bottoms.

THE CATAPULT POSITION

Notice that the pattern from the beginning of the year until the column marked "B" indicated the required down trend, the first rally followed by a technical correction which holds above the previous base level and then a succeeding rally which develops a catapult point, both of which are indicative of a trend reversal. Note in column "C" the full figure 34, indicated with an arrow. This is the most important of all signals given by the Point and Figure Method. It is a full true catapult point. Observe that ten points quick profit develops after a position is established at this point. An order placed to "Buy U.S. Steel on stop at 34," would show ten points quick profit without registering even a small paper loss.

THE SEMI-CATAPULT POSITION

The congestion area which begins to register in the column "D" and carries forward to the column "E" is a temporary halting of the up trend. It is the type of congestion area which develops a semi-catapult point. In column "F," full figure 45 develops to be the semi-catapult point and substantial profits accrue to this position without subsequently showing any loss to a position thus established. While the move from 45 was not as spectacular as the one from 34, nevertheless, it developed more than 18 points profit before the end of the move was completed.

CONSOLIDATING THE GAINS

Note the one point decline and subsequent rally plotted in column "G." Here is indicated a temporary supply of stock at the 49 level, which is blocking further advance. The stock reacts from 49, to 47, rallies again to 49, and then reacts to 46, in column "H." Column "I" shows good buying around the 46 level because the second decline fails to go lower and creates a double bottom at 46. Thereafter, the stock develops strength, and in column "J," a new semi-catapult develops. A reaction follows, in column "K." In column "L," it goes through to new high ground forming a new semi-catapult at 51. A small reaction then follows and in column "M" a new semi-catapult develops at 52. Now you will begin to notice that in the upper 50 zone the stock is meeting definite resistance. The moves are not nearly as sharp as they were previous to this point, and the progress, though it goes somewhat higher to approximately 65 or 66, is made with great effort and with many rallies and declines. New semi-catapults are developed in column "N" at 55, and in column "O" at 57, when a rally to 58 meets strong resistance and develops a double top, after which the first extensive reaction is witnessed which carries the stock in column "P" back down to the 51 level.

THE FINAL MARK UP

Here a sharp recovery takes place which is plotted in column "Q." Such a sharp recovery from a low of 51, indicates technical strength. The reaction from 58, down to 56, is another bullish implication because it is a normal correction. Then the stock rallies back to 58 making a quadruple top at this point. The subsequent decline to 54, where another double bottom is established, is bullish because it holds substantially above the previously recorded low point at 51. New semi-catapults develop at 59, and at 61.

THE END OF THE MOVE – A REVERSE FULCRUM

Figure 9.2 shows the continuation of the move of U.S. Steel which was carried forward from the point left off in Figure 9.1. Notice the congestion area which builds up around 65, and note further that for the first time we have a quintuple top and a failure to carry through the resistance level at 66 and 67. The actual top

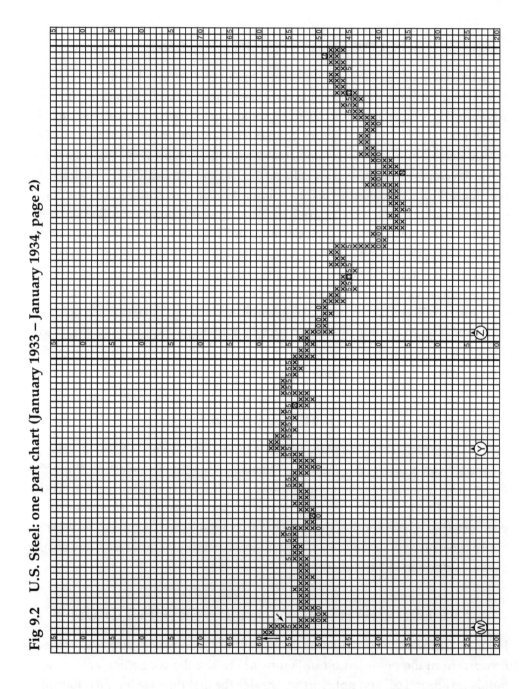

Fig 9.2 U.S. Steel: one part chart (January 1933 – January 1934, page 2)

of this move is plotted and indicated by the arrow at 67. Here is the end of the primary bull trend of U.S. Steel in 1933.

THE SHORT POSITIONS

From this point forward, the secondary correction commences, and we see between columns "T," and "V," the congestion area known as a ceiling or fulcrum in reverse with its top point plotted in column "U" and the reverse catapult position at 63, indicated by an arrow, in column "U." In column "W" at 56, a reverse semi-catapult position develops, and the profits of a down move quickly accrue. Examine, now, the extended congestion area plotted between the columns "W" and "Z." Here you see an indication of a close balancing of the forces of supply and demand. In column "Y," the failure of the rally to carry further is an indication of developing weakness. Notice the down trend which develops soon thereafter.

GEOMETRICAL CHARTS

In order that you may have an understanding of the application of the one point geometrical chart, we have plotted a part of the one point moves of U.S. Steel by geometrical technique. This is illustrated in Figure 9.3. Examine it carefully and compare it with the one point chart and with vertical line bar charts of the same move. This will give you a clear illustration of the advantage to be gained from the application of the Point and Figure Method to stock price movements.

THE TREND OUTLINE CHARTS

In Figure 9.4 we show the plotting of a trend outline chart of the three point moves of U.S. Steel. These charts, while not necessary in a technical analysis, are sometimes very helpful to students who will take the time to draw them.

THE THREE POINT FIGURE CHARTS

Figure 9.5 is a three point condensation chart compiled from the one point data of Figures 9.1 and 9.2, and shows the moves of U.S. Steel from the beginning of the year 1933, up to the end of September of the same year. Notice how the catapults and the semi-catapults develop on the three point chart and how they confirm the conclusions arrived at through the study of your one point charts. One

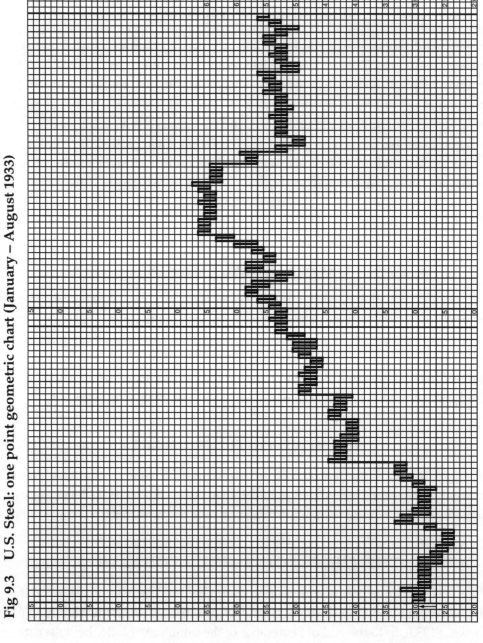

Fig 9.3   U.S. Steel: one point geometric chart (January – August 1933)

Fig 9.4   U.S. Steel: three point trend outline chart (January 1933 – January 1934)

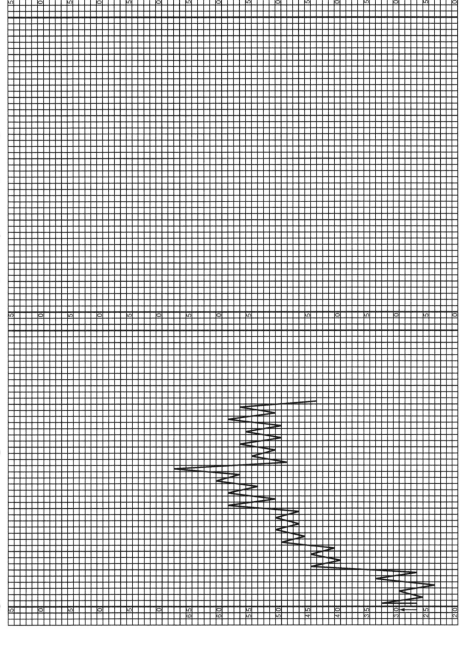

Fig 9.5   U.S. Steel: three point chart (January 1933 – January 1934)

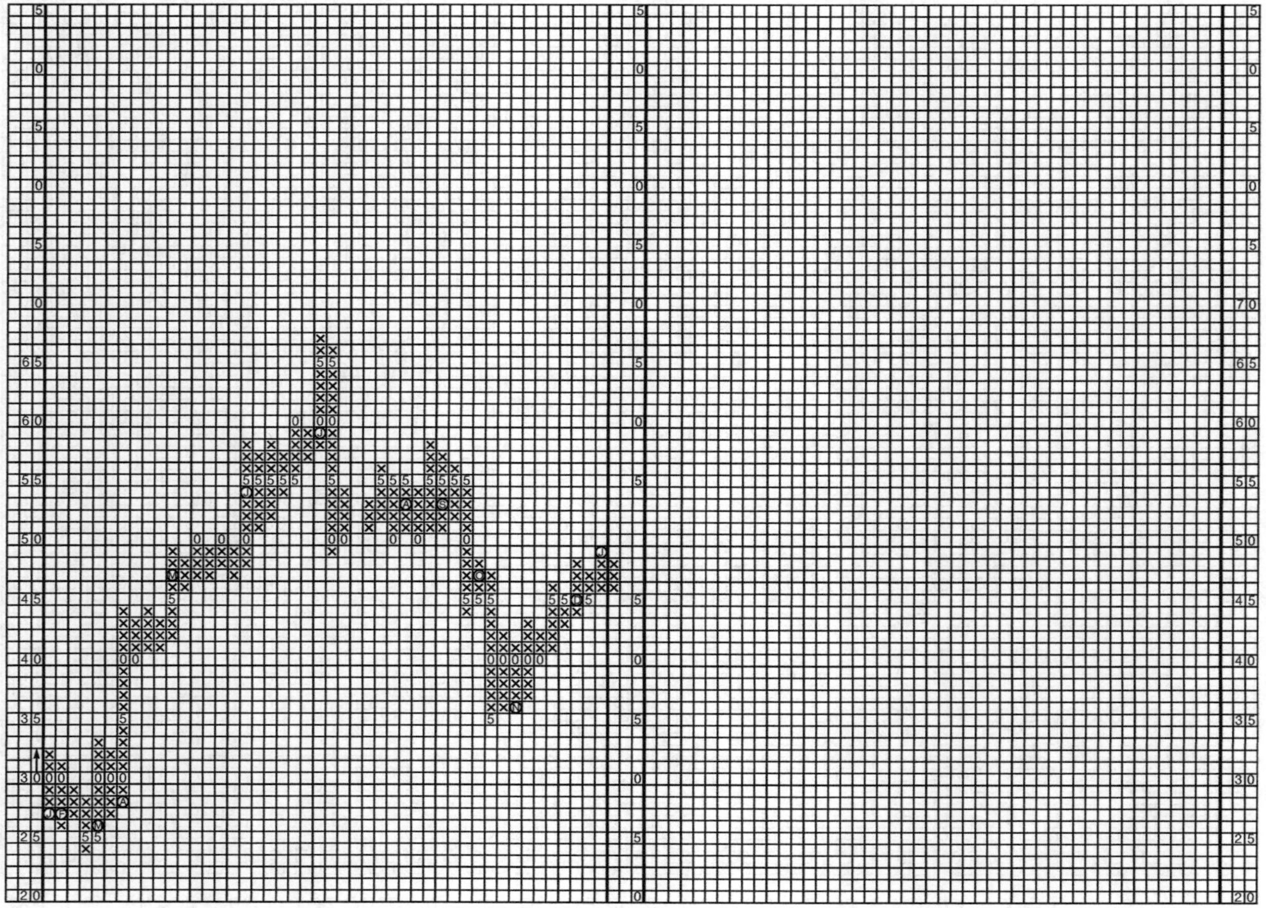

should always compile a three point chart for every one point chart that he keeps. One and three point charts are vital and essential to a proper application of the principles of this Method.

THE FIVE POINT CHARTS

In Figure 9.6 we show the five point moves of U.S. Steel. The five point data is obtained from the one point charts Figures 9.1 and 9.2. Five point charts are very helpful and show the broader zones of accumulation and distribution. They should always be compiled to show the moves of the main indexes and the volatile issues.

SUMMARY

When you attempt to establish a long position near the base of a fulcrum, your stop must be placed very close. Your position established at the catapult point must allow for a 50 per cent correction of the last advance. The same is true for the semi-catapult points. Note that the further the move has extended itself from the full fulcrum base, the more dangerous it is to establish a long position. After an extended advance, you run the risk of a more than normal technical correction touching off your stop. Be patient. Before you establish your position wait for the terminations of secondary corrections in a bull market. Analyze your formations carefully; then proceed with confidence as the full fulcrums and catapults develop.

Fig 9.6 U.S. Steel: five point chart (January 1933 – January 1934)

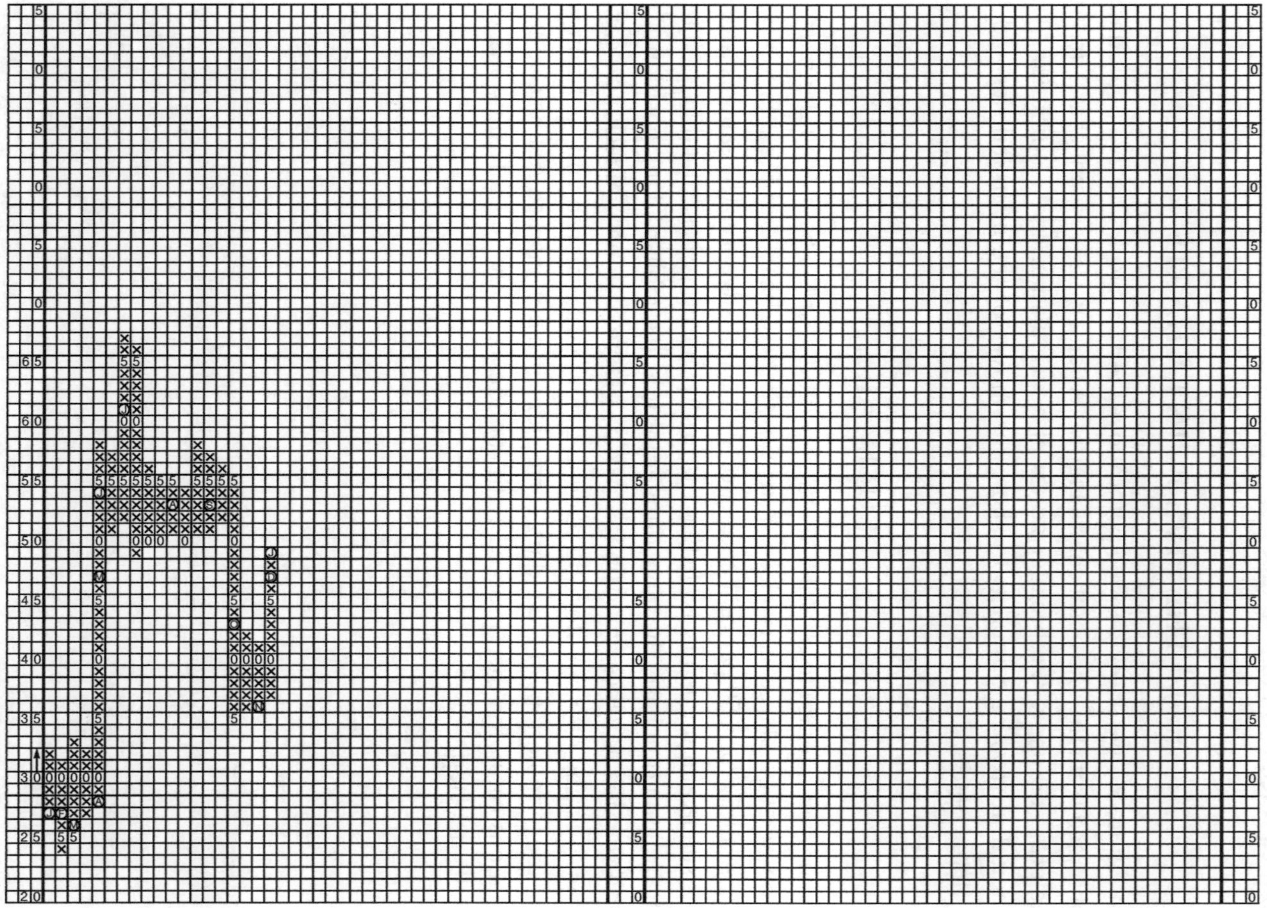

10

ANALYZING A CAMPAIGN IN WESTERN UNION

- Selecting the fast moving issues
  - The full fulcrum base
    - The catapult
  - The semi-catapults
  - The short positions
    - Summary

One of the most widely known multi-millionaire stock market operators, who lived and prospered at the turn of the last century, used to counsel his friends to buy Western Union Common whenever it was available around $50 a share. Western Union common has a $100 par value and formerly paid an $8 annual dividend. It was considered one of the prime blue chips. In the 1929 bull market, Western Union sold above $270 per share. In 1932, at the bear market low, its price registered $12.375. Hundreds of thousands of shares were turned over at price levels far below $50, which was the level at which the older generation of authorities counseled their friends to buy. It sold at one quarter that price at the bear market low.

SELECTING THE FAST MOVING ISSUES

In 1933, a remarkable campaign developed in this issue. It began around the end of February, or the beginning of March as shown on the chart, Figure 10.1. The stock was available between $18 and $20 a share for many days during February, March and April. In a very few weeks it advanced sharply and in a spectacular manner from the level of 18, to more than $75 per share. Here you have a move with a possibility of more than 300 per cent profit, since $1,800 invested in 100 shares of this stock would have grown to $7,500 in a short time. Notwithstanding such a tremendous profit percentage, there was nothing about the move which was not clearly indicated on the charts. You too could have had your share of those profits which were made by many who understood the technical condition of this issue. Your one and three point charts indicated the move weeks in advance.

THE FULL FULCRUM BASE

Figure 10.1 is a one point chart of Western Union. Observe that the down move was arrested near the end of February and the beginning of March and how a congestion area base with a flat bottom was built up between full figure 18 and 20. Note the sharp rally in the middle of the fulcrum when the stock advanced to 27, in one sharp, rapid up surge from the low of 18. Here was a sign of technical strength, a 50 per cent advance in the price of that stock within one day's market action. Surely no one could have failed to recognize such a definite signal. Its confirmation was had after the correction which held firmly in a double bottom formation established at 18, near the end of March and the beginning of April.

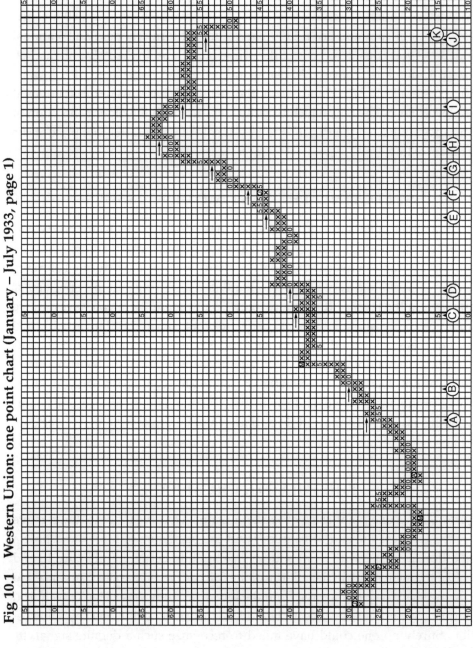

Fig 10.1   Western Union: one point chart (January – July 1933, page 1)

Here a new base builds up at a somewhat higher level and the formation begins to meet the requirements of the ideal full fulcrum. In column "A," when the stock has advanced to 26, this fulcrum is completed. The arrow in the next adjoining right-hand column pointing at full figure 27 shows the first full catapult position.

THE CATAPULT

Take particular notice of the firm and definite up trend which the issue establishes as it advances from 20, up through the catapult point and establishes another semi-catapult position at 30. This sharp up trend and its angle of inclination is a confirmation of the strength indicated in mid-March and connotes sharp continuation of the up trend soon to come. The advance begins to develop in column "B" from the semi-catapult point at 30. The stock soon rallies sharply to 38.

THE SEMI-CATAPULTS

A new semi-catapult position is developed at full figure 39, in column "C." Then follows a minor technical correction and a rally which establishes a new semi-catapult position at full figure 40, shown at the arrow point in column "D." The congestion area terminating with column "D," shows an excellent solid consolidation of the advance with the stock reestablishing a strong technical position and indicating a further sharp up move soon to follow. The rallies and declines between column "D" and column "E" create further consolidation, establish additional strength, and create a new semi-catapult at 44, shown in column "E." Another semi-catapult is shown in column "F," and still another in column "G." Notice how sharply the stock now advances. An additional semi-catapult position is shown at 62 in column "H." Here one must be on guard. The stock has advanced from 18 to 64, shown on Chart Figure 10.1, without a worthwhile technical set-back. Proceed, now, to Chart Figure 10.2. Observe that the correction sets in.

THE SHORT POSITIONS

A reverse fulcrum develops with a short position catapult indication at 58. This is indicated with an arrow in column "I." A reverse semi-catapult develops at 54, indicated in column "J." After the down move in column "K," notice the con-

Fig 10.2   Western Union: one point chart (January – July 1933, page 2)

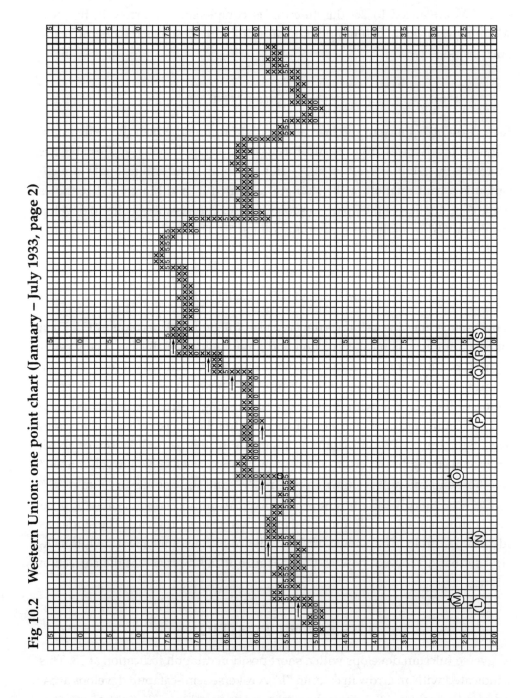

gestion area that builds up between the columns "K" and "L." This is an ideal full fulcrum, always a sign of developing strength, and an indication of the termination of an intermediate swing. It is always a signal to go long of the stock at the next catapult point. A catapult develops at full figure 53, indicated in column "M." Profits soon accrue as the stock rallies to 57 and a fraction. Some little resistance is met at that point, and the stock makes a double top at 57, after which it sells down to 53. In the zones between columns "M" and "N," one would be justified in being somewhat hesitant and in doubt about the technical position. The formation is a neutral one until a double bottom is established at 52. The decline which establishes the first 52, creates a new low after the 53, previously recorded and is to be considered a cautionary sign. However, when the stock rallies in column "N" and creates a new semi-catapult at 58, we have an indication of new strength developing. Notice the semi-catapult which is built up between column "N" and column "O," with its miniature full fulcrum at the bottom. Again an excellent semi-catapult position is built up at full figure 59, indicated with the arrow in column "O." The stock continues its advance, but meets with some difficulty, however, between the zones of 60 and 63. When it establishes a new low at 59, indicated in column "P," we must be on guard.

Any position now established must be stopped close beneath the low made on the move which was recorded at full figure 64. The zone from column "O," to column "Q," is a congestion area, of the type which sometimes develops to be the culmination of the move. Be on guard, however, when the stock develops a new semi-catapult at 64, in column "Q." It is a sign of strength. Congestion zone between "Q," and "R," is a consolidation of the gain, and a new semi-catapult position is established in column "R" at the 68 point.

From the base at 49 to 50 the stock has again had a 25 point advance when it establishes a semi-catapult position at 74, in column "S." The congestion area to the right of column "S" is a sign of developing weakness. Be on guard and ready to take your profits on further strength or when subsequent weakness reaches your stop order which should be advanced beneath the market as the move progresses upward.

SUMMARY

We are sure, that from a study of the one point moves in Western Union you would have been able to detect and take advantage of an exceptional campaign without the aid of tips, rumors or board room gossip. Examine your three point condensation chart Figure 10.3. Notice how readily these two types of charts are

Fig 10.3 Western Union: three point chart (January – July 1933)

used in conjunction with each other. See the indicated buying levels on your one point charts as they develop confirmations on your three point charts. We show them with arrows in columns "A," "B," and "C," in Figure 10.3. Compare them with Figures 10.1 and 10.2. From these charts you will learn that it is not necessary for you to listen to tips or rumors which circulate about the board rooms and are printed in many of your daily financial publications.

Study well and master the principles of this time tried Method and you will always be able to anticipate stock price movements weeks before the tips and rumors filter their way into the board rooms and financial columns.

11

JUDGING THE MINOR SWINGS

■ The half hourly index of the Dow Jones Industrials

■ The half point half hourly log

■ Half point technique

■ Scientific tape reading

■ Analyzing the half point chart

■ Ignore rumors and gossip

■ Summary

Elsewhere in the book, we have promised to give you the details and explain the methods used in compiling a *running action index line*, which is considered a vital aid by most experienced market technicians.

THE HALF HOURLY INDEX OF THE DOW JONES INDUSTRIALS

For the purpose of judging the day-to-day minor swings of the market, there is no technical aid as helpful as a one half point figure chart of the half hourly position of the Dow Jones Industrial Index.

For the purpose of facilitating the plotting of the action of this running line we have especially designed a one half point chart sheet known as #500 1.5. Students of the Method will find this sheet ideal for the purpose.

Messrs. Dow Jones and Company have recently inaugurated the policy of publishing the hourly position of their Dow Jones Industrial Index. Since the fall of 1931, your authors have privately compiled this important index at each half hour interval during every trading day. These computations form the basis for this exceedingly helpful half point half hourly index. The data for carrying this chart forward is supplied in the Full Figure Daily Data Service available from the publishers. This most indispensible index represents the fluctuations of the market as it actually moves from point to point during the day. Notice that the maximum high established in the newspapers and the maximum low are disregarded when we use a running action index line. We are concerned only with the fluctuations of the index as it moves in a continuous line throughout the day, and from day to day. The total of the maximum highs of the stocks which comprise the index highs, or the maximum lows which comprise the index lows, does not interest us.

We are concerned only with the relative strength or weakness of the rallies and declines as they develop and with the resultant congestion areas built up as the index line fluctuates during each market session. Of course, knowledge of the maximum high, the maximum low, and the close of each day is helpful in judging the technical position of the market; but more important for the technician is the information which is to be had from starting and maintaining this important half point half hourly running line index of the Dow Jones Industrial averages.

THE HALF POINT HALF HOURLY LOG

Turn now to Figure 11.1. The half point figure chart plotted here for you represents the technical action of the market, and, as continued on Figure 11.2 shows the action from the beginning of the year 1933, to beyond the top established in July. The chart terminates with the action indicated about the middle of August at the right-hand edge of Figure 11.2.

HALF POINT TECHNIQUE

Observe, here, that half point technique is exactly like your one point technique, the only difference being that the crossing of the half way zone and the full figure zone calls for a new symbol. Thus, a move from 101 to 102.56 would require "x's" in the lower half of the 101 square, in the upper half of the 101 square, in the lower half of the 102 square, and in the upper half of the 102 square, showing that the move had reached the half way point, or beyond. Should the move carry to 102.99, no additional symbol would be needed, but the moment it registers 103, we would be required to put a symbol in the lower half square of the 103 level showing that 103 flat had been reached. We feel confident that you will understand the technique of developing these half point charts, especially so if you are sure of your one point technique.

SCIENTIFIC TAPE READING

These valuable charts are very helpful to the board room trader and other who attempt to catch the shorter swings. They are far more reliable than an attempt at tape reading. This half hourly running line index plotted by half points is actually a picturization of the tape itself. It is dependable and helpful. It is far more reliable than trusting to memory or hazarding a guess. We urge upon every one of our readers to establish and maintain this half hourly log in half point form. It is a formidable tool and invaluable as an aid in recognizing the day-to-day trend of the market. As you proceed to study half point technique and its application to the running action line, you will begin to realize that the vital mechanical principles forming the basis of the Point and Figure Method, namely, the fulcrum, the catapult and the semi-catapult are clearly recognizable in your half point half hourly market log chart. Compile and maintain this chart. Watch the trend lines on it as they develop. Notice the congestion areas at the terminations of the swings as the market moves up or down the trend channel.

Fig 11.1   Dow Jones Industrial Average: half hourly by one half points (January – July 1933, page 1)

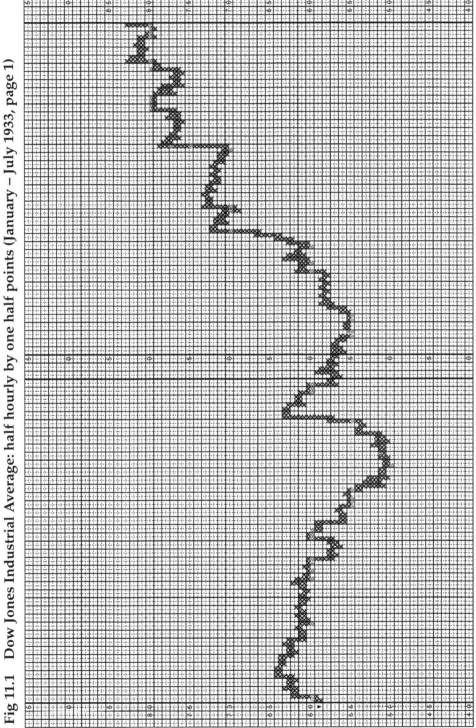

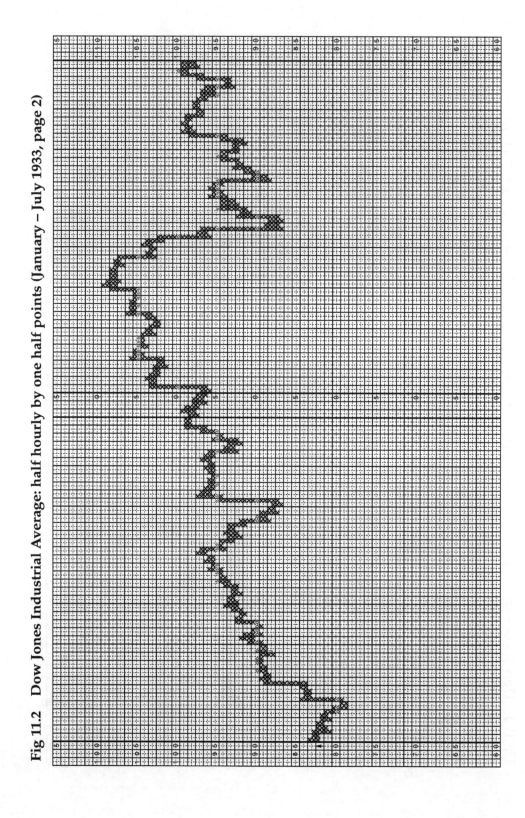

Fig 11.2   Dow Jones Industrial Average: half hourly by one half points (January – July 1933, page 2)

ANALYZING THE HALF POINT CHART

Be on guard after a sharp up surge when resistance to the advance is clearly indicated. Be ready to buy stocks after an extended decline when a congestion area builds up a fulcrum and a catapult develops. Consider the broader trend channels on this index to show you the trend of the market. The closer trend lines in the congestion areas will show you the danger zones after an up surge, and the point at which to liquidate your long position. The important buying levels indicated on this chart are in the bases formed after a down move when a full fulcrum or a catapult develops. Watch closely congested zones. Also, be on the alert to take advantage of the semi-catapult position which may develop in the price progression path of this important technical aid.

IGNORE RUMORS AND GOSSIP

If you maintain and study this chart you will soon be able to disregard the advice of your customers man or the board room habitues and the gossip in which they indulge. If, in the face of bad news and pessimism, this important half hourly index builds up a congestion area of accumulation, disregard the bad news, ignore the rumors, establish your long position, and have patience. Likewise, when all is enthusiasm and stock price advances get on to the front pages of our newspapers, your half point chart will either be showing a clear and already effected advance or the building up of a congestion zone. Congestion zones give implications requiring caution. Be ready to liquidate quickly at first signs of a ceiling developing even though the news and all about you are rampantly optimistic.

SUMMARY

It is well to remind you, at this time, that you cannot trade in index numbers. The half point half hourly running action index log is but a representation of the market. You must trade in stocks. When your index line is bullish, select the most bullish formations in individual stocks and place your position in those stocks. Use this valuable Half Hourly Log as an aid to reinforce your judgment. From it, analyze daily, the technical position of the market.

12

HALF POINT TECHNIQUE IN ATLAS TACK

- Historical background
- Analyzing the campaign in Atlas Tack
- Important signal during July break
- The first caution signal
- Board room observations
- The shorts began to cover
- Point and Figure analysis

In order that you may have an illustration of how the half point, Point and Figure technique is applied to an individual issue, we shall take you through the recent campaign in Atlas Tack. The sensational advance of this low priced stock which advanced within a few weeks from $1.50 per share to $34.75, attracted the attention of the Stock Exchange authorities and the Attorneys-General of several States.

HISTORICAL BACKGROUND

The Atlas Tack Corporation was first listed on the New York Stock Exchange at the beginning of the last bull market during 1920 or 1921. There are issued and outstanding 98,000 shares of common stock of no par value. The bull market high of 1929 was 17⅞. The low of that year was 5. In the period of 1930 and 1931, the high was 8½, and the low 1½. The bear market low in 1932 was 1, and the high of that year 3⅞. In 1933, the low was 1½, the high 34¾. In the month of December, 1933, the high was 34¾ and the low 10.

Here was an issue which presented an ideal opportunity for unscrupulous market operators to take advantage of the public. The small outstanding capital stock, with most of the stock closely held, and an extremely small floating supply, permitted easy manipulation.

ANALYZING THE CAMPAIGN IN ATLAS TACK

Turn, now, to the Chart, Figure 12.1. This is a one half point chart showing all the one half point changes in Atlas Tack from the high of the year 1930 to the low of the bear market and up to the high established on a recent date in 1933. Observe the zone between columns A, and D. Here you will see the type of fulcrum which will always develop in low priced stocks when you apply half point technique to their fluctuations. Give particular attention to that formation. Notice the difference between it and the one point fulcrums.

The sell off in column A, from the high of 8½, was quite sharp, considering the price level. At 1½, some resistance to the decline was met as the stock was picked up by the insiders. In the zone A, to B, the stock was several years under accumulation with very few transactions being registered on the tape. Little was heard or seen of Atlas Tack during 1932. In the last quarter of the year, during the months of October, November, and December, the stock sold down from 3½ to the actual low of 1¼, registered near column B. A few transactions were effected

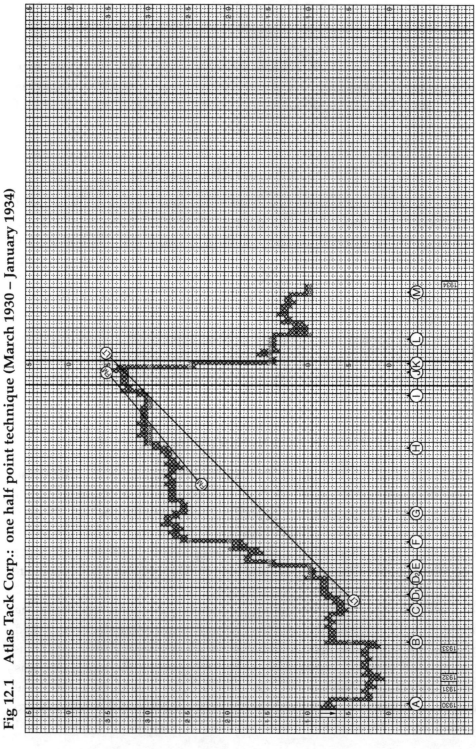

Fig 12.1　Atlas Tack Corp.: one half point technique (March 1930 – January 1934)

in the month of February, 1933, around the price of 1½. Later, a few thousand shares changed hands at 1¾, to 2, and in the month of April, we find a few shares changing hands during the first week of that month at $3 per share. During the month of May, the price of the stock advanced from 3 to 3½. Thus, you see, between the months of October 1932 and the end of April 1933, Atlas Tack had a very thin market while it was being accumulated by the insiders, when 7,500 shares comprised the total transactions. At 4, shown in column B, the stock was on the catapult. This was the first important buying signal.

Things began to happen during the last week of May 1933. It was at this stage, in the zone marked C to D2, that the manipulators begin to take a real interest in the issue. The advance from the bear market low to 10½ the top of the rally in column D2, is to be considered a normal one for a low priced stock of a company with fairly good prospects of future earnings. The zone from column B, to column C, represents the final stage of accumulation, C, being the June shake-out of the 1933, bull market run-up. In column D1, we find the first semi-catapult occurring at 8½ in this issue. Another developed at 9, in column D2. These two semi-catapults were buying points.

The action of Atlas Tack from the zone A to E represents a normal bull market action of a low priced issue. Low priced issues always have best percentage advances from a bear market low point.* Accumulation was effected in the zones A, to B, during the run-up in column B, and from B to D1. At the point marked E, we consider that the manipulators had completed their line and the stock formed a new semi-catapult at 11, which was another important buying signal. This took place during the month of August while the rest of the market was recovering from the drastic effects of the July break.

IMPORTANT SIGNAL DURING JULY BREAK

In the July break, while the rest of the market lost twenty-five percent of the average price, namely from 110.00 in the Dow Jones Industrial Index to 85.00, a net change of approximately 25 points, Atlas Tack had but a slight sell-off from 10½ to 9½, which constituted the technical reaction between columns D2, and E. That was an important and significant signal to the effect that big things were about to happen in Atlas Tack.

The negligible drop in the price of Atlas Tack during the July break was much less than normally would be expected and showed extremely strong sponsorship.

---

* See *Low Priced Stocks. When and How to Buy Them*, by Owen Taylor.

To those who observed its action by half point technique of the Point and Figure Method, the next semi-catapult point would have suggested an immediate purchase. Certainly, the fourth buying place, the semi-catapult at 11, would have been the best point at which to go long of this issue. The mark up in the zone column E, to F, was what might be termed "strong arm work." While the averages were still below their July tops, Atlas Tack was in this mark up phase. The ability of this issue to continue its advance and to hold its reactions at less than normal correction levels was indicative of a continuing strong sponsorship, especially when one considers the fact that the price continued to advance persistently during reactionary periods of the market.

THE FIRST CAUTION SIGNAL

The first cautionary signal came at the zone G. There, when the stock reacted from 28½ down to 25½, we had the first sign of a change in the technical structure. However, sponsorship was still apparent in the zone F, to G, and, in fact, it continued until around the columns J and K. Some distribution was going on in the zone G to K. Note, however, that the sponsors were buying the stock on minor reactions and distributing it at the upper levels, they were buying and selling on balance, meanwhile reducing the size of their long position established in the zone A, to D2. A new semi-catapult developed at 29, in column H. After the reaction at G, all stops should have been advanced to a point close below the low established on that sell-off. Subsequent to the semi-catapult at 29, one should have been on guard. Stops should have been advanced close beneath the market. Surely one should not have allowed such an issue to come back more than 2½ to 3 points from its last high. Positions established at 4, at 8½, at 9, at 11, at 18½, and at 20½ all would now have shown substantial profits and should have been closely guarded by stops. Notice, here, that the main trend line "LT," intercepted the work area in column I, when the stock backed and filled in the 30 level. That was the final warning. Stops should have been advanced to just below the price of 30, and, on subsequent strength, moved up close beneath the market. Compare the mark up trend pitch with the pitch of its predecessors. The final mark up trend line, "FM," clearly showed that the insiders had distributed a great part of their stock to the public and were standing aside. The public then held the bulk of the floating supply.

BOARD ROOM OBSERVATIONS

The mark up in column F, when the stock advanced from 18 to 26, occurred on increased volume, and it was there that many board room habitues, customers men, and others were attracted to the performance of Atlas Tack. The churning in the zone between F, and H, represented distribution on balance by the insiders and some short selling on the part of the more experienced board room traders. The mark up in column I, occurred on terrific volume. There was another sign for board room traders. Great turnover in the number of shares of this stock, many transactions in this issue which had theretofore been extremely scarce, and rarely printed on the ticker tape as it unrolled from day to day, were indications to the more informed tape readers and board room observers that the end was close at hand in Atlas Tack. Many began to sell the stock short from column H to column J. This condition is always apparent on Point and Figure Charts when many half point changes are recorded.

THE SHORTS BEGAN TO COVER

In the zone K to L, some board room traders who shorted this issue began to take in their short lines, and the sell off in the stock met temporary support due to short covering. However, the less cautious ones stayed short, for they knew that even at $15 per share the common stock of the Atlas Tack Corporation was still high in price. After the temporary demand on the part of shorts who were covering around 15, was met, further supply carried the stock down to 10, and, in the zone L to M, this issue found a normal level consistent with its actual value and reasonable prospects.

POINT AND FIGURE ANALYSIS

Notice that the zone H, to K, represented a large number of figure changes while little progress was made in the advance of Atlas Tack. This occurred during a period when the balance of the market had shown considerable strength. The opposite technical action occurred during the July break. That was the final signal for students of the Point and Figure Method to close out their positions. Increased volume with lessened progress, and sluggishness in the advance, were all definite signs that the sponsors had unloaded their stock on the uninformed public. It was time to get out of the issue, and, as a matter of fact, to look for the first opportunity where the price broke a previous support level at an inverse catapult or semi-catapult and there go short of this issue. The sell off in Atlas

Tack from the actual high of 34¾ to 9½, was indeed dramatic. On Saturday, December 16, Atlas Tack opened at 33½ and soon sold down to 32¼. Trading in the issue was temporarily halted. The next sale recorded was 4,800 shares at 25. That day, the stock closed at 21⅝, and a few days later declined to the low of 10. Thus, you see that no matter where your stop would have been in Atlas Tack, the positions established at the catapult point or at any of the semi-catapult points before the advance would have netted you $25 per share, a handsome margin of profit from the first position established at 4, the second at 8½, the third at 9¼, or the fourth at 11. Of course, there is a big difference between $34 per share near the high and $25 per share, the point at which the first block was sold after trading stopped. It is an indication of the danger involved using stop orders in a thin market stock. Nevertheless, it permitted the taking of mighty fine profits for those who took advantage of the signals as they were clearly developed by Point and Figure technique.

13

THE MAIN TREND AND MAJOR CYCLE CULMINATIONS

- Critical culmination points easily detected
- The one point chart – the basis for analysis
- Interpreting an intricate major culmination
    - The first temporary top
- Semi-catapult point – unusually bullish pattern
    - Strength carries through objective level
        - The change over of technical action
    - The top of the move clearly indicated
        - Indications of a major culmination
            - Bear trend technical action
        - The investor or long term trader

In order to illustrate how the Point and Figure Method will aid you to judge the capital movement trend and the major cycle crucial turning points, we have added Figures 13.1 and 13.2, one point charts of the New York Times Average from June 1929, to the now historical break which occurred in October of that year. Figure 13.3 is a three point condensation chart of the same move and Figure 13.4 is a five point condensation chart. The data used to prepare the three and five point charts was taken from the one point moves as plotted on Figures 13.1 and 13.2.

CRITICAL CULMINATION POINTS EASILY DETECTED

The four illustrations, Chart Figures 13.1 to 13.4, represent the top zone of the biggest bull market ever witnessed in the entire history of finance. That top represents an important and critical zone in which an ideal test of this Method may be demonstrated. We have stated that the Point and Figure Method provides the means for judging the major as well as minor culminations of price movement trends. We add to this statement that this is the only Method which will always aid you to recognize the turn of the major cycle when the market changes from bull trend to bear trend.

THE ONE POINT CHART – THE BASIS FOR ANALYSIS

Figures 13.1 and 13.2 depict all of the one point moves of the New York Times Index during the critical period from June 1929, to the break in October of that year. In those few weeks some of the issues on the big board fluctuated over a range of hundreds of points. The market from June, to September, offered exceptional opportunities for profit on the long side and the breaks of September and October duplicated those opportunities on the short side. Not only did this Method clearly show the top and the reversal from bull to bear trend at that time, but it will continue to do so again and again as the price path leaves its tracings for posterity.

INTERPRETING AN INTRICATE MAJOR CULMINATION

The fifty stocks which comprise the index compiled by the New York Times, and which we use for the purpose of illustrating the reversal of the technical action in 1929, were a fair cross section of the market, when it was fluctuating around

Fig 13.1   N.Y. Times Average: one point chart (May – October 1929, page 1)

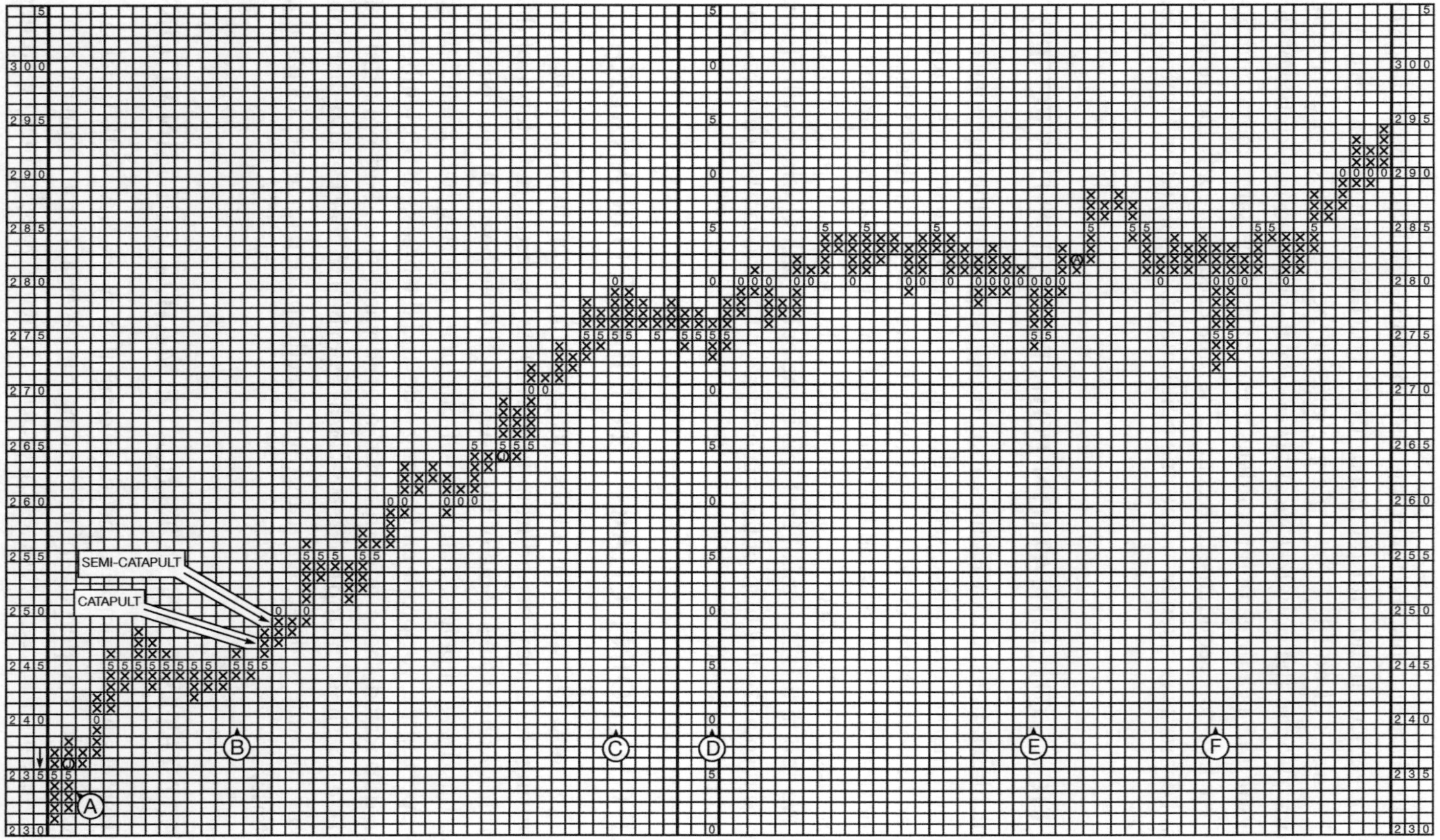

Fig 13.2 N.Y. Times Average: one point chart (May – October 1929, page 2)

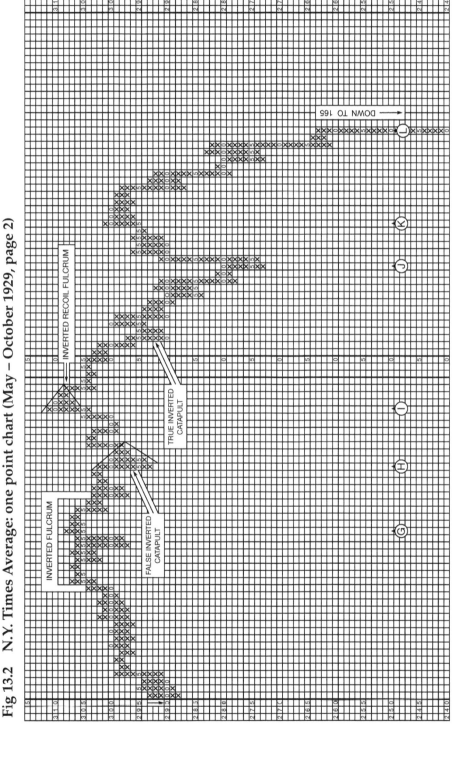

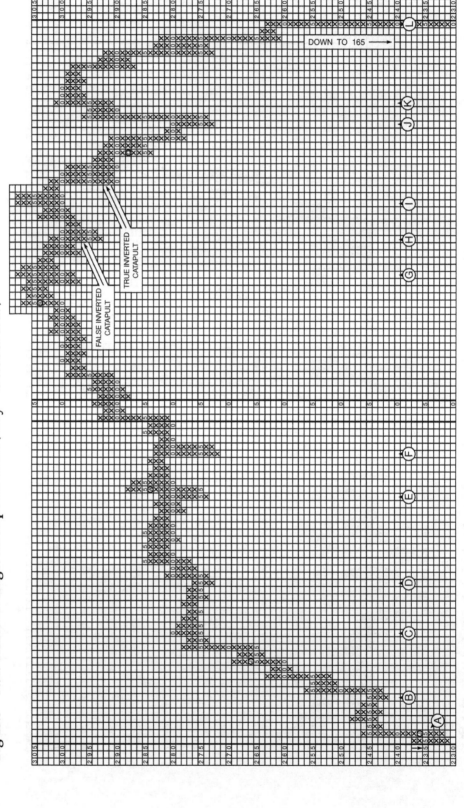

Fig 13.3   N.Y. Times Average: three point chart (May – October 1929)

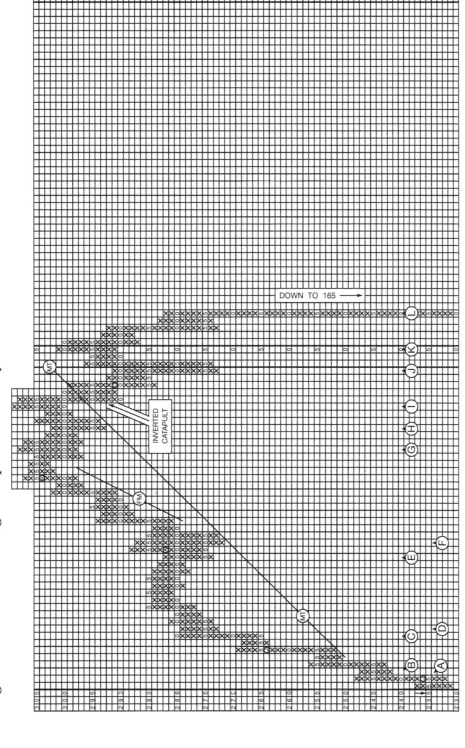

Fig 13.4 N.Y. Times Average: five point chart (May – October 1929)

the higher zones during the period under consideration. Any of the popular averages could have been used for the same purpose – either the Dow Jones Industrial group, the New York Herald Tribune, or the Standard Statistics group of ninety stocks. Point and Figure Method technique may be applied to the movements of any market composite index. For best results, we suggest that you be sure the index you use is a true representation, a reasonable cross section of the market, that it is fairly accurate and compiled by a responsible organization.

THE FIRST TEMPORARY TOP

In the Spring and early Summer of 1929, several widely known organizations began suggesting the liquidation of long positions and the establishment of short positions in anticipation of a major trend reversal. The vertical chart formations of the action of some stocks during that time began to appear as though the end was near to hand. You will see from the following discussion that the Point and Figure Method would have prevented such conclusions on the part of those who understood its technique.

We ask you now to turn to Chart Figures 13.1 and 13.2. In Figure 13.1 the zone A, to B, represents a trading area in the month of June which misled many vertical line technicians. We are sure that you will recognize it as a Point and Figure pattern with a *bullish* implication. The run up from column A, to the high at 248, in the middle of the zone was a sharp one, and a reasonable reaction should have been expected to correct so sharp an up move. Therefore, the declines which terminated at 242, are to be considered normal in view of the nature of the previous run up. It is true that the small air pocket which occurred beneath the work area around the figure 245, might have been considered a minor bearish implication, but only so if the reaction would have carried substantially lower, cancelling more than 50 per cent of the previous rally. In the area above column B, however, you will notice a few rallies and declines which began to show important bullish signals.

The bottom at 242, was tested, and the decline stopped at 243. Thereafter, the succeeding decline stopped at 244, and the future rally created a catapult at 247, and a major trend semi-catapult at 249. No student of the Point and Figure Method would have failed to recognize the bullish implications of market action at that time. No one would have sold out long positions or established short ones. The technical action was decidedly bullish and, in addition, the theory of "the Count" applied to the congestion area between A, and B, implied substantially higher prices.*

SEMI-CATAPULT POINT – UNUSUALLY BULLISH PATTERN

The congestion area A, to B, with its semi-catapult point at 249, was an unusually bullish pattern. It implied substantially higher prices, and the run up B, to C, followed. This mark up B, to C, was a spectacular run in of the shorts who had established their positions during the Spring and early Summer prior to the zone marked B. Those sharp advances are typical of major operations and in this case they proved to be the means of obtaining front page publicity for the market and an invitation which carried many of the public at large, head over heels into the biggest bull market ever witnessed.

STRENGTH CARRIES THROUGH OBJECTIVE LEVEL

The implications of the congestion area A, to B, suggested that the rally would run to at least 266, or higher, and it is at that zone that you would have had reason to begin to look for a possible top of the bull market.

In the zone 265, to 270, however, the market continued exceedingly strong and no danger sign occurred until the price area 275, to 280, began to develop. From the last starting point, 242, at B, to the temporary top, 280, at C, we have had no correction of consequence. Examine the three and five point charts, Figures 13.3 and 13.4, and notice the sharp trend of the rally B, to C. Active short swing traders, basing their judgment on the one point moves, would have liquidated positions around the 275 zone, side stepping the market until either a correction was witnessed or until the semi-catapult point at 281, was registered. The rally A, to C, required either a congestion area of re-consolidation, or a reaction sufficient to correct so sharp an up swing. The reaction which came was of minor consequence, however, as is shown between columns C, and D. It was clearly indicated at this point from the bullish pattern and the solid formations which were witnessed between C, and D, that a further advance in prices was in prospect.

THE CHANGE OVER OF TECHNICAL ACTION

Observe carefully the zones between D, and E, between E, and F, the final mark up F, to G, the minor correction G, to H, and the false rally H, to I, with its inverted recoil fulcrum. Note the signs of distributions subsequent to the zone

---

* The Count method is more fully described in *Advanced Theory and Practice of the Point and Figure Method*.

marked D. Observe that the highest squares between the work areas are massed solid with the oft repeating sharp declines followed by sharp rallies. These are always signs of the beginning of distribution and the weakening of the technical structure of the market. Stocks in this zone began to come out of the strong boxes, to pass from the hands of the insiders and long term holders into the floating supply and to the inexperienced public who buy at the top of rallies and sell on the declines. Notice that the zone from D, to I, repeats again and again the elongated hollow areas beneath the work zones as the price path pattern progressed slightly higher and moved across our chart. Notice the absence of solid zones of consolidation. Observe that the move was struggling and meeting additional resistance as it worked higher.

Note carefully that patterns which have the form of the character "M," with the congestion work areas at the tops of the "M" loops, when repeated many times in rapid succession, are always to be considered of *bearish* implication. On the other hand, patterns which have the form of the character "W," with the congestion work areas at the bottoms of the "W" loops, when repeated many times in rapid succession, carry *bullish* implications.

The one point moves as depicted on the charts, Figures 13.1 and 13.2, show many repetitions of the "M," pattern in the zone D, to I. This, in accordance with the theorem set forth above, implies a weakening technical condition and constitutes an important cautionary signal.

On the three point chart, Figure 13.3 the dips columns E, and F, indicate the beginning of a weakened technical position of the market, but the unusually sharp recoveries imply that the main top and reversal is to come from higher levels. In column I, you will note the reverse of these dips when the list rallied to 311, and quickly backed away. The action that quickly followed confirmed the last inverted catapult which had developed at 296.

Compare the one, three, and five point charts at this point. Notice, on the five point chart, Figure 13.4, that the final mark up trend line "FM," is soon intercepted by the price pattern just above the 300 mark.

THE TOP OF THE MOVE CLEARLY INDICATED

The intersection of the price path pattern, by the final mark up trend line "FM," on the five point chart was the all important danger signal, the final caution. That signal was confirmed by the nature of the patterns on the one point chart, from zone D, to zone G. This, together with the failure of a mass zone of consolidation to develop between G, and I, were all to be considered as warnings of the impending reversal. The patterns recorded from column D, to I, constituted a change in the type of technical action and were caution signals for students of this Method to liquidate all long positions and stand aside until the previous rally, A, to H, was fully corrected. The correction could have been effected by either a congestion zone of consolidation or a reaction.

INDICATIONS OF A MAJOR CULMINATION

Notice carefully the peculiar and extremely nervous state of the market as was indicated on the one point chart between zones G, and I. Observe the triangles on the one point chart between zones G, and I. Observe the triangles at H, and I. Consider the fact that no consolidation of the final mark up appeared. Consider the inverted fulcrum at G, and the false inverted catapult at 296. Notice that the last push through at I, was accomplished without the previous formation of a firm solid base at 300. Also, consider the inverted catapult point at 292, between columns I, and J. These were all vital and important signals for students of this Method; they clearly indicated the top of the bull market and its impending reversal.

BEAR TREND TECHNICAL ACTION

Having reached the conclusions outlined in the foregoing paragraphs that the zones D, to I, represented a change in technical action, no student of this Method could have failed to recognize in the sell off from I, to J, and the rally J, to K, definite signs of an impending bear market and bear trend technical action. The top at I, is a typical inverted recoil fulcrum which you will recall always implies swift action. On the way down in the decline, full figure 303, represents the inverse catapult point. An additional inverse catapult is developed at 298. Certainly the failure of the decline to hold 299, and consolidate above that zone is an exceptional example of the imminence of a big break and an additional confirmation that buying power had been exhausted.

You will remember, that a recoil fulcrum, whether upright or reverse, always connotes a sharp move impending. Therefore, either at 303, or at 298, you would have established short positions, especially so, if you were trading for the shorter swings based on conclusions and analysis of the one point moves as depicted in Figures 13.1 and 13.2.

THE INVESTOR OR LONG TERM TRADER

The longer term trader, although he would have been out of the market, might have waited for further confirmation or an opportunity to analyze subsequent technical action before establishing his short position.

The decline I, to J, which started in September, and terminated temporarily in the beginning of October, was typical bear trend action. The recovery J, to K, was final and definite confirmation that the bull market was finished and the bear trend started. The congestion area which built up after the rally in column J, in the zone around 295 to 300, above the symbol "K" showed definite resistance and plentiful supply of stock for all buyers who wished to take it. The failure of the rally J, to K, to penetrate the main trend was a final confirmation of the bear trend even for the more cautious long term traders who would have been out of the market during the decline I, to J. After the rally J, to K, with its inverse catapult at 289, inverse semi-catapults at 286, and 272, none could have doubted that the bear market was under way.

14

TECHNICAL INDICATIONS
AT A TURNING POINT

- The change to an up trend
- The change to a down trend

By observing the number of full point or half point changes recorded daily, either by individual issues or by a market index, and by studying the technical action throughout the day's trading and its relationship to immediately preceding market action, we are able to judge minor swing turning points.

THE CHANGE TO AN UP TREND

After a period of decline in a bull market, a turning point from *down trend* to *up trend* usually develops in the following manner:

1. The number of full figure changes dries up (lessens) on the declines.
2. The number of full figure changes increases on the rallies.
3. A test of the last established low point follows, which test must hold at a level above the last low or at the same point as the last low. The latter technical action is known as a double bottom, the former as a higher bottom.
4. After the test establishing a higher bottom or a double bottom, the succeeding rally develops sufficient strength to penetrate the preceding rally top.

(Students will note that the foregoing type of technical action exactly meets the requirements of the Point and Figure fulcrum formation.)

After a period of decline, it is customary, during periods of accumulation, for market activity to subside to such a degree that often many days may pass in succession wherein only 20 or 25 issues of the 100 most actively traded will show but one full figure change daily. Students must remember that a limited number of full figure changes after a decline is an indication of an impending turning point. In such a period, one should not feel that the market is inactive, or to use the colloquial expression, "doing nothing." It is at such times that important accumulation is being completed.

Changes in trend occur when the half point half hourly index hovers around a given level and builds up a congestion area from the few half point changes which register each day. This is especially indicative of a change over of trend when it occurs at or near one of the trend lines.

THE CHANGE TO A DOWN TREND

After a period of advance in a bull market, a turning point from *up trend* to *down trend* usually develops in the following way:

1. The number of full figure changes increases within a congestion area while the rest of the list rallies – buying power is temporarily exhausted as stocks pass into the hands of weak holders.
2. The number of full figure changes increases on the successive declines.
3. A test of the last established high point follows, which test must fail at or lower than the last high point. The former technical action is known as a double top, the latter as a lower top.
4. After the test, the succeeding decline gathers momentum as it goes down and breaks the support point of the last previous decline.

(Students will recognize this to be the type of technical action which meets the requirements of an inverted fulcrum.)

After an advance, it is customary, during periods of distribution, for activity to increase. In such periods, stocks fluctuate with increased numbers of full figure changes but make little further progress or the rate of progress is greatly reduced as the number of fluctuations increase.

CONCLUSION

Success in every field of endeavor is but the result of assiduous effort towards a definite objective. In order to attain success, we must apply the principles which have aided others. In applying these principles to our own problems, we are, in effect, making the experiences of others our own.

Oft times the progress is slow and discouraging moments arise. When such obstacles do occur, the mettle of the individual is put to test. If he permits discouragements to impede his progress and concludes that he is incapable of accomplishment, he drops by the wayside and is overtaken and passed by those whose tenacity of purpose and determination to succeed is uninfluenced by temporary discouragement. To the successful these obstacles are merely additional incentives.

In the preceding chapters, we have endeavored to teach and to illustrate the basic principles of the Point and Figure Method of anticipating stock price movements. This Method has run the test of time and has not been found wanting.

Since a proper assimilation of the principles of this Method and their correct application to market action are the keystones to the mastery and acquisition of a knowledge of a stock market technique which cannot but pay handsome dividends, we urge you to keep the following guides before you at all times:

1. Apply yourself to a serious study of this Method. Ground yourself thoroughly in *all* of its principles and their application as set forth and illustrated in the text.
2. Apply the acquired knowledge to past as well as present market action. Test and retest your reasoning and conclusions. Money need not be involved at first. Theoretical trades will be found interesting and instructive. They will give you the required familiarity with the proper application of the principles, and thus you will be instilled with that confidence so essential to success.
3. Having acquired a mastery of the principles of this Method, and a knowledge of their correct application, be sure to follow their implications. Have the courage of your convictions, and do not permit yourself to be influenced by outside opinions, rumors, or gossip.

The success achieved and the profits derived from your stock market transactions will be in proportion to

- the enthusiasm with which you study the principles of this Method and their application,
- your understanding of the technical action of the stock market,
- the intelligent application of these principles to your own market operations.

ADVANCED THEORY AND PRACTICE OF THE POINT AND FIGURE METHOD

VOLUME 2

by

Victor DeVilliers

and

Owen Taylor

1

PREREQUISITES TO SUCCESSFUL TRADING

- Develop proper mental approach
  - The value of isolation
- Proper and adequate physical equipment
  - Technical knowledge and equipment
    - The importance of selective data
    - Tape watching or active trading

Keen judgment is absolutely essential to success in any field of endeavor. It can be easily developed by training, and will improve with practice. Successful trading or investing, whether by this or any other method, depends for the greater part upon an unemotional analysis of known facts and future reasoning. We therefore deem it necessary to outline the proper approach to the development of such judgment.

Preparation for success resulting from stock market operations, whether large or small, falls into three distinct categories. They are (1) The Proper Mental Attitude; (2) The Maintenance of Sound Physical Condition; and (3) A Thorough Understanding of Market Technique.

DEVELOP PROPER MENTAL APPROACH

One should always regard the action of the Stock or Commodity Markets from the point of view of the professional trader. The mind can gradually be trained to analyze and observe market action without emotion and in a cool and detached manner. The professional trader regards market action as complete in itself, and always indicative of the future. He does not vacillate, one moment hoping, the next fearing. He does not seek tips, nor eavesdrop when rumors are prevalent. All these are best summed up as mere guesswork.

The professional trader also avoids the timid, fearful, and amateur board room habitue, who at best is engaged in guessing and hoping that he is guessing correctly. The professional analyzes, makes plans, bides his time, and acts when the proper moment arrives. If the route is not clearly defined at first, he stays out of the market, until it clarifies itself.

Education, that is, a college or highly specialized training, as such, is not a necessary prerequisite to a development of a keen mental equipment, marketwise. Neither is it desirable that one be of the so-called shrewd or clever type. While a trained mind is helpful, market education is more important to the prospective successful market operator than an intensive study of higher mathematics, or an inexhaustible knowledge of the classics. Some of Wall Street's most successful investors and traders were neither professional men nor college graduates. Most of the successful operators were and still are practical and painstaking people of average mentality, who are able, at all times and under most trying conditions, to control their emotions and exercise keen judgment marketwise.

THE VALUE OF ISOLATION

Always keep in mind that the market is a logical and deliberately organized series of events. It will serve one best if he recognizes these facts and guides himself accordingly. While fast action may be necessary at times, nothing can be gained by a constant *desire* for action since this urge may lead one to an illogical act which will surely prove unprofitable.

Another desirable attribute of proper mental approach and the development of the professional attitude, is to be able to cast out, eliminate now and for all time, the old habits of investing and trading that one has followed in the past, and which have proven unprofitable. One must not follow the crowds. He must neither buy at the top, nor sell out at the bottom. He must trade by method, by reason, by plan, and in a logical manner. It is not only necessary for one to disassociate himself from former bad habits, but in addition it would be well for him to avoid the persons and influences which have caused him to err in the past. There is an old adage, "He travels fastest, who travels alone!" Heed it. It will aid materially in the development of one's confidence in his own judgment.

The value of isolation and self-study cannot be over-emphasized. Opposing opinions make the market. Where some gain, others lose. Remember there would be no fluctuating markets and no profits were it not for opposing opinions prevailing at the same time.

The reasons for the varied opinions are as many as their proponents. One should keep his judgment to himself, and not permit it to be clouded by others. As a serious student of market technique, one cannot afford to mix a lay opinion with his own, be influenced thereby, and run the risk of having his own good judgment upset. The serious study of this Method is an indication of your intention and desire to acquire a professional mind – the only proper mental approach to stock market profits.

As you proceed with your studies, the conviction will grow upon you that the average person with whom you converse, most of the customers men in board rooms included, knows absolutely nothing about stock price movements and their motivating influences. Observe, study, analyze, plan, then act. You will soon be possessed of the proper mental attitude to properly gauge stock price movements.

PROPER AND ADEQUATE PHYSICAL EQUIPMENT

It should be unnecessary for us to call to your attention the importance of physical well-being. As an element to stock market success it is most important.

A sick or tired person cannot exercise unemotional, and cool judgment. A mind irritated by extraneous matters, is not a proper adjunct to a calm, deliberate study and analysis of the implications, of Points, Figures, Lines, Volume, Time, Triangles, and the other numerous technical indications influencing one's judgment. A robust, cheerful smiling individual, in full possession of good health and all of his faculties can be either bullish or bearish, as the occasion requires. His nerves will not override his judgment, if his market position is in harmony with the indicated trend.

We have digressed a moment to comment on this aspect of physical equipment, because it may, at some time or other, interfere with your judgment. If physical condition distracts one from the proper exercise of keen judgment, it is always best to take a rest, for "the market will always be there." Absence from the market for a short period, relief from the tension and anxiety regarding one's commitments, will strengthen one's judgment and ultimately result in greater benefit. The market's most successful operators, relax completely before and after each major campaign.

TECHNICAL KNOWLEDGE AND EQUIPMENT

Whether one is a trader or investor, of large or small means, the third and most important factor for success is a development of a thorough knowledge of market technique, coupled with a proper marshaling of facts upon which to exercise such knowledge.

While in the past you may have relied upon others for market advice, your study of this Method, evinces a desire to develop a technical knowledge of price movements.

By means and methods, other than the Point and Figure Method, a trader or investor will require copious historical reports, records of dividends, earnings, wordy and lengthy investigations of corporate personnel, a knowledge of seasonal trends of the particular issues under consideration, as well as a record of the movement of the stocks and earnings in question over past periods of years. However, by the use of the Point and Figure Method of anticipating stock price movements, the technician is able with but few and simple records, easily compiled, to so time his commitments as to synchronize them with the plans and campaigns of the insiders, thus anticipating the news and statistics later to be released. He will thus *buy* when the insiders buy and *sell* when the insiders sell.

The days when fundamental statistics were considered essential to market profits are past. Many will continue to insist that basic fundamentals be their guide to stock market commitments. It is our contention that those who rely on technical indications to guide their trades will profit more and sell out while the fundamentalists may find themselves in a position of being long of stock in a declining market.

Up-to-date methods require that judgment be based upon the technical action of stocks and the market. In that way one will be enabled to avoid losses and plan most commitments in a logical and professional manner.

THE IMPORTANCE OF SELECTIVE DATA

It is essential to start and keep up to date a graphic summary of the action of a number of important market averages from which we judge the future probable technical action and present technical positions of, (1) the issues in which we are interested and, (2) the market as it is represented by the important indices.

When one understands this Method and keeps the suggested data, losses will be moderate and can only arise through faulty interpretation, or because stops are touched off, which stops were placed to limit the risk at the time of the establishment of positions.

These losses, if any, are not to be considered as such. They are really premiums paid for insuring or protecting capital. Perfection is impossible of achievement. Our mission is to make the profits exceed the losses and to keep reducing the percentage of errors.

After one has mastered this Method, attendance at the broker's board room will be unnecessary and, as a matter of fact, detrimental. The tape and board room gossip has caused more losses to traders and investors than most all other reasons combined. Avoid therefore the board room and tape reading; start and maintain the necessary data, recording all the full figure changes on important stocks and averages daily. You will soon find a majority of trades developing good profits, in place of the losses previously suffered.

TAPE WATCHING OR ACTIVE TRADING

It is not necessary to watch the tape, nor is it necessary to trade actively. You must, however, avoid outside influences. You must analyze the technical implications of your recorded data. You must have your own opinions and be guided by them to the exclusion of everything else.

In the following chapters we explain for you in detail, the many ways of analyzing the implications of chart formations as applied in the study of technical market action.

Apply yourself assiduously to a proper understanding of these principles and their applications. Study first and practice afterward, always remembering that skill results from constant practice.

2

BASIC PRINCIPLES – THEIR APPLICATION

- Basic principles underlying this method
  - The trading range – accumulation
    - The fulcrum
    - The mark up
    - Distribution
    - The trend line
  - For long term main trend operations
    - Plotting the trend line
    - Technical position
- Determining the technical position of the market through the use of the five dominant positions
  - Resume

We have outlined in Chapter 1, the needed prerequisites to successful trading and investing. Students of the Point and Figure Method, who have progressed in their work to the extent of studying this book should now be in full possession of a complete knowledge of the basic principles underlying the Point and Figure Method. These principles were fully discussed in Volume 1.

BASIC PRINCIPLES UNDERLYING THIS METHOD

In order to successfully analyze the technical position of individual stocks and the market, one must keep and maintain a suitable number of one and three point figure charts. The data for compiling these charts can be secured from the ticker tape. In order to obtain the fullest benefit from the formations created by the movements of stocks and the averages, one must record each full figure change on the one point charts, each one half point change on the one half point charts, and each, and every, full three point swing on the three point charts. If we compile and study the developing formations as they appear on our records, we will soon have no difficulty in analyzing the technical position of stocks, and in recognizing suitable signals which will be sure to develop profits.

THE TRADING RANGE – ACCUMULATION

The most important formation, in which we will be interested, is the congestion area or trading range. The congestion area is created on our charts when a stock fluctuates up and down in a trading area. These congestion areas on the one point charts develop to be either zones of accumulation or of distribution. In future chapters in this book you will learn how to recognize and detect whether these zones of congestion are to become areas of accumulation or distribution and then you will be able to adopt positions in accordance with your conclusions. Second in importance is the type of pattern formed. That is, the pattern created by the action of the stock before, during, and after these congestion areas. As the stock fluctuates in a trading range, creating these patterns, it indicates either accumulation or distribution, and develops either a base or a ceiling. You will soon be able to recognize which pattern is under formation.

THE FULCRUM

Where a base is under formation, the most important pattern to watch for is the full fulcrum. This is a very strong type of base and always implies substantially higher prices. It is the first important point at which long positions should be established. The fulcrum is fully described in Volume 1. After the fulcrum has been completed and in many instances after other types of bases have been completed, a stock moves out past previous resistance points onto the catapult. The catapult point is the second important place for the establishment of long positions. These two indications always develop after a trading range has been built up. They offer splendid opportunities for quick substantial profits.

THE MARK UP

Second in importance are the types of patterns which occur after the base has been laid. The mark up or push up is the move wherein the sponsors or manipulators of the stock force it into higher grounds on and up to a new zone where another trading range or congestion area is to be built up. On the way up, in many cases, a third important group of formations develop. Included in this group is the semi-catapult. This pattern is more fully described in Volume 1. One may in most instances establish long positions at the semi-catapult point, with confidence that profits will soon develop. After the mark up we must be on the lookout for distribution in order to determine a point at which to sell out long positions. We must lay out our trend line, continuously check the trend, and be on guard to catch the first signs of inside distribution.

DISTRIBUTION

After the period of accumulation, comes the mark up. Stocks are accumulated and marked up for the purpose of selling at much higher prices. When an advance of from 15, to 50, points has been effected, we must begin to be on the alert for signs of distribution. The patterns created on our Point and Figure Charts, from which we can recognize distribution, may occur as one of three types, (1) the ascending steps which intercept our trend line and show a diminishing velocity of advance, (2) the formation known as a trading range or congestion area at the upper level after an advance, and (3) a group of descending steps formed after a culmination point known as a vertex, or the descending steps formed after a definite double top has been registered.

The first type shows distribution during the advance, the second distribution within a narrow trading range near the top, the third skillful distribution on the way down after the high has been established.

THE TREND LINE

We stated in the last paragraph, that it was very important to continuously check the trend since individual stocks, and the market in general, go up or down, from the congestion area or trading range to another. The question of trend lines and their uses should be understood by most of our readers. Trend lines when used in conjunction with conventional vertical bar charts, have very often proven themselves to be grossly unreliable, especially when students and technicians attempt to apply them too closely to the technical action of the stock, inasmuch as they consider the fluctuations day by day. It has proven to be the undoing of many traders when they have tried to use trend lines on a stock as it breaks out of a triangular formation on the down side, breaking the trend line, and then suddenly reverses its movements and develops a sharp and substantial rally. Trend lines have their best application when used in conjunction with the full figure changes as required for the proper application of the principles of the Point and Figure Method.

Trend lines may be drawn to show the immediate short term swings in stocks of from three to seven points, the general intermediate trend, and the main long term trend. Each type of trend line has its limitations and its special uses. These lines, as applied to our one point charts, are especially helpful in judging the pressure behind the movements of stocks, on the upmoves and on the downside. They are also a great aid in indicating points at which to take profits after a stock has had a substantial move and reaches a tentative congestion area. Trend lines used in conjunction with one point charts will show the beginning of accumulation, the force behind the move during the mark up, and in addition will indicate the point to sell.

FOR LONG TERM MAIN TREND OPERATIONS

The use of trend lines in conjunction with our three point charts will indicate periods of accumulation, direction of the main trend, and zones of distribution.

PLOTTING THE TREND LINE

We have stated that trend lines have their limitations. Therefore, in plotting them, we must keep in mind and make due allowance for the manipulation of the sponsors and insiders. We do this on our one and three point charts by allowing one full square from the low of one shake-out, and the low of the next higher shake-out, which we join up and use to indicate the pitch of our projected trend line. Detailed illustrations appear in many chapters throughout the book. This principle should be applied to trend lines indicating the intermediate and the main trend.

When we use this line to gauge the pressure of the mark up, and to indicate initial signs of distribution, we do not make these allowances, but connect them with the corners of the last points of a reaction and project forward a degree of pitch, which is obtained from the plotting of the line connecting exact corners of the lowest squares. Trend lines drawn above the line of action of a stock to indicate the trend channel should always provide the one point leeway described above. Trend channels with their upper and lower lines are always helpful to gauge the probable culmination of the move both on the down side, as well as on the up move. In a bull market the important line to watch closely is the lower trend line, drawn beneath the points of reaction. In a bear market the important trend line is the upper line drawn connecting the points of resistance on the rallies.

TECHNICAL POSITION

At any moment the market action of every stock can be classified and will fall into one of five important technical positions. A careful study of a Point and Figure formation using a one point chart together with close drawn trend lines to indicate the immediate move, in conjunction with the count system, more fully described later in this book, will indicate to you the probable extent of the next immediate move in the stock under consideration.

We indicate the technical position into which stocks group themselves with the five letters A to E inclusive. They are as follows:

A. In position A, a stock indicates that a minor rally of from 3, to 8, points is due. This is best estimated by past performance of the stock together with a consideration of its characteristic rallies and declines.

B. In position B, a stock indicates a major rally due, of from 10, to 20 points. Here in gauging and judging the move, we resort to trend lines, its past performances, its characteristic rally and decline range, and the count.

C. In position C, a stock indicates the opposite of position A, namely that a decline, correction or reaction, of from 3, to 8 points, should soon occur.

D. In position D, a stock indicates the opposite of position B, namely, that a major reaction of from 10, to 20 points should develop soon.

E. All other stocks will fall into this fifth grouping. In this group are included the stocks in which the future immediate probable move cannot be determined.

DETERMINING THE TECHNICAL POSITION OF THE MARKET THROUGH THE USE OF THE FIVE DOMINANT POSITIONS

At any time during the progress of market action, you can easily determine its technical condition by drawing off a balance sheet on which you will list the above five positions. Should the number of issues falling into columns A and B, be substantially in excess of the number falling in C, D, and E, the market would be in an extremely bullish position. An excess of listings in columns C, D, over the columns of A, B, and E would indicate a substantial reaction to be due. A great percentage in position E, would indicate the market at stalemate either under accumulation, or distribution. When the columns of C, D, and E, are in excess of the totals of A, and B columns, it would indicate distribution; time for a correction. At such a time be on the alert to liquidate your long position.

RESUME

We have discussed briefly herein a few of the important principles to be detailed for you in this book of *Advanced Theory and Practice of the Point and Figure Method*. In subsequent chapters we will show the application of these principles to individual stocks and the averages. We will take you through a number of actual campaigns, so that you may understand, in a more thorough manner, the fundamental principles involved. You will be taught how to coordinate the one point indications with those shown on the three point charts. You will be able to recognize the important signals given at the catapult, at the semi-catapult, and the implications to be drawn from the action of stocks on dividend days, and on ex-dividend days. In many issues, a full campaign of accumulation, mark up, and of distribution will be described to you. Finally, before we conclude this work, we will tell you all there is to know about the principles underlying the count, which indicate the extent of the probable future move in the stock you have under consideration. Study carefully and apply yourself diligently. You will have no regrets for the time spent in mastering these basic principles of the Point and Figure Method of Anticipating Stock Price Movements.

3

CHART FORMATIONS INDICATED THE INCEPTION OF A MOVE

- The value of charts
- One cardinal principle which must be understood
- A necessary premise
- Wait for signs of accumulation or distribution
- What to look for
- Await previous support
- How the move begins
- Establishing a long position
- A practical example
- Dead center
- The use of the stop
- Ultra-conservatism

In our first chapter we have emphasized the value of proper preparation for the development of accurate market judgment. As we proceed, we shall attempt to develop your ability to recognize the technical position of stocks and the market, so that you will be able to anticipate the next move and profit therefrom.

THE VALUE OF CHARTS

Students who have read Volume 1, have mastered the theory and understand how to prepare the necessary graphic records required for the observation of the action of stocks. Permit us to again impress upon you the importance of collating and maintaining a full set of data, graphic records (charts, as they are sometimes called) of the action of at least one hundred stocks and four or five averages. The neater and more careful the preparation and maintenance of the graphic records, the more able will you be to recognize quickly the important formations indicating wide moves either up or down. The best reasons for maintaining a set of one hundred stocks and averages are, additionally, (1) the increased number of opportunities presented, (2) the larger variety of confirmatory or contradictory signals available.

Of great importance is the ability to recognize formations indicating accumulation, which usually precede important upward moves. Next in importance is the ability to recognize distribution. Both of these formations must form on our one point charts. We will endeavor to show how stocks are marked up and finally distributed, after which a reaction or sell-off invariably follows.

ONE CARDINAL PRINCIPLE WHICH MUST BE UNDERSTOOD

Before one can hope to profit from his commitments, whether trading from the tape or charts, or investing for the so-called long pull, he must be willing to concede that a good deal of market action results from artificial stimuli, manipulation, if one chooses to so name it. We do not necessarily mean to imply that all moves, either up or down and in every stock that fluctuates, result from the plans and machinations of individuals or groups; but we do insist that the influence of floor traders, specialists, board room speculators, and others, is such that the resultant action is best anticipated and understood, if this principle is subscribed to and recognized.

A NECESSARY PREMISE

The world is long of stocks; everybody owns some, and will continue to acquire them, and in greater quantities as confidence develops. Stocks in American corporations represent equities in the plant and earning power of these corporations and in American enterprise. The majority of those who trade and invest are always long of stocks. By the majority we mean not only the small investor and trader, but the big interests as well. The big interests constitute the bankers, the insurance companies, the many types of holding companies (trusts), the large and vested estates; in short – the mystic composite entity usually termed "they."

It is necessary to recognize this premise in order to estimate the market's position and be able to judge its probable future movement. It is also necessary to take for granted that seasoned stocks will always find buying and develop a sound base at a level in the price structure, where the present or estimated future income from dividends will exceed the annual return from other sources, wherein the same amount of capital may be employed.

This confirms the accepted theory, that values in common stocks will eventually be asserted; that no one should doubt the recuperative ability of sound investments; and that as a consequence, so-called bull markets must succeed so-called bear markets, with far higher values eventually prevailing for the proper type of stocks.

The trader or investor should be alert to gauge the correct moment in order to participate in that advance, to recognize the proper psychological moment at which to establish a position. This position may either be long or short, and we must be willing to go either way because (a) we miss fully 50 percent of all opportunities when we stay either bullish or bearish at all times; and (b) we are actually buyers, whether we go long or short, since as bulls we merely buy first, then sell, while as bears we sell first and buy at a later time. Eliminating the time factor, both transactions are exactly alike, justifiable technically, legally, and morally.

WAIT FOR SIGNS OF ACCUMULATION
OR DISTRIBUTION

New moves are always in the making. Stocks will always fluctuate. They go up or down, and are never stationary. A trading area or price band in which stocks fluctuate within narrow limitations indicates accumulation, distribution, or consolidation. When stocks are obviously undervalued and have had a good decline, the subsequent inclination is to go up. It is then that we should be on the alert to seek buying opportunities. When stocks are high in price and have had a good advance, their subsequent tendency is to react or decline. We must be ever alert to seize the opportunity to take our long positions or to sell short.

The trained technician never buys or sells on hunches, tips, rumors, or because brokers are bullish or bearish. He seeks only the opportunity to study and analyze the facts – the formations of our Point and Figure Charts. They will tell all one can wish to know, and all that is needed. A like cause results in like effect. Experience will teach you just what to expect from each of the relatively few important types of formations.

WHAT TO LOOK FOR

When a new move is about to begin, the forces of supply and demand are about evenly balanced. When supply overcomes demand, stocks go down, and similarly, when demand overcomes supply, they go up. However, when supply and demand are about evenly balanced, fluctuations narrow down. All types of charts present graphic representations of these phenomena.

Fig 3.1   The chart of the pendulum swing

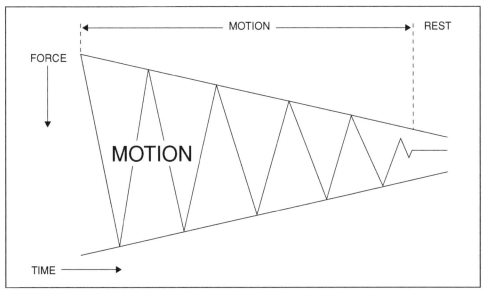

The simplest form of chart which we can apply to the theory of supply and demand, is one representing the movements of a pendulum (see Figure 3.1). As a free pendulum is started by a motivating force, it travels through a wide arc, which narrows down gradually until the pendulum comes to a stop. The forces of supply and demand can be plotted, and the results portrayed will greatly resemble the chart of the swing of the pendulum (see Figure 3.2).

Fig 3.2   The forces of supply and demand

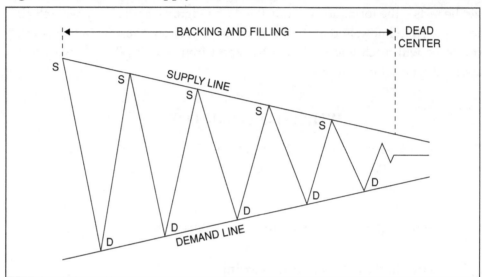

Neither an engineering, nor a scientific education is necessary in order to realize that market charts are the outcome of attempts to record, in graphic form, movements having a natural basis. The Point and Figure Method, of recording movements in graphic formations, has a close relationship to the forces governing the influence of stock price movements. The forces of supply and demand, which create stock price movements, can be plotted so that one may observe the phenomena, and by this Method detect the inception of the moves.

AWAIT PREVIOUS SUPPORT

Not until we have a clear indication that a move has begun, are we justified in establishing our position. Before we take a new position, we must estimate the probable future extent of the move, the risk to be assumed, and the possible resultant profit. If the prospective profit is not substantially greater than the assumed risk, the wise trader stays out.

Authorities are of the opinion that estimated profits should always be at least two to three times the risk involved. All is speculation – even life itself – therefore do not hesitate. When the indicated probable move warrants the risk, have the courage of your convictions; assume it fearlessly, and act accordingly.

HOW THE MOVE BEGINS

Refer now to our chart, Figure 3.2, illustrating the pendulum-like manner in which stocks swing up to the supply point, and then down to the demand point. Compare this with our one point charts and you will notice that a similar condition develops, where the range of a stock and its swing narrows down to a pivot, or point, that roughly marks the dead center of the arc representing its former broad move. Figure 3.2 may be considered a minor cycle, which is a movement of anywhere from 20, to 50 points. As the momentum diminishes, volume will, in all probability, decline until the last phase is reached, that is, where a trading range of from 3, to 5, or 7, points develops. The extent of these varying swings depends upon the volatility, price, and characteristics of the individual stock. In many cases the culmination of the move is finally confirmed by subnormal volume and the development of a pivot or dead center, with narrow daily fluctuations and very few full figure changes.

It is now nearing the psychological moment to act. That is the time to establish your position. The stock is technically on a pivot of dead center, as illustrated in Figure 3.2. It is more easily recognized when charted in the conventional manner as required by this Method, as shown in Figure 3.3. If this condition exists coincidental with subnormal volume, an ideal signal is indicated – namely, it is time – *be ready to act*.

While a signal is a command to act, no signal can be regarded as certain. Insiders act on signals, and as you may have read, they are by no means always 100 percent correct in their trades. We have no reason to expect better results. But it can be fairly stated, without fear of contradiction, that the majority of signals given by this Method prove more reliable, more practical, more dependable, more logical, and in the end, more profitable than any other plan or method for stock trading that we know of.

ESTABLISHING A LONG POSITION

After determining that many stocks have developed bases, we refer to our charts in order to ascertain the probable trend of the market. We try to be certain that the majority of the groups are in harmony with our findings, and that the individual stocks in which we are interested have reached, or are nearest to, dead

Fig 3.3   Atchison: move following a balance at dead center

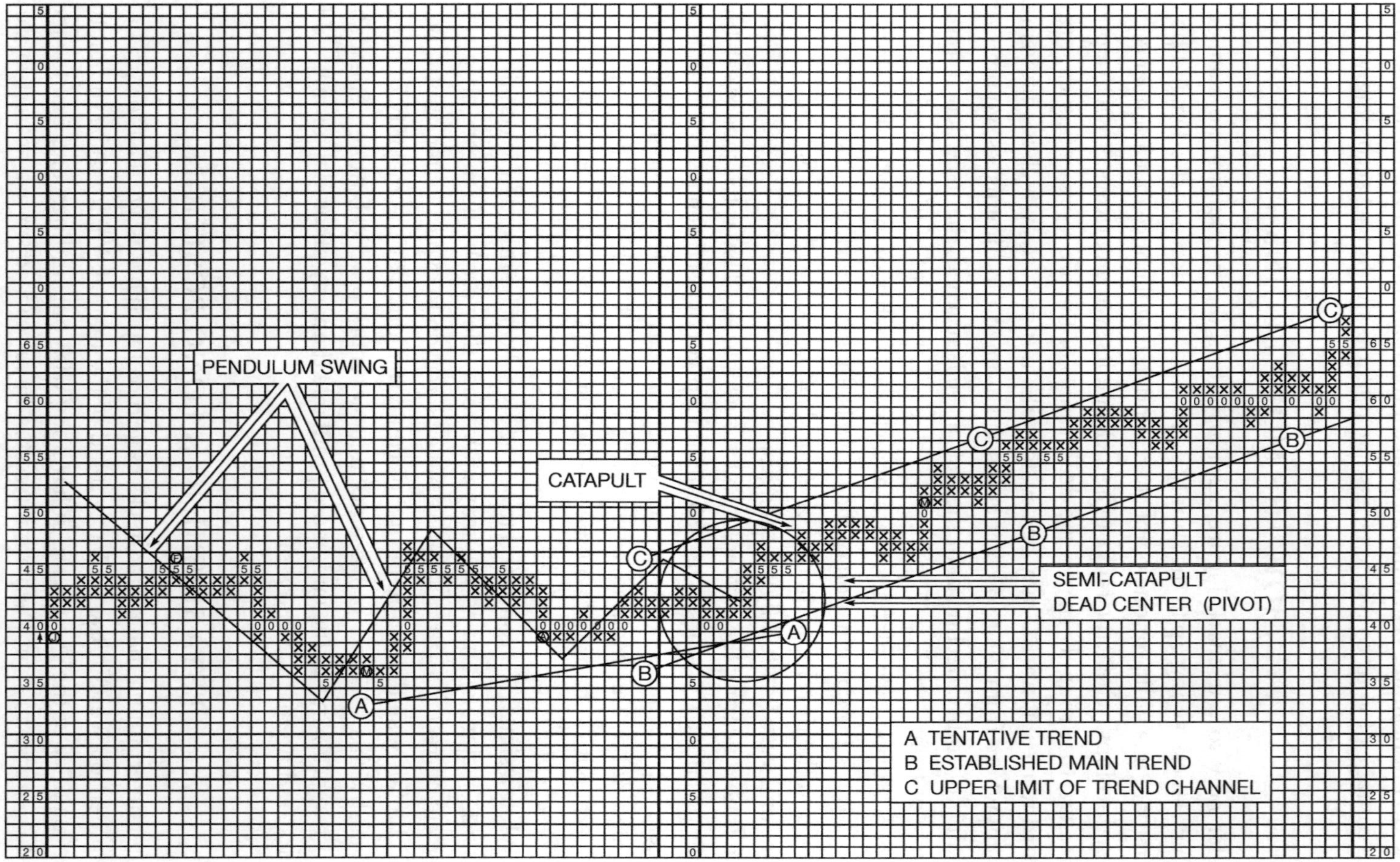

center, which, together with a study of volume, confirms our tentative diagnosis of dead center or culmination. Where the Point and Figure Method, by its one point charts, indicates a satisfactory base or congestion point, such a signal is good enough to follow in establishing your position, protected by a stop placed at a point below the congestion area, to protect your capital until the stock gives indication of ability to move up from the point of dead center, out on the catapult, then off to higher levels.

A PRACTICAL EXAMPLE

The one point chart of Atchison, Figure 3.3, from January 1, 1933, is an instructive illustration, not only of the move following a balance at dead center, but also of another principle of frequent value, namely the half-way rule.

The New Year began with the stock at the full figure 39. By mid-February 46, was reached at three different times. The failure of the stock to go through the resistance point of 46, after the third attempt, was a bearish signal. The formation became dubious at 43, and was more strongly emphasized at 42. The stock had no rallying power. It was apparently headed for a major decline of about 15 points from 45. However, volume on the decline dried up, and a stubborn barrier – base – was set up in the 35, to 37, zone. The 37 figure was repeated 8 times, counting in one blank. The formation had changed from sagging vertical which was bearish, to a drawn out horizontal which is bullish. The stock stood the mid-March test splendidly, and its quick advance to 47, proved that the floating supply had without doubt passed into strong hands, that is, the right people held the available supply stock.

By this time, on this formation alone, without reference to previous formations or the influence of other factors or the time element, we have a set of known facts, which we now analyze for you. The very bearish indications of mid-February, 42, to 46, zone had been offset by the excellent support at 35, to 37. The ability to rally 12 points, 35, to 47, was equal to 33⅓ percent of its price, and must be interpreted most favorably. The decline of 8 points was from a new high 47, and might logically have stopped at 40, to 41, half-way! The additional two points on the down side was no worse than that of the averages, and was as good or better than, the performance of most stocks. The stock showed tremendous resistance in the 40, to 43, zone, which was the half-way point, and the previous drop below 41, was then amply atoned for.

DEAD CENTER

Dead center, or pivot, of the entire formation from January to mid-April, 1933, was 41. This happens to be the half-way point of the previous swing. It is also the center of the arc bounded by figures 35, and 47. Any point above or below the trading range at the seventh 42, in the center of the page, was to be our signal. At 40, came a full three point reaction, which was normal. We were still in doubt despite a previous bullish formation built up since April 1, which had established eight 40s, up to that time. The recovery from the ninth 40, to 44, registered at the middle of the page, was another bullish signal. Dead center or pivot is being left behind, and we must get aboard Atchison at 44, or at 44, "on stop."*

There were no further selling signals in this stock. One must stay long from 44, to 67. As a matter of fact, the stock reached the full figure 80, in July, but many selling signals appear around 70, in June.

THE USE OF THE STOP

In this illustration, an excellent and unusual full catapult formation developed at the first full figure 48, a most favorable point to go long of the stock "on stop." A subsequent decline of but two points after our purchase, with previous strong support at 45, to 46, should not have caused the need of stop order protection below the flat 46, say at 45⅞, until after 50, was made. Then a stop placed at 49, would have been logical.

By using the most conservative stops throughout, whether on our long commitment taken at 44, which was after dead center or pivot, or at 48, when the stock passed out onto the catapult, the formation shows clear support at 51, at 55, and at 58. Stops should be placed below those congestion points on the way up. The chart moves off the pages at 67, without indicating the next logical point for our stop order. Those who have recorded the subsequent action of Atchison will agree that a stop was called for at 68, and was proper even though it was later caught and thereby clinched a gross profit of 20, to 24 points.

ULTRA-CONSERVATISM

In the foregoing illustration, ultra-conservatism was followed throughout. The real move in Atchison began at the first 38, following the decline to the second

---

* Method explained later.

35. The latter figure was a clear double bottom. Conformation at that point was had from the low volume of transactions and the fact that the closing of all the banks in the United States had failed to force this stock below its former full figure low.

We will now show the reasons of this interpretation. At the first 35, the stock had a major decline of 11 points or 25 percent in its value in a short time. At the second 35, its failure to go lower under the most adverse conditions must be interpreted as a favourable indication. It is here, at 35, that the stock begins to show resistance, for at 38, we witness the best rally in some time, namely 3 points, following a series of 2 point swings. At 39, the rally of 4 points from bottom is slightly more than normal and the formation is decidedly bullish at 40, after 38, followed by 39. At the 40 point, we had clear evidence that the move was begun at 37, to 38, which was the place to have taken an initial position. Our start around 44, was ultra-conservative yet it nevertheless developed substantial profits.

Examine your chart very carefully and note the bullish fulcrum formation. See the sharp run up which followed as soon as the stock moved out "on the catapult." After the first reaction the work or congestion area between 39, and 43, creates another bullish signal of the type which should never be ignored. After the move sets in no danger signals appear until resistance develops at 70, and the congestion area builds up between that point and 68. These signals do not appear on the chart, Figure 3.3; they register immediately after the last 67, as shown.

4

RECURRING OPPORTUNITIES DURING THE MOVE

- Study creates skill
- Recognizing opportunities
- Dividend absorbed
- A long position established "on stop"
- Judging the move
- Confirmation of the move
- A critical analysis of trading zones
- How to plot new trend lines

Throughout the course of the intermediate moves, and at any stage of the minor speculative cycle, which includes the intermediate swing and its trading area, countless opportunities for profit occur again and again.

We have advocated calm, isolated study of the Point and Figure data. It is from these carefully prepared records, detailing every relevant move of stocks and the averages, that you will be able to recognize and profit from recurring opportunities. Start and maintain complete sets of both one and three point charts of as many stocks as you have time to keep current and to study.

STUDY CREATES SKILL

You should study carefully full figure one point charts of five selected averages and active leading stocks, for through this work you will familiarize yourself with the oft recurring formations, and you will learn to profit from them. Some of these charts are reproduced here either in whole or in part, as illustrations for this text. Study them carefully for they record actual past performances and similar formations will and must recur again in the future, and when they do, similar opportunities will be available. When you have studied these completed movements and have grasped the principles of the Point and Figure Method, you will then be able to recognize future possibilities.

The patterns we describe in this chapter are those which occur at other than the ideal points of "at dead center" and "on the catapult." These opportunities are clearly supplementary. Basic formations need not be awaited, since they may develop at any point and at any time.

RECOGNIZING OPPORTUNITIES

Let us go through the chart of American Sugar Refining (ASR) in Figure 4.1. Here is a striking illustration of the simplicity of the Method and the clarity of its signals. Note between the levels 25, to 70, the freedom from confusing formations and the numerous commands to trade, all of which resulted in fine opportunities for profit. On the one point chart of ASR, no true pivotal formations are indicated, but notwithstanding the absence of these basic formations the action is replete with profitable opportunities all clearly indicated.

On January 3, 1933 our chart starts with the first full figure 22, and at 27, it reached an apparent ceiling, or resistance point. After the fourth 27, was registered, preliminary diagnosis would indicate that point as a ceiling, however the

Fig 4.1   American Sugar Refining

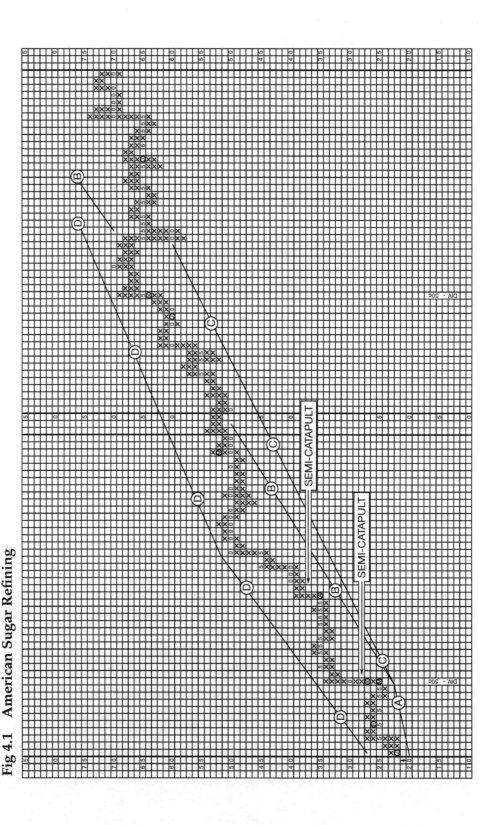

situation changes thereafter. The decline to 24, a 3 point correction, was normal. Let us here impress you that we have always regarded a three point reaction in a stock selling between 20, and 60, as normal. In the higher priced issues selling let us state from 60, to 100 and over, it is well to consider a 5, or 7, point correction as normal.

After twice registering 24, ASR advanced to 27, starting the move on the first day of March when it sold, ex-dividend. This was a most important signal. A quick advance to 28, and a new high for the move followed. These facts contradicted the previous tentative diagnosis wherein we concluded that 27, was a ceiling or resistance point. ASR, at 28, is in a strong bullish position and now the previous resistance area 24, to 27, is converted to a base. The stock had evidently been under accumulation in the 24, to 27 zone. The reader is now advised to take a blank sheet of paper and cover up the action subsequent to the fourth 27, and begin to read the current movement just as though it is happening at present. We wish to be entirely fair and will not permit our knowledge of the subsequent move to influence our diagnoses and subsequent conclusions. We will hereafter reason out the move with you by the Point and Figure Method exclusively without the aid of other factors. In so doing we feel you will learn how to analyze similar moves for yourself.

After the fourth 27, is recorded, a normal 3 point reaction to 24, a negative, tentative bearish signal is recorded. At the fifth 27, ex-dividend, shown on the chart encircled, the 3 point recovery, also normal, partly cancelled any bearish signal justifiably created before this point. A new high would of course be bullish, especially after its ability to hold at 24, when it formed a double bottom. The first angle formed where trend lines A, B, and C meet is bullish because the line A, which is a diagonal base, created by joining the last full figure 22 with the last full figure 24, is changed to a steep up grade, by line C, which is the line formed by joining the last full figure 24, with the 52, in May. A change in the pitch of a trend line from a lesser to a greater pitch as occurred at line A is always bullish. It indicates additional pressure behind the new buying power, and therefore behind the move.

DIVIDEND ABSORBED

Note that the one-half point dividend indicated on the chart is absorbed in the move at 27. At this point two possible positions are clearly created, the first very bullish at 28, with the second bearish at 23. In addition at 28, the rally from 24 would be greater than normal, that is 4 points. If the stock were in a bearish position it would not rally more than 3 points, that is to say, it should not go above full figure.

A LONG POSITION ESTABLISHED "ON STOP"

Correct procedure at the point 27 ex-dividend, would have been either to buy on the new high 28, a semi-catapult position, or to buy "on stop" at 28. The order to the broker in the latter case would read, "Buy——shares ASR, at 28 stop." This would instruct your broker to purchase for you only if the stock actually sold at full figure 28, and not otherwise. Had ASR merely bulged to 27⅞, or lower, or turned permanently downward from the ex-dividend 27, the investor or trader would not, and could not, have been long, when following this procedure.

The stock is in a bullish position at 28, whether bought at the market or on stop. It was a decided struggle for the stock to climb from 21, to 28. It took eight weeks to complete that short move and came after weeks and weeks of work between 25 and 27. It proved profitable as it most always does, to get aboard at 28. The dividend factor added interest to the move.

In our first book we explained that fractions must be disregarded. The full figure 28, or better, was needed to complete a bullish formation for ASR. The public is prone to buy on fractional bulges in new high ground believing it a sign of strength; this same group usually sell out on fractional declines, creating new lows. Such policy is always a mistaken one. By our Method, ASR could have fluctuated between 26⅛, and 27⅞, without altering the principal formation. These minor fluctuations totaling 1¾ points, take on an apparent significance by any other method and are the principal causes for most of the losses of the average "in and out" trader. It is a fundamental principle that stocks must fluctuate – we must allow for these fluctuations.

JUDGING THE MOVE

The strength and pressure behind ASR now becomes clearly apparent for it rallies sharply to 34, an advance of 10 points. This issue participated in the inflation move of March 1933 with enthusiasm. The student of this Method had no occasion to seek reasons, news, tips or to concern himself about fundamental economics, for the technical action of the stock itself was decidedly bullish and our Point and Figure Method clearly reflected its position.

No selling signal had appeared as yet. Up to the fourth 36, we have had simply a series of 2 and 3 point fluctuations, all normal, none altering the bullish formation from 28. We *must* stay *long*. Our Method involves no guesswork, we await signals. We are probing ASR, with the future work covered over, therefore we are not sure about the formation at 33, to 36 – it may be distribution or accumulation. Is the formation bullish or bearish? Tentatively it is bullish; let us examine why. (1) The stock held far above the former critical point at 28; (2) it moved 8 points higher to 36; (3) at the new high point its fluctuations have been normal, 3 points or less; and (4) the drawn out work around 33 to 36 gives us confidence.

April 1, the stock registers a full figure 35; at 37 we would have another semi-catapult, a new high, and a most logical point to buy again. Here we may again buy either at the market at that price or buy "on stop." Additional buying on the way up is called pyramiding, a procedure some technicians regard with awe. When using this Method one may proceed with assurance and confidence. If ASR is strong enough to make a full figure 37, it is an opportunity similar to the situation at 28; one may buy with confidence whether the first commitment was made at 28, or not. With the formation preceding 37, one may buy any stock with confidence. Thereafter the stock makes 37, advances to 39, and reacts one point twice. This action is decidedly and emphatically *bullish*.

CONFIRMATION OF THE MOVE

When ASR breaks away from the 33 to 36 zone into new high ground the trend or direction becomes clear. Here we can lay our trend line by joining the first 25, registered in March with the first 35 made in April. Trend lines are at the best an approximation, and therefore in practice we have found it advisable to allow a margin, or leeway, of one full square below or above the figure. This is in our opinion good practice. It allows for errors, manipulation, and other contingencies. Following this procedure we get our new trend line BB.

All action above the line A, and BB, on the one point figure chart of ASR is to be considered *bullish*. Action developing below the line BB, would be *bearish*. This foregoing principle is not absolute in its operation because, one point conclusions may be modified, delayed, or reversed, as result of the implications to be had from a consideration of our three point charts. It will be noticed that even if we adhere to our one point conclusions without considering the three point implications, trades from signals of the Point and Figure Method are far more profitable than can be had from other methods.

A number of three point illustrations will be given later from actual examples of current movements and will clearly show when latitude may be allowed in the indications of the one point trend lines.

ASR resumes its upward course, well above the trend lines to 50, without altering in the slightest its bullish formation. After the first 50, a normal reaction occurs and then the stock makes a 52. Thereafter we get our first caution, a 6 point reaction to 46.

What does the Method now indicate? The stock has had a 100 percent rise and is entitled to a reaction. Pool operations obviously began in the 27, to 37, zone; the average price for the stock in that zone would be 32, and that is where the insiders have averaged their positions. Without referring to volume let us examine the shake-out from 52, to 46. We cannot object to this nominal reaction after a major advance from 22.

A CRITICAL ANALYSIS OF TRADING ZONES

The Method here suggests an examination of the various trading zones or steps in the advance. This examination is necessary so that we may get a fair idea of the pressure behind the above moves, and thus be able to appraise its future possibilities. The ascent from 22, to the first 52, is indeed a very bullish formation. The reaction to 46, is the first fair set-back in three phases of the move up from 22. These three phases are one – the work from 22, to 27, the accumulation zone; two – the 33, to 36, area wherein a consolidation of the gains was effected; and the third, now forming, 46, to 52, which may be either another consolidation or a zone of distribution.

Between these three stages in the move, nothing of any importance has happened. It was a continued advance, and the decline to 46, is only a fair correction of a big rise.

There was no half way correction from the first to the second zone, 22, to 36, and we might have expected a correction of from one-third to one-half between the second and third zones, 36, to 52. A one-third decline would be 5½ points, and would be to a full figure 46. Half way decline would carry down to 44. Either of such corrective or conventional reactions would by no means have altered the implication of a continued uptrend. In addition, the decline to 46, is still substantially above the new trend line BB. Therefore, after duly weighing all factors we must conclude that the implications to date as reflected by the charts, are still very bullish.

The strong recovery, 46, to 51, substantiates our previous conclusions. Now a trading range builds up above the BB line. The initial full figure for May is 52, a double top and a full recovery of the previous decline, then comes a new high at 53, a three point reaction to 50, which has now registered eleven times and still above the BB line. Thereafter comes a one point rally and decline which touches our line at the twelfth 50, then a new high at 54. This confirms our previous bullish diagnosis and shows a strong line of support at 48, to 50. Anything coming below that area, would now be of bearish implication and signal a change of trend. This is emphasized as the stock reaches into new high territory at the first 55 where we still have a diagonal bullish upward sloping formation. Another new high is now made at 58, and we must begin to look for another 3, to 5, point reaction. The reaction goes down to the previous support zone 50, to 52, a signal that shows we must now be on our guard.

It is now time to search for a proper point from which to plot a new trend line.

HOW TO PLOT NEW TREND LINES

The greatest amount of work, churning and congestion, has up to this time occurred in the 50, to 57 zone. This horizontal formation stretches out for about 30 squares, from the first 50, to the last 52. It would seem to be distribution were it not for the fact that the angle of inclination of the trend is still decidedly upward. We have three distinct stages, each rising higher than the last, each bottom showing higher support.

ASR now has a strong 5 point rally to 57, a one point decline which is decidedly bullish, and then a new high is registered at 62, all of which confirms its up trend.

The formation is perfectly clear at this point. We have no doubt as to the direction of the trend, and proceed to plot our new line CC. We join the first 25 in March, to the last 52 in May, with the leeway of one square beyond each full figure. Now anything forming above CC is bullish and below it would be bearish. It is a fair appraisement of the move and in accordance with this Method. The only possible and permissible modification on this conclusion would come if the three point chart should show a positive contradiction.

The stock rose to 70 in a very bullish manner. At this phase (please cover rest of work) the stock stays in bullish position only under two conditions, namely, that it fails to break below the strong support at 65, to 66, or, that it stays above the trend line CC. The next four point decline and three point recovery are normal. Several plans of procedure are now open. We now have about 41 points profit on a stock that cost around 28. What should be done? We may place a stop immediately below the support points 65 to 66, or we may set a deadline at one point below our trend line CC. In addition we may allow ASR a one-half reaction from upper to the immediate lower congestion area, which would be at about 61.

Frankly, it is simple to look back and write about price movements and we cannot now state which of the three plans we would have adopted. No method can chart a course in the stock market which would be 100 percent correct. In this instance under consideration all three plans would have closed out the positions and all with substantial profit.

This campaign in ASR, by the Point and Figure Method if skillfully and professionally conducted, would have indicated a commitment around 28, and a sale between 61, and 64, with a gross profit of from 33 to 36, points, which would be in excess of the original cost of the stock. Moreover it took a reaction of 12 points to shake us out of our positions and close the opportunity to further profit.

5

THE ONE POINT CATAPULT AND SEMI-CATAPULT

■ Strong signals

■ Illustrations of catapult and semi-catapult patterns

■ Broad fulcrum desirable

■ Catapult and semi-catapult not the same as the conventional "new high"

■ Tracing a move in DuPont

■ The ladle formation

■ Confirmation

■ How to analyze the trend

■ Watch the trend line and use stops

In our first volume* we pointed out the exceptional opportunity afforded by taking positions when a full catapult, or semi-catapult is formed. These types of patterns were carefully explained, and a theoretical, but ideal example was given to illustrate the scientific basis underlying them. They result from the operation of the inevitable law of supply and demand, and operate as naturally and surely as the sunshine that follows the rain. We do not mean to infer from these statements that our methods, or any signals or formations can be considered infallible. Nothing is sure in stock market operations except that we must pay taxes to the State and Federal Governments, and that we must also pay the broker his commissions.

STRONG SIGNALS

The patterns known as the catapult and semi-catapult are to be considered exceptionally strong signals, and should be followed each time they occur. These can develop only under the following conditions. In a bull market, after a period of major or minor reaction, or after a period of consolidation, when sufficient accumulation favors a further major upmove. These designs develop and imply higher prices soon to come. The reverse is true in a bear market, when the implication is that lower prices must soon follow. For the purpose of this discussion, and in order to make it clear to all readers, we shall now explain these formations only as they develop in a bull market with long side operations. In a later chapter we will deal with these patterns as they develop on the short side where they imply lower prices.

Most investors and traders are inherently bulls. They, as a rule, dislike short side operations, and justly so, for whenever they attempt to profit from short positions, adopted as the result of guesswork or tips, they are sure to lose their capital. We agree that constructively, the long side of the market is the most congenial in which to operate, although both long and short positions alike give excellent signals, when judged from the point of view of the implications of the Point and Figure Method. When you have become adept and skilled in the use of this method, we urge you to take advantage of your knowledge and skill and operate both on the long and short sides of the moves.

We will, in this chapter, give illustrations showing how to recognize opportunities through the use of the full catapult and the semi-catapult patterns. However, before studying these two examples, we ask you to refer back to the one

---

* Chapter 9, *The Point and Figure Method*, pages 95, to 106. Please study Figure 9.1, page 97, very carefully.

point charts, of Atchison, Figure 3.3, and American Sugar Refining, Figure 4.1. In tracing the action of these two stocks in our previous chapters, we did not fully point out the advantages of the catapult pattern which developed in these issues. We urge upon you to study and learn to recognize these important patterns. Take advantage of both the catapult and the semi-catapult whenever they appear. If in doubt about their implication, adopt your positions "on stop."

ILLUSTRATIONS OF CATAPULT AND SEMI-CATAPULT PATTERNS

Refer to your chart of Atchison, Figure 3.3. This stock was really on the catapult at 44, and again at 48, as was clearly labeled on the chart. Please note that the actual formation in Atchison, from about the second 35, to the last 49, is almost identical with the theoretical illustration of the fulcrum and catapult in Volume 1, on page 97. This formation of Atchison might be considered ideal and almost classic, even though it is not always encountered. At 44, and at 48, it has the following merits, which may be considered in conjunction with this and other opportunities indicated by this method.

BROAD FULCRUM DESIRABLE

When a fulcrum takes form it is always desirable to have it develop a broad base. The broader the base, the more positive the signal and we may be more sure of the advance. The fulcrum is often in two parts, as indicated in our illustration. Atchison shows a continuation of the first base with higher supports in a rising diagonal direction. The highest support does not in any way impair the continued horizontal formation which develops around the clearly indicated base.

Atchison's base started around the full figure 35, and by continuing upward at 39, 40, 41, and 42, served to greatly fortify that base.

From the second 35, to the last 41, we had a clearly defined diagonal base AA, that should be considered as a continuous formation.

We consider 35 as the original fulcrum, then 39 and 40, as a continuation of that foundation, and offering higher re-enforcement to the first point. From this it can be seen that a fulcrum does not have to be flat or mathematically horizontal. In this connection let us now consider American Sugar Refining, Figure 4.1. Here, we do not find such typical examples of full, catapult patterns. However, ASR, on the chart, indicates several instances of the formation of excellent semi-catapult patterns.

Here we consider the last 37 – a sufficient catapult signal to justify action. It was safe to go long at this point because: (a) the trend was clearly defined through typical tentative channels DD and later BB; (b) the highly uncertain and panicky situation of January to mid-March was dispelled; (c) the group into which ASR is classified developed excellent strength during the inflationary move. One could go long of ASR, either at the market when it registered 37, or at 37, "on stop." In either case it would be good practice to place a limit loss stop 3 points down at 34. This safety stop would not have been caught, and could have been moved up to protect capital soon after the rally started.

Here then is another illustration showing that the students using the Point and Figure Method need not pay any attention to news, fundamentals, or other statistics. Such factors confirm our judgment of the trend. At that point the Method indicates "the trend is up," and if major fundamentals agree with diagnosis, we have additional confirmation for our optimism. Should the Method show the trend to be "up," and major news items and fundamental statistics indicate the contrary, we, as technicians must give the weight of authority to the Method because it indicates that the major operators (the insiders) are using the current adverse news to complete their accumulation.

Another true semi-catapult was formed in ASR, at 53. Strong bases had been formed in each of the foregoing instances, which resemble the typical fulcrum, and under which the leverage was clearly sufficient for constructive market forces to continue their campaign for the rise.

CATAPULT AND SEMI-CATAPULT NOT THE SAME AS THE CONVENTIONAL "NEW HIGH"

For many years we have seen many people lose considerable money through the practice of buying at new highs and going short at new lows. The general practice of doing so, without other indications, is not endorsed by the authors. It seems too easy, in the first place, and we of the professional mind in Wall Street, always look with suspicion on commitments which seem to indicate easy profits. Money so risked is usually lost as a penalty for insufficient technical knowledge.

In the preceding example, and in the additional examples which follow, it must not be concluded from the fact that any particular catapult or semi-catapult pattern is formed at a new high, that additional and substantially higher prices are indicated. It is indicative, but by no means conclusive evidence, that the advance will continue. Occasionally a full or semi-catapult may develop at the very top of a move. Constant analysis, careful interpretation and the use of stops, will prevent unnecessary losses at these points. We must have in mind that occasionally the insiders also make errors at the top of swings, but since they have more capital than the average trader, they are able to see their commitments go from 30, to 50 points or more against them, and each of their transactions is only a part of a full campaign. When using this method, and stop orders in conjunction therewith we will never suffer such paper loss.

Let us turn now to DuPont, Figure 5.1, herewith for illustrations of the full catapult and semi-catapult patterns, both of which offer fine opportunities for profit.

TRACING A MOVE IN DUPONT

A perfect fulcrum was built up through the first quarter of 1933, which was completed around mid-April. We outline and describe the fulcrum, in Volume 1, pages 67–72. Here it is formed with a strong foundation at full figure 35, which was repeated ten times. It is confirmed by a test of the low and a repetition of the full figure 36's. It was developed after a good decline, and conformed in every way to the requirements of a perfect fulcrum. The advance at 34, 35, and 36, with no reaction was indeed a strong signal. The bullish diagonal lengthening of the base up to the last 35, 36, and the extremely harmonious continuation of the same formation in the same direction is further confirmation of the strong signal and is to be considered a classic example of one of the strongest types of patterns created by this Method.

THE LADLE FORMATION

The ladle shaped pattern, described in Volume 1,* appears at least in part. Let us omit the enthusiastic rise in the center of the ladle occurring from 33, to 43. It was a ten point upward surge, created as a result in the change of outlook when the New Deal administration was inaugurated in Washington. The down trend,

---

* *Editor's note* At this point the text refers to an earlier edition of Volume 1, no longer in print, which included what is reproduced here as Figure 6.2 on p. 69. The accompanying discussion was as follows: "From 63 top to first 50 we do not know as yet whether the decline will cease, or whether it will have really started at 50. The 50 line spreads. Then 51, 52, and 53 each get longer. Is this going to be a new ceiling or another floor? At 53 the rise goes through the down trend line A. At 55 we have a rather promising looking ladle shaped picture suggesting that major interests have scooped up everything from 50 to 53. Trend channel is changed here to an upward tilt, and at 57 there is no doubt the former bearish picture is altered completely."

Fig 5.1 DuPont: full catapult and semi-catapult positions

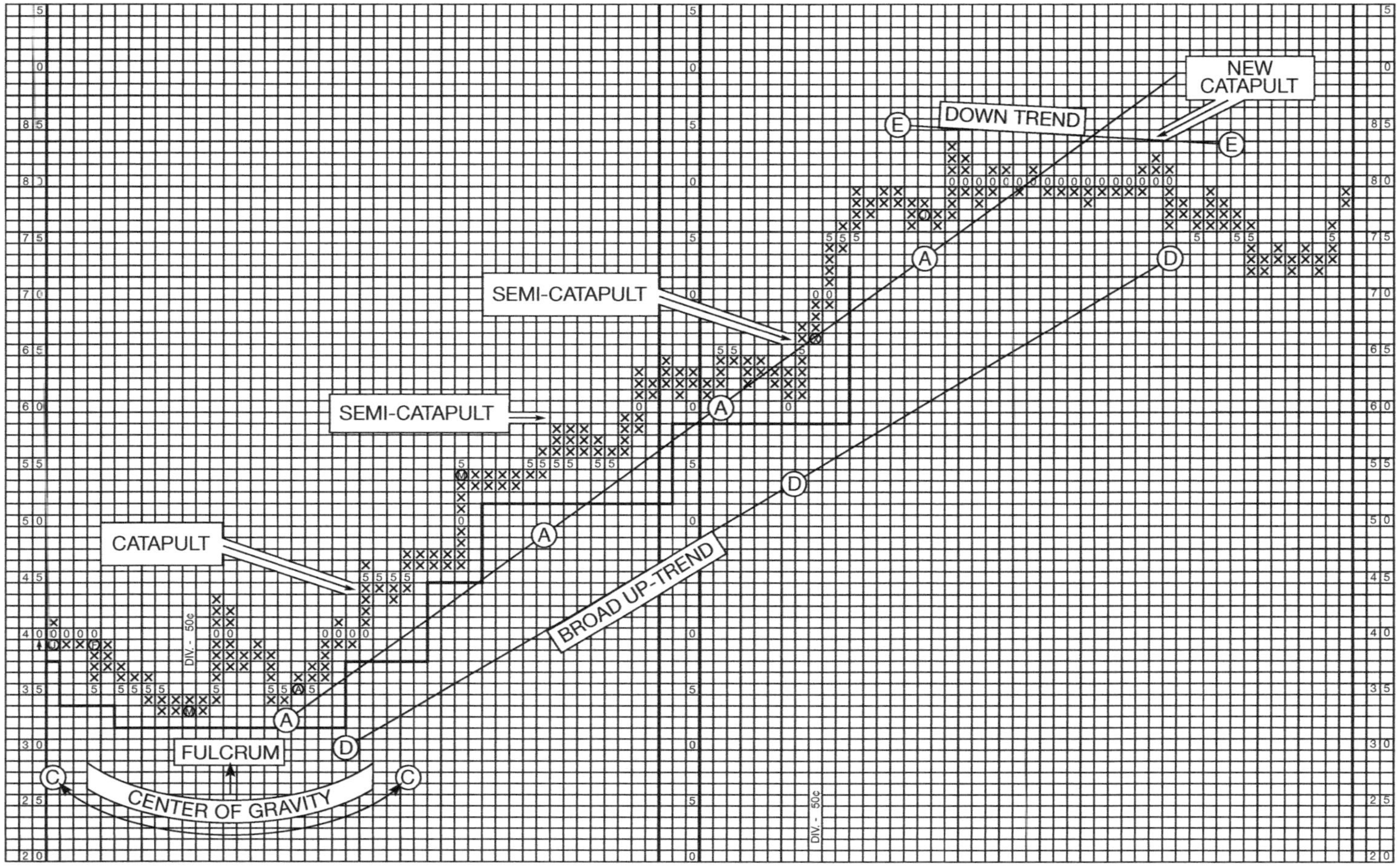

which we require before the completion of the ladle-shaped pattern appears on the chart from 41, down to 33, a correction of the abnormal rise to 43, stopped at 34, and must be considered bullish because it stops within the trading range 33, to 37, which has already been diagnosed as bullish. When a rise of ten points in the price of a stock constitutes a 33 percent advance in its price, we must consider the stock to be in a bullish position. The hesitant investor or trader might have overlooked the implication of support at 33, to 35, the ability of the stock to rally more than 3, to 5, points, and to hold a higher level after a nine point climb to 43, and a reaction, with no evidence whatever of distribution. If he failed to get aboard, on the long side, at any stage between 34, the place of evident support, and the last 36, the point where the Point and Figure Method pattern turned bullish, he could have waited for the completion of a full catapult.

CONFIRMATION

A true catapult pattern was clearly indicated at 44, as is so marked on the chart. All the necessary essentials confirming this to be a true catapult position are in the pattern. We now have the ladle-shaped confirmation, a double bottom, at the 34, and a double top at 41. In addition there has been plenty of preparation for a new advance. In fact, more than three months passed during which accumulation continued with a sharp advance, and a similar sharp correction. This indicated the stock to be in a bullish position until it arrived on the catapult at 44, in April.

From that point onward the ascending stairway formation as outlined by the draftsman is a clear picture of strength. With this you will agree, we are sure. No student of this Method could go wrong after the clear implications at the full figure 34.

The semi-catapult was formed at 59. It is a semi-catapult because there is no antecedent work to create a full catapult. It may not be considered merely a new high, because of the unusual amount of preparation preceding its formation and the excellent base between 50, and 60, all appearing in the diagonal formation way above the broad outline of trend line DD.

A tentative trend line AAA, projected conventionally, according to the principles of this Method is likewise indicated on the chart. The catapult at full figure 59, is well above the safety line. Should one have been confused at this point, and if the stock had not progressed further, it would have been policy to place a stop 3 points down, which would not have been caught and would have protected the position. Another clear bullish semi-catapult position was indicated at full figure 66.

HOW TO ANALYZE THE TREND

In our previous chapter, we have pointed out that a decline of from 5, to 7, points in a stock which sells in the price range from 60, to 100, is to be considered a normal reaction. Many traders adopt the practice of following up profitable commitments with stops at logical points.*

After having placed our commitments at 59, it would have been prudent, to place a stop at a point or so below the last clear level of support, especially so in view of the fact that the move started from 33, and now shows a 26 point advance.

In this case, by covering up the work after the semi-catapult at 59, we get a better picture of what should have been done. Previous support is indicated at 55, to 56. Thereafter it was hard work for the stock to get through the 61, to 65, trading or congestion area. After the new high was established at 65, it was time to stop, look, and listen. We could tentatively allow a 3 point reaction and see what happened.

It came and carried the stock down to 62, with the rally recovering to 64. Then another 2 point reaction, a point below the tentative trend line at 62, with a one point reaction. All these rallies and declines were sub-normal. The major pattern has not changed in the least. A new line of support is clearly indicated at 61, with a tentative congestion area developing at 64, to 65. If by chance one had become skeptical of the move between 61, and 65, he would now be ready to re-establish a new position. Should that new position be long or short? The stock cannot alter its main up trend unless it abandons its indicated strength in the 60, to 63, zone. Should it break below 60, and fail to rally at least 3, to 5 points promptly, the trend would thereafter be downward.

The new 5, point rally to the third 65, prepared us for a semi-catapult position. This was clearly indicated, and could not be considered a conventional new high because of the strong antecedent work and the support at 60, to 65. Note the substantial base appearing above 60, and the ample consolidation around the new tops at 62, to 64. Note also, that this is clear and far above the broad trend line DD.

Here we may go in again, either at 66, or at the market, with a stop, as heretofore explained. There is no definite change in the pattern until 79, is reached. Here usual sub-normal trading reactions occur and soon 83, is registered. Now we again have an indicated gross profit of 17 points. A 5 point normal reaction comes carrying to full figure 78, and is followed by a series of 3 point or less ral-

---

* See *Stop Orders* by Owen Taylor, Stock Market Publications.

lies and declines, to the last 80. That figure was repeated sixteen times. The high was 83, and the strong rally to 82, after a 5 point reaction from 83, to 78, was roughly a double and lower top. Conventional as this may be, it is a signal, and a reminder to us that we have excellent paper profits which will only be cash profits, after we close out the position.

WATCH THE TREND LINE AND USE STOPS

The work may now be covered up again with blank paper about half-way, into the 80s, for the sake of practice and fairness in studying the formation. The new catapult, if it were to come, should be created at 84, where we could expect to witness some fireworks on the upside, because if 75, to 81, is an inside accumulating zone, the insiders need at least 15 to 20 points more in which to close out their operations.

A continuation of our trend line AAA, here cuts completely through the full figure 80 squares. At 82, a double and lower top is indicated; we mark the trend as tentatively down by connecting the line EE. AA, and EE, intersect, at about the full figure 82, to 83, tentatively indicating safety above the 80, to 83, mark on the long side and of danger below. The line of squares is now drawn out, 17 times at 79, and 13 at 78. This horizontal formation around the 80, line is the longest congestion area, which has developed up to this time.

A logical stop would be at a point or so below the strongest lines of support, around 79, to 80, particularly after the 14th or 15th full figure 80 is recorded, and after the last 82 is reached. The stock must go through this time to catapult at 84, or higher. Now, we can allow nothing more than a nominal reaction of 3 to 5 points. Our stops must be placed either at 78 or at 76. It would not have been logical to carry the stock lower. The gross indicated profit on the position last taken is now at least 10 points, even though we be stopped out at 76, or 78.

6

GAUGING THE VOLATILE ISSUES

- A fast mover
- An unusual and unique device
- Individual characteristics often repeated
- Long positions
- Consolidation zone
- Three point summaries should be consulted

Let us now illustrate how the Method works on fast moving issues. As long as a stock is reasonably active, and has a bid and asked price, of not more than 2, to 3 points apart, it is not dangerous if you judge it by means of this Method. On the contrary, such a stock furnishes greater and wider opportunities for profit. All stocks may be gauged by this Method – but, best signals are created by those which trade actively. The majority of persons would rather buy, or go long, of volatile stocks, than sell, or go short of them. This Method handles either side with impunity and impartiality. There are few, if any, treacherous or difficult stocks, which cannot be analyzed by the implications of their Points and Figures.

A FAST MOVER

Auburn Automobile has always been regarded as a stock dangerous to trade in. Closely held, with a comparatively small capitalization, about one half of which is held by its subsidiary, the Cord Corporation, and a restricted floating supply, its market gyrations have traveled over a range of hundreds of points. Investors and traders have had their fingers burned in AAC, where anything but Method was applied to gauge transactions in it. We will see whether or not trading in it is dangerous when it is placed under the rigid analysis of the Point and Figure Method.

The graph of AAC's, moves from January 1933, to beginning of May 1933, Figure 6.1, will show that in the first quarter of the year the stock moved widely. It declined from 56, to 32, a drop of 24 points in that short time. This was equivalent to about 50 percent, of its price. As we recall it, AAC, began its career around the 30s, when it came from the Chicago Stock Exchange to the Curb Market, eight years ago. Since then it has crossed 510, on the N.Y. Stock Exchange in 1929, and dropped below 30, in 1932. From that point it recovered to 84¼. The graph (Figure 6.1) represents a complete bear cycle double bottom.

The January–March 1933 decline in Auburn was greater than the averages, and more acute than the majority of stocks in the 50s. Few issues declined over 50 percent of their value.

An examination of the pattern will reveal that according to this Method there was nothing particularly dangerous in going short of AAC, when support was first withdrawn in the 50, to 56, zone. From 56, down to 32, the formation was certainly most clearly a bull market in reverse. This will be easily demonstrated, as we proceed.

Fig 6.1   Auburn Automobile (page 1)

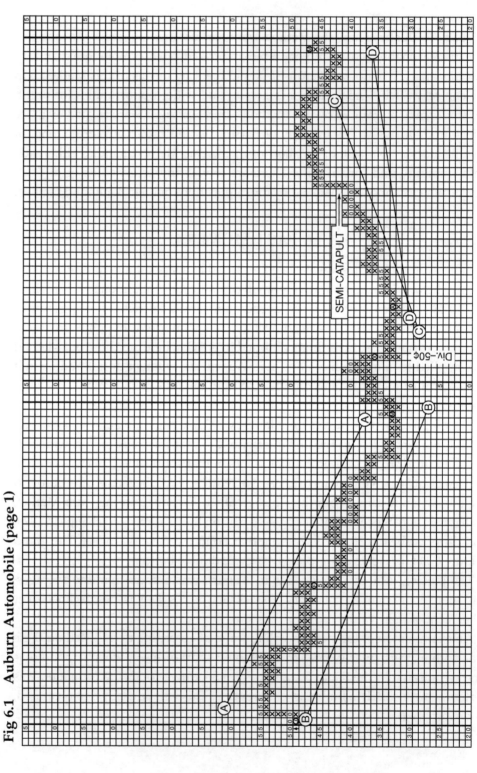

AN UNUSUAL AND UNIQUE DEVICE

Recalling our interpretation of bull trends by the ascending ladder, trend lines and semi-catapults, the reader is requested to look through the graph of AAC, against strong or artificial light upside down, through the back of the paper.

By this means, which may be unfair to AAC's manipulators, but permissable in diagnosing its action by the Point and Figure Method, the simple character of the steady liquidation in the stock through January and February 1933, becomes readily apparent. In the next chapter we will explain how a campaign on the short side could have been conducted in AAC, with absolute safety from the upper limits of the congestion area 53, to 55, to the final point of support at 32, to 33.

On the long side, AAC, failed to give a single catapult or semi-catapult signal at any stage of this decline. The trend lines AA, and BB, were straight down. But, the trend channel between A, and B, as stability began to show up in the 32, zone, began to narrow down. The trend lines began to converge and a bottle-neck pattern formed at the obvious points of support, in the lower 30s.

AAC, participated rather half heartedly in the enthusiasm of mid-March 1933. It advanced 9 points, from 32, to 41, failing thereby, to rally half way, by 3 full points. This was a tentatively bearish signal in a volatile stock, especially after so drastic a decline.

To have acted bullishly, AAC, should have advanced to the 44, or 45, zone without much difficulty, where it might have encountered some resistance, and selling by longs previously tied up in the stock. Sponsors must have encountered major offerings above 40, and with their known shrewdness and experience, pulled away from the 40, mark as gracefully and as quickly as possible. This false move failed to make a catapult or semi-catapult, which was another warning of weakness.

The decline brought AAC, back to the point from whence it began. Another period of excellent preparation was begun in AAC, at the bottom, at 32. No doubt, its sponsors were taking no chance this time. By April, the stock was still at its base 32, for the tenth and last time. However, this base was 23 squares long counting in the blank 32's. This was indeed a good sign.

INDIVIDUAL CHARACTERISTICS OFTEN REPEATED

From here on, AAC, began to duplicate its action on the return trip with a pattern formation curiously identical with its previous decline. It is difficult indeed to find a material variation in the tactics of its movements. Note the identical for-

Fig 6.2 Auburn Automobile (page 2)

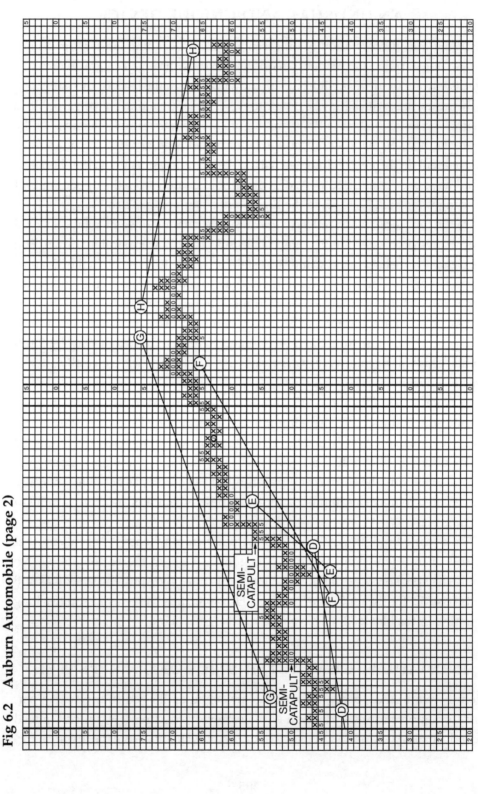

mations to the left and right of the middle of the page with the middle 41, considered as the center.

This move is a most bullish one because (a) it follows ample preparation, (b) a very long base has been laid, (c) ample evidence of accumulation at 33, is apparent, (d) a more harmonious pattern for a bullish formation with the diagonal sloping up trend in the right direction at CC is formed, (e) the strong consolidation at 35, to 38, on the way up, and (f) the general action of the market and of the automobile group as a whole at that time.

Anybody who failed to take advantage of the change in trend from the last 36, where the inclination to continue the rise was clearly established, and when only a single 3, point reaction had taken place up to that time, could have waited for a catapult formation.

A semi-catapult was formed at 42. It would have been a full and complete catapult at that figure but for the strong resistance and barriers set up in the 40, to 45 zone from the beginning of February onward. From that point the stock had a rapid advance to 49.

LONG POSITIONS

There were two opportunities in AAC, on the long side throughout the move, namely, at the last two 34s, or at 36, on stop, and at the semi-catapult at 42. There were major opportunities on the short side, which we will discuss in an ensuing chapter.

Auburn has been the kind of a stock that dislikes conforming to the conventions of the stock market. Probably for this reason it later broke through the strong support at 45, last quarter of page, declining to 41, which was a 7 point reaction, below the tentative trend line CC. Whether the holder of long stock at 34, or 42, followed up his advantage with stops "at a logical point" or was stopped out, is immaterial.

The continuation of the stock's subsequent action herewith reproduced, Figure 6.2, furnished more opportunities. The reader must note that the major advance from bear market low 32, to the high at 49, was 18 points. A justified half-way correction of the entire move would be 8½ points. Auburn declined only 7 points and began to make a base at 42, and a more stubborn one at 43, to 45, at which point, the implication is clearly bullish. If the second sheet be placed alongside the first, the excellent new formation at 42, is emphasized. It is clearly a new base with the main support around 45.

CONSOLIDATION ZONE

Now we note the lengthening consolidation zone from 45, upward, the latter figure being recorded fifteen times. A semi-catapult is formed at 50, and if the stock can go through that mark, a new deal in AAC, is to be anticipated. The full figure 50, is duly reached, with 54, quickly following. After that a 4 point reaction was quickly corrected by a 3 point rally. Then a 2 point reaction occurred followed by a 4 point rise from 51, to 55, and a new high was then made. All of this is bullish.

Double bottoms were clearly made at 32, and 42. These can now be joined to indicate the broad main trend DD, that will be tentative, (a) while the angle continues in the same direction, or, (b) until the angle of direction rises or falls sharply.

By this time we know that AAC, can reverse itself from 7 to 9 points counter to its apparent inclination and still follow its main trend. It is a volatile stock and acts accordingly. Its trend channel is wider and we must allow more leeway – more latitude than that of standard stocks. In popular language "its swings are wide" and we must be guided accordingly.

The 8 point reaction from 55, to 47, comes to a clear vertex with a single 47, forming the head of an inverted triangle. This is a bullish formation, and also occurred at the last 42. The decline to 47, still registers higher support. The angle of inclination, upward, is growing sharper. It is noted at EE. This is not the true trend line; it is merely a guide to the temporary trading direction of the stock. Another semi-catapult is formed at 56; the work here is harmonious and creates confidence – three 55s and three 56s with no decline – an extremely bullish indication. When the stock has a quick run up to 61, there should be no occasion whatever to carry it below 55, again.

THREE POINT SUMMARIES SHOULD BE CONSULTED

Our main trend line is still DD, but we watch the angle of inclination EE closely for a clue of the trading direction. At 65, we are "in the clear" again, so far as our semi-catapult commitment at around 50, is concerned. A trading area is formed from 62, to 65, with lengthening base from the first 60, to the last 62, at the middle of the page. Now, the angle of inclination is not so sharp. It is merely diagonal. Our main trend line is now justifiably altered to FF, by joining the last 47, and the last 62, one square outside the range, as explained heretofore. The line FF, is the real and true continuation of DD, and is a compromise of the angle formed by DD and EE. Our entire attitude towards the stock market should be one of compromise and latitude.

Whether we should have waited for the tentative trend line DD, or EE, to be violated is somewhat irrelevant. Had we decided that everything below FF, is bearish a stop around 67, or 68, would have been caught, which is satisfactory considering that 73, was the extreme high for the move.

The narrowing bottle-neck formation of the trend channel between FF, and GG, is another signal of the approaching culmination of the uptrend. It is the reverse of AA, and BB, in Figure 6.1. The action at the bottom and top of Auburn should now be carefully and promptly compared. No signal should be disregarded.

At 72, AAC, had a typical 7 point downswing and a 7 point recovery, then a 3 point reaction and a new high at 73. A drastic break took place at this point to a final low of 54, almost immediately after the violation of the trend line FF. A distinct head had formed in the 72, to 73 zone, with considerable churning in a fairly narrow trading range around the top. A previous new base was 60, to 61, and new high at 73, a 12, to 13, point swing that would allow a 6, to 7, point normal decline to 66, or 67.

The trend of AAC, turned downward when supported around 65, was abandoned. The recovery from 54, to 68, decline to 63, and rally to 67, still left the stock in a doubtful position for the long side. The series of lower tops like HH, is usually ominous. Your three point charts would have confirmed the change in trend.

In every case of doubt or hesitation, in any volatile stock, after a substantial rise or decline, the three point charts should be consulted. They define the intermediate trend for the more volatile issues.

7

HOW TO RECOGNIZE ADDITIONAL OPPORTUNITIES IN VOLATILE STOCKS

- Low priced stocks
- Avoid guesswork
- Erratic stocks not dangerous
- Consider the unexpected
- Conservation pays
- The importance of dividends, extras, and rights
- Watch "ex-dividend" dates
- Limit losses let profits accrue
- Continually analyze the formations

Occasionally volatile stocks and issues in the specialty group develop spectacular moves, either up or down, which are occasioned by causes not apparent until months after the move has been completed. Later, when the reason for the move is disclosed and becomes known and understood, the general optimism or pessimism created thereby causes widespread public participation in the issue involved.

LOW PRICED STOCKS

The stock, if it be a specialty, may have formerly been considered in the "cat and dog" class, and carefully avoided by speculators, investors, and traders alike. These issues, which nobody would buy when they were selling below 10, or 20, assume an importance in the market after a big advance, often far out of all proportion to their true value. Participation by the general speculative community will usually begin after a 20, to 50, point rise has been effected. For strange reasons traders begin to take up such an issue and attempt to scalp a few points profit at the time when the issue is obviously at a danger point and perhaps at the very top of its move. This seems to be due to a subconscious impulse on the part of traders and others who have not participated in the advance, to rush in under the belief that the issue will go on further. Great volume, activity, with spectacular and irregular moves, up and down, distinguish this kind of an issue, especially after a good advance has been witnessed.

Conversely, there is a strong temptation to go short merely because a stock has had a 30 point advance. Such a move usually invites uninformed traders to sell the issue short merely because it has had a steep advance, and they do so at a point which is neither reasonable nor logical according to this Method of gauging the action of the stock. These mis-informed traders, who sell an issue short merely because it has had an advance are the very ones who help to create the sharp move often witnessed in this type of stock.

Without method, or logic, it is foolhardy to participate either way in such a stock unless, and until, you understand its action through the aid of some scientific method of gauging its technical condition.

AVOID GUESSWORK

The uninformed public cannot help losing, as long as they insist upon placing their commitments in the market based upon guesswork. Pool operators and manipu-

Fig 7.1   ACF Industries (page 1)

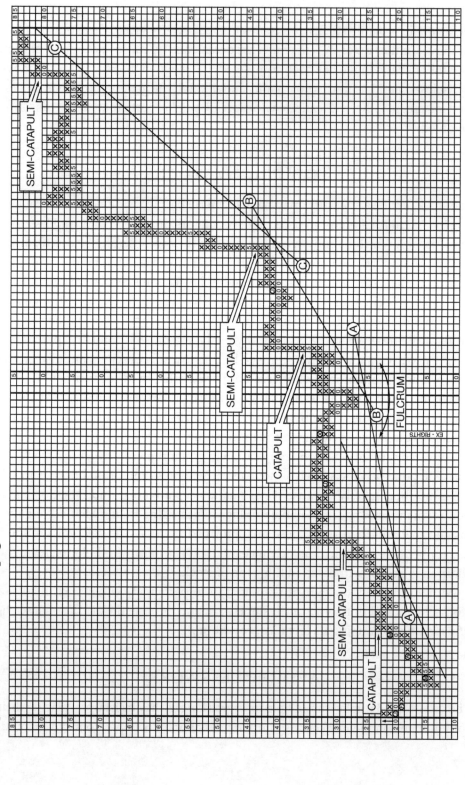

lators are always anxious to invite participation by such foolhardy traders. It is a simple matter for the uninformed to misjudge a move, especially (a) on the long side after a fair rise, (b) on the short side when the initial up-swing has not completely exhausted itself, (c) on the long side again in new high ground after an incomplete technical correction, and (d) on the long side while a volatile stock or specialty is completing its major process of reaction and consolidation. ACF Industries, Figure 7.1, affords an excellent illustration of the many opportunities available for those who understand how to recognize them. It is also an ideal and typical lesson for the demonstration of the many great opportunities, which may be recognized when one trades in harmony with the trend and in addition emphasizes the serious danger of trading against the trend.

We wish it were possible to trace, point by point, all of the moves in U.S. Smelting & Refining, Ingersoll Rand, Industrial Rayon, National Distillers, U.S. Industrial Alcohol, and other non-standard stocks, which in recent months have advanced sharply largely, because of their limited floating supply and the lack of information on the part of the general public as to the character of their movements and their susceptibility to manipulation. Have in mind as you trace ACF, with us, that the foregoing and similar specialty issues are influenced in approximately the same manner.

ERRATIC STOCKS NOT DANGEROUS

Specialty and volatile issues need not be avoided by the student of the Point and Figure Method. One need have no fear of these erratic movers, as we will endeavor to show through a critical analysis of the move in ACF. The movements of these stocks, when examined by any other method, would appear unusual when compared with standard active leaders. However, when we analyze and compare the move of these issues through the application of the Point and Figure Method, we begin to realize that even these wide movers and erratic specialities are relatively easy to understand, since the technique of handling them is exactly the same, as that used to judge the more normal issues. In short, there is nothing particularly difficult in their action when one plots and analyzes the pattern formed, according to the principles of the Point and Figure Method.

Let us examine the one point chart of ACF, from a critical and analytical viewpoint. For the longer range or investment position, we should refer to our three point chart, since only on this chart do we find clear indications of long range accumulation or distribution. The one point chart, however, is very dependable as a guide for intermediate trading and for close critical analysis.

The move from January 1933, follows the typical lines of the averages for that period. Quiet and inconspicuous moves, of this stock during the period of January to May must have misled a great many people. Those who established long positions unquestionably had their patience tried and probably sold out during the reaction in late February. The pattern gave no clue whatever to the spectacular moves that were to follow in the ensuing months and as a matter of fact, which were to start in a very few weeks after the first full figure registered in the month of May.

CONSIDER THE UNEXPECTED

Take nothing for granted. Always look for the unexpected in the stock market. Remember the rankest mining promotion has on numerous occasions found gold. Occasionally a wild cat oil promotion actually strikes oil. Therefore, always have in mind that you must be prepared for the unexpected in the stock market.

The only hint of developing strength in ACF, was the initial rise from 12, to 25. Examine the chart, and see the broad developing base around the 20 zone, and the trading area 20, to 25, with no single hint indicating the fireworks soon to come. A semi-catapult was formed at first full figure 23. At that time the stock looked far more bullish on the tape and in its daily action than it did on our full figure one point chart. There was nothing in the pattern on these charts to arouse enthusiasm. The partial catapult at 23, was weak and inconclusive. The amount of previous work was insufficient to justify full confidence in the issue. However, the formation began to change at the third 25. The angle of inclination was decidedly bullish, since a steady diagonal up trend was forming between the work, 20, and 23, in the month of May, and which was now beginning to look promising. This backing and filling at this point is a clear indication of major accumulation. Such a formation always develops near the beginning or near the end of a major campaign. If the stock made a new high at 26, it would have been reasonable to expect a reaction of at least 2, 3, or possibly 5 points. A minor correction of normal proportions is witnessed after the new high of 28, which is followed, by a sharp advance of the stock after it moves out on a new semi-catapult at 29. The point is clearly marked on the chart by an arrow.

CONSERVATION PAYS

At this point the average trader or investor may not have cared to consider the adoption of a position at 29, a catapult. The advance had been too abrupt and came without the formation of a full fulcrum, which is so essential for a safe long position. It would have been prudent in this case to await the reaction. Let us caution you here – it is usually better to miss an opportunity than to be imprudent. It is well to remember that there are many stocks. If you are keeping your data on 100 issues, you may have signals, which give you more confidence than the one here shown in ACF. However, when the full figure 30 is registered, no further doubt could exist as to the invulnerable bullish position of ACF. It was reasonable to assume at this point, that the floating supply was in the hands of the right people and if this were the case, subsequent action of the stock would confirm that fact. It is clear now, that the accumulation in ACF, took place on scale down around 15, and on the way up to 25, in the zone 20, to 25.

After the semi-catapult at 29, the stock rises to 35, perpendicularly. Not a single normal reaction was registered from the time the stock left the last full figure 21. It has now advanced about 15 points and should be in position for a technical correction. What is the implication here? Bullish? Decidedly so. Let us show you how this conclusion is justified and confirmed. With the view of gauging the possible extent of a reaction and the plotting of a trend line, we could have placed a tentative line under the work to date. This line is laid by joining the 12, square below the low at 13, together with the 20, square below the 21, low in May. This line projected forward would intersect the work at approximately 31.

The main trend is by no means clearly defined at this point. The indications are from technical action, and the laying of the trend line, that the trend is up. We cannot rely too greatly on temporary or tentative lines. A serious reaction must take place in ACF, before we can plot a dependable line. We must await a more than normal reaction.

First congestion point in the move of this stock is the trading range, which is built up between 30, and 34. The advance from 13, to 35, totals 22 points. A one third correction of this move, would be a reaction to 27, or 28, a full half-way correction would be to full figure 24. Examine your chart and note that the decline is checked at full figure 27, which is exactly a one third correction of the run-up. This shows the stock to be in an exceedingly bullish position, since it indicates that the insiders were still holding the bulk of the floating supply. This, in itself, is a confirmation of the extreme bullish position of ACF, and justifies the anticipation of more than an ordinary further advance in this issue.

THE IMPORTANCE OF DIVIDENDS, EXTRAS, AND RIGHTS

Attention is here called to the congestion area in the move beginning and ending at the first and last full figure 30. This was a 5 point trading range, which proved to be extremely stubborn.

We know now that it was probably an area of consolidation and reaccumulation, but in any event the range 30, to 35, proved to be a strong resistance level. Let us call your attention to the fact that in this area, ACF sold Ex-Rights on June 14. This is indicated on our chart by the lettering "Ex-Rights" vertically appearing in the proper column. This notation also indicates the point where the stock first sold with "rights off." A circle around the full figure 33, marks the point clearly. It is good practice to mark the date on the chart as well. Some technicians use a blue, green, or red crayon indicating such special situations. These special occasions indicate a signal, and always an implication for which one must carefully search.

WATCH "EX-DIVIDEND" DATES

It has been noted elsewhere in this book that the dividend period, which is likewise clearly marked on our charts, usually denotes a phase or period in the formation of the pattern of the movement of stocks, which have important significance. This important significance also applies to rights, which are extras or privileges and have a value analogous to extra dividends.

We often attach important significance to such a period in the pattern of a stock's progression. We invite you to make particular note of the fact that a major rise takes place almost immediately after the rights were taken off this stock. This advance was almost a straight vertical movement from 34, to full figure 80.

Now let us return to our critical analysis of the chart formation. From the shake-out to 27, the stock rallied to 34, a bullish 7 point recovery, then reacted 4 points to 30. This reaction gave us the point to plot our trend line. We plot line B, connecting one figure below the previous reaction together with one figure below the reaction to 30, and get our trend line BB. If the stock holds above this line, we may be certain that the uptrend is confirmed. From this point onward, the technical action of the stock creates confidence. When it moved out, onto full figure 36, it was on the catapult, and in a very bullish position. This point is considerably more bullish than the previous semi-catapult at 23, or at 29, because of the antecedent work immediately preceding it. This antecedent work is in the nature of a full fulcrum formation. At this point, there are indications that the insiders, who control the floating supply of the stock, have locked in a substantial short interest in the shake-out zone, from 33, to 27, in the middle of the fulcrum. The new catapult of 36, is followed by another typical "push-up," which action is fully explained in our first book. This type of action is created by the stock sponsors, partly for advertising purposes, and partly to further embarrass the hemmed in shorts, who will now have to pay dearly in order to extricate themselves. This type of run-up also results from the natural insistent and urgent buying, following such indicated strength. Remember, if you will, in placing your commitments that clever professional traders, who are responsible for the movement of volatile stocks, can also read the implication of the Point and Figure Method and know just when to stage such a mark-up. At 42, a new high, some little resistance develops and a normal reaction takes place which is less than a half-way correction from the previous consolidation area 30, to 35, and a new trading area from 30, to 43, develops. The work of this new trading area, occurring as it does well above our BB trend line, implies that the stock continues in bullish position. In addition, the reaction having been less than normal, confirms this diagnosis. Here we must conclude that long positions must be carried further, because the move is not yet over. Substantial profits have now accrued to either of the three positions, which were clearly indicated by the Point and Figure Method.

LIMIT LOSSES LET PROFITS ACCRUE

We believe it is proper at this point to comment upon the wisdom of letting your profits accrue and of following up your trade with stop orders,* placed at logical points so as to insure further profits accruing, so long as the stock continues in its bullish technical position. Avoid the policy of taking small profits, and remember that to profit from the stock market, we must limit our losses, but let the profits run. Remember that most people who take small profits usually sustain large losses in their commitments.

CONTINUALLY ANALYZE THE FORMATIONS

Cover the chart over as far as the square indicating the first transaction in July, which is carried on the 41, square. Observe carefully the formation of ACF, up to

---

* See *Stop Orders* by Owen Taylor, Stock Market Publications.

this point. Go over your three point in conjunction with the one point chart. Examine them carefully and impartially for possible indications of distribution, for now the stock has advanced about 30 points, and we must be on our guard.

As the move progresses, ACF, gets out of range once more on the upside at 45, and at 44, a new semi-catapult is created with a clear and decidedly bullish implication. Our new trend line BB, assures us that the trend is up and that the stock continues its extremely bullish technical condition. The rise proceeds to 53, and a trifle less than normal reaction is followed soon by another wild advance to 66, then a 4 point reaction after which the stock advances sharply to 80.

There are few traders indeed, who could claim that they would have stayed long all the way through this major spectacular advance in ACF. Hardly one in a thousand would have done so, yet it was clearly indicated that the stock would have a spectacular move, since at no point could we find sufficient distribution to indicate that the stock sponsors, loosely and ordinarily called manipulators, had begun to liquidate and unload on the public. By following the principles of this Method, together with the use of stops advanced beneath the working areas, we were sure to ride with the move. Implications were clear and logical, and pointed definitely to a big move for this stock.

At full figure 80, a broad trading area commenced to form. The first 6 point reaction, considering the scope of the previous advance, is considered a normal one. The stock continues to be in bullish position. We must at times make allowances for stocks such as ACF, when we are attempting to gauge a normal reaction or rally. A 7, to 8 point, correction at this stage of the advance could easily have been considered normal and here is where the student must commence to use his judgment. The Point and Figure Method and its principles are not fully mechanical. However, they do train you and develop your judgment. Therefore, at this point, your judgment should be exercised. The advance has been so steep that no nearby trend line can help us judge this trading area easily. A series of rallies and declines now create a trading range from 80, to 73. Examine carefully the work at this upper trading area, notice that a complete catapult and a good one is formed again at 81. Now we are once more in a position to plot our new trend line CC. Everything appearing above the line CC is to be considered bullish. Tentatively at least any work appearing below could be considered bearish.

By following the implications of this Method we have carried up our profitable position anywhere from 49 to 62 points. Considering that ACF, began its career at 12 when it was in the "cat and dog" class, we must concede that the Method has clearly pointed the way to large profits. A discussion of the further progress of ACF, is explained in our next chapter.

8

CULMINATION, LIQUIDATION, PROFIT TAKING, AND THE SHORT SIDE

■ When to take your profits

■ One point signals on the short side

■ The reaction pattern in ACF

■ Signal for the short side

■ Watch for signs of absorption

■ The inverse catapult

■ Signals for short and long positions

■ Analyzing a stock for technical position

■ Signs of culmination

In the preceding chapters we have traced the patterns of stocks as they develop during the periods of accumulation and mark up. We will now try and show you how to proceed with the analysis of formations for the purpose of detecting liquidation, the culmination of the move, and of determining a point at which to close out your long position. It has been said, "stocks are put up, but they fall down." An advance that takes many months to establish can be wiped out in a few days. A bull market enduring two, three, or more years, is followed by a bear market lasting as many months. A price level established for a stock resulting from skillful manipulation, which took many months or years to attain, will fade away rapidly, when, as the influencing factors change and sponsors withdraw their bids, weak holders are wiped out literally overnight.

WHEN TO TAKE YOUR PROFITS

How then may we be sure to close out our long commitments before these calamities occur? One of the three types of patterns which we discussed in Chapter 2, of this book, will, as a rule, develop in a sufficient degree, to permit the recognition of distribution, culmination, and the end of the move, in time to close out long positions before the wash out.

Let us examine now Figure 8.1, ACF, which is a continuation of the work drawn on the Chart Figure 7.1. Note carefully the new catapult at 81, on Figure 7.1. Examine also the congestion area between 75, and 80. Notice the pattern between 80, and 85, and the fact that the new full catapult position had great difficulty in breaking through the 80, to 85, zone and finally, on a nominal two point reaction, touched our trend line C, at 83, which is the first time that the pattern came within a full square of our trend line CC. From the low of 83, the stock rallied quickly to 89, and had another six point reaction back to 83, this time penetrating our trend line CC. Here is a signal indicating that major distribution has been taking place. The insiders were getting out of ACF. The congestion area 74, to 80, on Figure 7.1, together with the further congestion between 80, and 89, on Figure 7.1, and, 8.1, represents major distribution. The penetration of our trend line CC on the reaction from 89, is a signal to get out of long positions, whether established at the semi-catapult points 81, 67, 54, 44, or catapult at 36, or at the semi-catapult at 23. The signal given when the reaction from 89, passed through our trend line at 84, is the indication "sell out." If we note that the stock has had a rise from 44, to 89, without having had a full corrective reaction, that is, a reaction of at least one third of the previous rise, we have two more reasons for

Fig 8.1   ACF Industries (page 2)

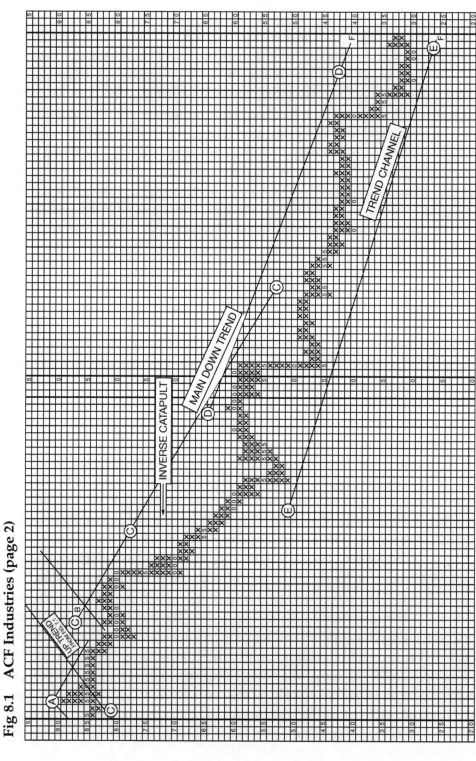

closing out long positions: (1) the stock has not undergone a corrective reaction during the move from 44, to 89, which places it in an extremely vulnerable position, and when it does undergo a reaction, it will be more severe than otherwise would have been the case, (2) a corrective reaction amounting to one third of the move from 44, to 89, 45 points, would have called for a reaction of at least 15 points, which was worth avoiding by selling out. The distribution as indicated from the action of the pattern of ACF, Figures 7.1 and 8.1, falls into Group 2, outlined in Chapter 2. The backing and filling action of the stock between 74, and 89, is a sign of major distribution. Other illustrations to be explained in later chapters will cover this phase, types 1, and 3. ACF, which was one of the market leaders during the latter part of June, and July 1933, was one of the first stocks to crack wide open in this break. Now let us consider the composite pattern that this stock created from January 1, 1933, until the bottom at this point.

ONE POINT SIGNALS ON THE SHORT SIDE

Many traders and investors fear the short side of the market. On the question of short selling* we will be brief. Short selling was justly criticized during the World War. For obvious reasons short selling was denounced at the time by the federal government. Recently during the years 1931, 1932 and 1933, in an effort to control short selling, further pressure against the practice has been attempted. Many critics of speculation, claim that short selling is a menace to the security price structure. Proponents of this theory claim that concerted drives against one or more stocks, tend to undermine the technical condition of the list, thus forcing lower prices and creating a vicious circle of liquidation.

If short selling were entirely prohibited the market could no longer be called a free and open market, and would not function as smoothly as it does now. Trading would certainly be diminished in volume, and price fluctuations would probably be much more volatile than at present. We must bear in mind, that short selling is but the reverse of buying. Those who sell become potential buyers. All serious students will agree that the short interest serves to cushion the list because on any sharp weakness those short of the market, place their buying orders and thus help support prices. We will leave the question of morals and the philosophy of short selling, and proceed with the investigation of ACF, for the purpose of determining how the Point and Figure signals develop for short side operations.

---

* See *Short Selling* by Owen Taylor, Stock Market Publications.

THE REACTION PATTERN IN ACF

The rise from the first full figure 30, to 89, – see Figures 7.1 and 8.1 – took about two full months. The reaction from 89, back to 30, happened, and was completed in three market days. The subsequent recovery from the low at 30, to 66, was accomplished in short order, and gave a clear bull signal after the base had been formed in the lower 30s. The head and shoulder tops in ACF, created from the full figure at 74, up through the top to 89, and back down to the inverse catapult of 72, creates a perfect head and shoulder formation with a true vertex indicated at A, on the chart, Figure 8.1.

If you can, lay copies of Figures 7.1 and 8.1 together so that the pattern is joined at 85, creating one continuous formation for both pages. Here you have a picture of a full, perfect, and ideal, bull and bear cycle. Every phase of a complete cycle is shown, accumulation at the left of Figure 7.1, the mark up, and consolidation between 30, and 35, another mark up to 42, followed by another period of consolidation and the violent push up, from 40, to 80, where distribution began to take place. After a good portion of the insiders' stocks had been distributed in this area another mark up was staged to 89, where selling on balance was completed. From the vertex at A, in three days' time, the sell-out created a complete bear cycle which terminated at 30, near the right-hand edge of Figure 8.1. These two figures together represent the actual movement of a stock during the last bull move and the drastic shake-out of July. Please study it carefully. We could not have conceived a better example to give you for study.

SIGNAL FOR THE SHORT SIDE

Let us now examine the pattern for the purpose of studying and determining points at which short positions could safely have been adopted. This stock advanced from 13, to 80, in short order, and the question arises how far back should it go. In theory, we know how far down a stock can go. No stock can go below zero. Therefore the fullest possible extent of any bear move is from the high or current level to a point where it will be driven off the board. There is a theory in Wall Street, that we never know how high a stock may go. Some stocks have moved from below one dollar a share, to sell at over three hundred dollars per share. Many instances of this type have been recorded in the past. A few have risen from less than a dollar to more than five hundred dollars per share. Here then on the long side lies the romance of fortunes to be made in Wall Street. In the July 1933 bull market, the wet stocks led the advance on the last up swing.

Tremendous paper profits were created in a short time. On the 17th, or 18th, of the month a few of the wet issues on the Curb Exchange, developed extreme irregularity and trading was temporarily suspended in some of them. This was the signal. Like a mad fever it spread to the wet stocks on the big board and then to the entire market. As the market collapsed on the 19th for the most drastic reaction on a percentage basis witnessed since the big break in 1929, paper profits, as well as original capital, were wiped out in short order. The break was of terrific proportions. Students who followed the implications of the Point and Figure Method were out of the market, of course.

WATCH FOR SIGNS OF ABSORPTION

When the list reaches a point of absorption, we must be on the lookout for signals, so that we may liquidate our upside long positions and catch important indications of signals for short positions. Short sales are made either for profit or to hedge.* Any student of this method who followed the signals given on the long side and took his profits somewhere in the zone 75, to 89, in accordance with the indications given by this Method, did better than the average trader or investor. He had taken the bulk of this 75 point move with little risk involved at any point on the way up.

If one is willing to take the indications given by this Method and sell short at the important point, he is helping to dampen the action of stocks by selling at the top and becoming a potential purchaser at the bottom. This type of intelligent trading would prevent the excesses of both the bull market 1929 peak, and the bear market 1932 low. The head and shoulders pattern which was formed in the zone 75, to 89, is always an ominous indication, not because this Method prefers any particular type of formation, but because technicians and market operators, as well as casual traders attach a great deal of importance to this type of pattern when it appears on their conventional vertical line charts. We watch its action, therefore taking advantage of our knowledge. The vertex A, being the vertex of an inverted triangle at the top of a move is easily plotted by joining the first 85 square to the 89, and thence to the last 85, on the down side. This inverted triangle with its vertex is always an important signal. Exactly above the right shoulder work at 80, another inverted triangle with a vertex B is created.

---

* A temporary short sale made for the purpose of protecting or hedging against long stock held in a vault, this being consummated with the idea of covering the short position as soon as the market stabilizes. The hedge is more fully described in the book *Short Selling* by Owen Taylor.

By placing together Figures 7.1 and 8.1 we begin to get an important short side implication. After inverted triangle vertexes A, and B, are plotted, the next sell off gives us a complete head and right shoulder formation, head at A, and right shoulder at B. Examine carefully this pattern and consider the work in the trading area 74, to 89, and the line of full figure 85, all of which indicates a diminishing ratio of strength. Pressure behind ACF is gone. Insiders are out. It is now time to establish short positions.

Forecasting the market is not an exact science. Its action is ofttimes harmonious, subject to repetition and strongly susceptible of logical interpretation. It may be easily diagnosed and analyzed by empirical methods. As to the double vertex formation A, and B, they are clear implications of a decided down trend for ACF.

THE INVERSE CATAPULT

At full figure 72, a new formation appears. It is called the inverse catapult. Examine the pattern at the full figure 72, where this phenomenon develops. This pattern is exactly the same as the full catapult on the long side previously described except that it occurs in reverse. A fulcrum in this instance is all of the work comprising the head and shoulders top with the fifth 85 and the run up to 89, representing the inverse center of gravity. If you will reverse your charts and look through them from the clear side of the sheet against a strong light you will recognize this position immediately. You will see and recognize the struggle of the forces of supply and demand, with demand overcoming supply and the implication of lower prices to come. Those who had not taken their profits above the 85, level, should have done so here after the action of the stock has created the inverse catapult and broken below 73. The 12 point break, from 89, down to 77, was, of course, far more than a normal reaction of the upmove from 75, to 89. Our limit to a normal reaction, you will recollect is a correction of from 5, to 7 points for this type of stock and its current technical action. A ten point maximum for a highly volatile stock may on rare occasions be considered a tolerable allowance, but it must be considered an exception rather than a rule to be followed.

Let us assume for the purpose of argument, that the student would allow ACF, plenty of latitude, then he must have had a stop either at 79, which is 10 points down from 89, or at 72, in accordance with the principles above stated.

After the sell off of 12 points, the rally of 6 points in ACF, was less than normal under such conditions, and was another bearish indication. It was a strong signal to close out long positions and to go short on a subsequent rally. At this point notice a so-called "air pocket." This is not what might be considered the dangerous "arched ellipse" mentioned in our first book, which is always an ominous indication. This is created by the work above 75, on both sides of the line in which the run up to 89, is plotted.

After further weakness we begin to look around for logical points on which to plot our bear trend line. It is always well to lay in your lines as they are a strong check up and aid in recognizing the technical position of the stock under consideration. The method of plotting trend lines has been carefully explained to you elsewhere in this volume.

SIGNALS FOR SHORT AND LONG POSITIONS

On the short side it will be well for you to continuously examine your charts, turned upside down against a strong light, and read from the back. If you are familiar with the method on the long side, read short position exactly in the same manner through the translucent paper. Plot your trend, and regard your signals with the same confidence you had before.

Watch carefully for the change in the pitch of your trend and the converging of the upper and lower lines of the trend channel. The line limitations on the upside of the main down trend, are herein indicated as DD, and EE, the line of support on the downside. When the trend lines converge, and the narrowing thereof creates a bottle-neck formation, as the extremes of lines FF, are approached, it is a signal that stabilization is nearing, the bottom is near at hand, and that a new fulcrum may be formed which would give a signal to cover your short positions and go long of the stock.

Full figure 30, proved to be the bottom on July 21st. It also proved to be the base of a new fulcrum. A new catapult was formed at 35. Here then, full figure 35, was the place to cover all shorts at any cost, and go long of the stock once more. It is the first opportunity on the long side which permitted students to profit from a quick move of 37 points to 72.

Now turn to Figure 8.2 which records the action of DuPont from approximately mid-June 1933 until mid-August. It includes the major break of July 19th. This actual example of stock market action is a typical representation of distribution type 1, described in Chapter 2. Notice how clear-cut are the ascending steps together with the uptrend channel lines converging in the circle at the intersection of lines AA, BB, and CC. Here is another clear example that the student of this Method need never follow fundamental news, or other statistics. It emphasizes the fact the market by its technical action reveals that the averages

Fig 8.2 DuPont: one point chart mid-June to mid-August 1933

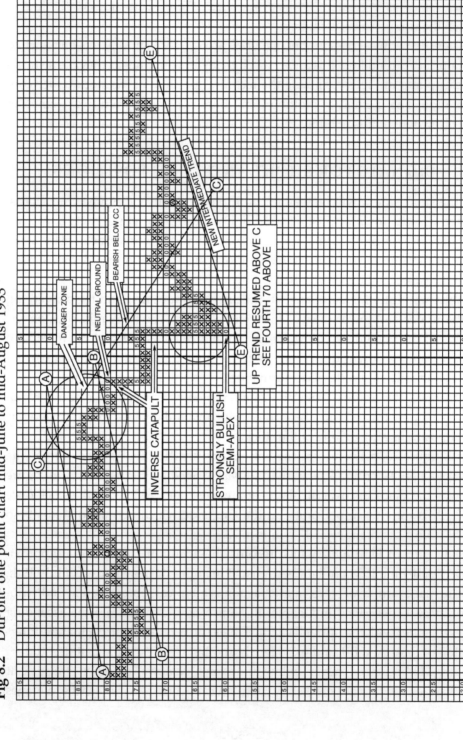

and individual stocks anticipate everything that may occur at a future time. The principle of judging future market action from its present technical condition is the soundest one upon which to base your stock market commitments.

ANALYZING A STOCK FOR TECHNICAL POSITION

Let us break up the action of DuPont into its component parts for the purpose of studying its technical position at any point along the pattern as it develops on Figure 8.2. Note now the trend lines we have plotted, AA, and BB. This represents the bull market uptrend channel which culminated in mid-July. BB, was the main or intermediate trend line on which the pattern of the movement of the stock must stay in order that it remains in its bullish position. A careful examination of the pattern as it backs and fills in the trend channel between AA and BB, will show clearly the ascending stair formation above referred to. The line AA, represents the upper limit of the rally from which the pattern begins to recede as it rallies a second time to 84, before making the high at 85, within the circle shown on the chart. Here is a clearer indication of distribution by insiders on the advance together with signs of diminishing strength as the move progresses.

SIGNS OF CULMINATION

As the trend lines AA, and BB, are projected you will note that they tend to converge. As the work progresses it is leaning more and more toward line B, with the rallies failing to carry to line A, definitely indicating progressing weakness. This is our strong warning signal. Get out of long positions. When the reaction from the triple top 85, intersects our lower trend line BB, at 81, we have a final definite signal that the end is here.

The area within the circle at the intersection of trend lines AA, BB, and CC, is the danger point for long positions and the beginning of opportunities for short side profits. Some support is indicated at full figure 79, when the stock rallies three times from that level after the sell out from the triple top. Now is the chance to establish short positions during the rally which failed after the last triple support at 79. Go short here or at 78, on stop with a stop-loss protection stop above the rally point at 82. This three point stop-loss order is a practical policy to follow. While stops are dangerous to use at times, yet here was a case where a three point margin proved ample and a good insurance against loss.

At 78, an inverse semi-catapult develops where short positions should have been adopted, on stop with profit protecting stop placed at 82. Note here that the true and full inverse catapult appeared at full figure 72. Even from that low point in the reaction, a good profit was easily to be had for the stock sold off to 60 flat before it rallied.

Our Chart Figure 8.2 is so clearly marked for our readers that there seems little need to go into a detailed discussion of the formation. Note that the trend line CC, could have been plotted and projected soon after the first rally failed. Connect the first square above the last 85, with the first square above the 81, and project this line forward. All the work appearing below the line CC, could be considered bearish and the first intersection on the upside is to be a bullish sign of developing strength. Also note another important principle in connection with analyzing your Point and Figure patterns. On previous work in DuPont, zones of congestion and support were built up between full figures 55, and 65. We must again expect some support at these points when the stock reaches there. Note that the sharp sell-off terminated at 60, and that the next reaction stopped at 63, the third at 62, the fourth at 63, then the formation tapered out to a triangle at 64, and 65. Note carefully these rallies and declines from the bottom low at 60. This type of formation shows good support on the decline and is a very bullish signal.

9

THE THREE POINT CHART

■ How to prepare the three point chart
■ Averages a confirmation
■ Watch for the balance of forces
■ The importance of seasonal trend
■ Three point analysis

Our discussions in the preceding eight chapters together with the explanations given in Volume 1, clearly show the scientific basis upon which the Point and Figure Method rests, its theory, and the many principles upon which its signals depend. Through copious illustrations, we have applied these principles to actual chart patterns created by stock movements shown on one point charts.

You will recollect that the Method teaches us to ignore fractions. On our one point charts we regard only a change of one or more points in either direction. This particular principle reduces the confusion, which causes many students of other methods to err in their judgment of technical position and future probable action. However, the one point charts record all of the relevant moves which appear on the tape and which have a bearing on the action of a stock or the averages, whereas our three point charts are a condensation of one point transactions. We are able through the use of the principles of the three point charts to get a more comprehensive picture of (1) more volatile issues, and (2) the broader or intermediate swings of the market.

HOW TO PREPARE THE THREE POINT CHART

Just as a one point chart disregards the irrelevant fractional moves, so does the three point chart disregard the intermediate one and two point moves.

On our three point charts we disregard all moves of less than three full points in the direction opposite to which the last trend was established. After a run up to any particular level, a stock may go down 2⅞ points without registering a down move on these charts. Then, if it recovers 2⅞ points to the previous high, no change would be indicated. However, should it rally beyond the previous high point, touching on the rally a full figure above the last full figure which has been previously recorded on our charts, it would then be added to the column of previously recorded transactions. Thus you will see that our three point condensation charts disregard moves of 2⅞ points. From this explanation you should be able to recognize the valuable aid that three point charts afford in showing you important areas of accumulation and distribution. The principle here involved also eliminates false signals created by shake-outs due to artificial manipulation.

Note here, that while we disregard the decline of 2⅞ points in the opposite direction of the movement we are plotting, we record a recovery which would carry the original move a point or more further than previous; thus it will be clear to you that although we say we disregard a move of less than 3 full points, it is not strictly true when the move comes in the same direction as the previous move which we have been plotting. When our chart indications are moving upward, 2⅝ points reaction would be disregarded. Also when we are recording a down move, a rally of 2⅝ points is ignored. The data from which you compile your three point graphs is obtained from the movement of stocks as indicated on your one point charts. It is not safe or logical to compile your three point charts from any other source.

Turn now to Figure 9.1. It is a compilation of the famous Dow Jones Industrial Averages, followed by investors and traders all over the world, probably the most popular and best known index of the market. Study carefully this chart. It shows all the relevant three point swings of this important index for the years 1932 and 1933 to date.

Our chart of the Dow Jones Industrial Averages records the Spring advance of 1932. The base was made in December 1931, with the beginning of the rise starting in January. Note that no Spring rally developed in the year 1933. The Spring rise of that year was evidently dampened by the attempt of the insiders to liquidate their holdings in anticipation of the bank runs that were to come in February. After the Spring rally in 1932, an air pocket occurred at just about the 80, zone. A trend line plotted would have intercepted the work at the last 80, or 79, and given indications of the final down, swing of the great bear market.

AVERAGES A CONFIRMATION

Here was a confirmation from the averages, of an impending bear move which should have been a check on the bear movements which were indicated in every individual stock. You could have gone short at the 79, level of the Dow Jones Industrial Averages with confidence. A new bear market was on. The shake-out which followed represented the greatest percentage decline that was witnessed since the big break of 1929. Notice that on the way down a slight rally of 5 points in the index started from the full figure 60. This was not a normal 50 percent recovery, nor anywhere near it. One could have stayed short of the market, with a confident feeling that lower prices were to come.

Note on the chart the congestion area built up during the month of June, and for the first part of July. Here then is a mirror of the market. The indication given by the leading stocks through the implications of the Dow Jones Averages on three point charts clearly showed that stocks were under accumulation. We must follow these implications, cover our short positions and go long without hesitation. We see that the base at 45, is broader and shows more work than at any other point on the chart. This is another bullish indication.

Fig 9.1   Dow Jones Industrial Average: three point chart

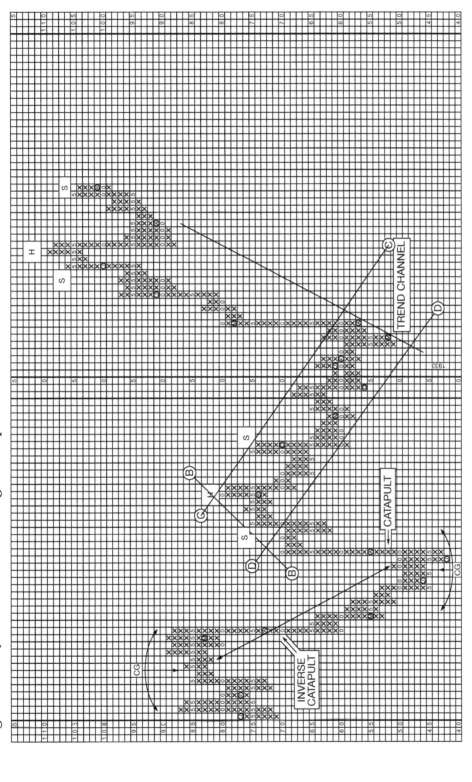

WATCH FOR THE BALANCE OF FORCES

The forces of supply and demand are always operating in the market. Note on our three point charts the inverted full fulcrum as indicated by the first CG. The center arrow indicates the point at which the forces of supply and demand balance. A similar formation occurs at the bottom. Notice the arc CG, at that level. These arcs indicate the conventional three point fulcrums.

Note that the technical action during the accumulation period between 42, and 51, completed a congestion area and formed a three point fulcrum. Here at 52, the market was again on a catapult formation. Thereafter occurred a perpendicular advance in the nature of 23 points without a 3 point correction. The check which our three point charts of the averages gives us on the trend of the market is here particularly emphasized. Let us now follow our pattern from figure 42, to the top, full figure 80. No reaction of sufficient proportions took place which could have been considered a full correction of the previous advance.

THE IMPORTANCE OF SEASONAL TREND

The top of the first bull swing was made in September, 1932. Generally, September of each year is a crucial point for the stock market. As a rule, business is on the upgrade in the Fall of the year, and the market has in most cases, been advanced in anticipation of that business improvement. The top of the first recovery from the bear market low in 1932 came around Labor Day. Our one point chart gave good indications of distribution at that level. Observe now the top of the advance in 1933, and note also that the peak was made in mid-July, in this case just six weeks before Labor Day. A similar parallel exists in 1929, when September marked the high point of the big bull market. Our one point chart of the market averages plotted in 1929, clearly indicated the end of the bull market at that time.

THREE POINT ANALYSIS

Study carefully the trend lines and the formation of the top of the move indicated by the perfect vertex of the inverted triangle on bottom and perfect triangle at the top. We have marked the head H, and the shoulders S. It is by joining up the top of the move H, with the tops of the shoulders S that we create the triangular top known as the perfect vertex top. After you have studied the formation at the top of the 1932 Fall advance, notice how the sell-off from September, 1932 to the low in February, 1933, confined itself within the limits of the down trend channel between the lines CC, and DD. A study of the action of the down trend in the trend channel will show clearly strong support beginning to come into the list around the 60 level. Observe the rally which came into the list from 58, and carried to 68. Notice at this point that the force of the down move began to lessen as the work moved over toward the upper end of the trend channel. It is reasonable to suppose that the shake-out which occurred toward the end of February and just before the 1st of March, was a drastic shake-out from the 60 line accumulation area, effected for the purpose of shaking weak holders out of their long positions. When the upper trend line is intersected by the full figures 63, and 62, it is an indication checking the bullish implications that were given by our one point charts.

10

COORDINATING THE ONE POINT WITH THE THREE POINT CHARTS

■ Three point chart a check on the one point chart
■ Illustrations of coordination
■ Inside accumulation
■ Manipulator's campaign
■ The manipulator's methods
■ The false start
■ Pool switches to short side
■ A new angle on narrow fluctuations

There should by now be no doubt in your mind that three point charts should be kept and maintained in order to aid you in judging the action of the market and individual stocks. Their value as intermediate trend guides cannot be too strongly stressed. One glance at a number of three point charts is all you need, to recognize the tremendous value of such an aid to your market operations.

THREE POINT CHART A CHECK ON THE ONE POINT CHART

There is a distinct advantage in having both one and three point charts of the stocks you are watching, as well as of the principal market averages. The one and three point charts used in coordination, form the keynote and the principal basis upon which the Point and Figure Method rests. While it may be said that the three point charts are not an absolute necessity, let us urge you to make and keep them. They are vital and important checks on your one point charts and are the principal means through which you may get the action of the more volatile issues. As intermediate trend indicators they cannot be surpassed.

ILLUSTRATIONS OF COORDINATION

For the purpose of convincing yourself of the value of keeping three point charts* in addition to your one point charts, compare Figure 10.1 with Figure 4.1. Figure 10.1 represents a three point chart of American Sugar Refining, and covers a greater period of time than that shown on Figure 4.1. On Figure 10.2 we show a three point chart of ACF Industries. Compare this with the one point charts Figures 7.1 and 8.1. As a further illustration of the value of coordinating the one and three point charts, we add one point and three point charts of Commercial Solvents, Figures 10.3 and 10.4. Examine carefully on Figure 10.4 the three vertical columns showing fluctuation from 4, to 13, in this stock. From the first full figure 10, registered in March, the bear market low was indicated in a straight down run without a full three point rally, and was made during the month of May. The July–September 1932, bull market carried CV, to a high of 13, the October reaction to a low of 9, after which it rallied to 12, and then declined, making a double bottom at 9, in February.

---

* Three point charts cover all three point moves from January 2, 1932 to September 11, 1933. The one point charts cover all one point moves from January 3, 1933 to August 21, 1933.

Fig 10.1   American Sugar Refining: three point chart

Fig 10.2   ACF Industries: three point chart

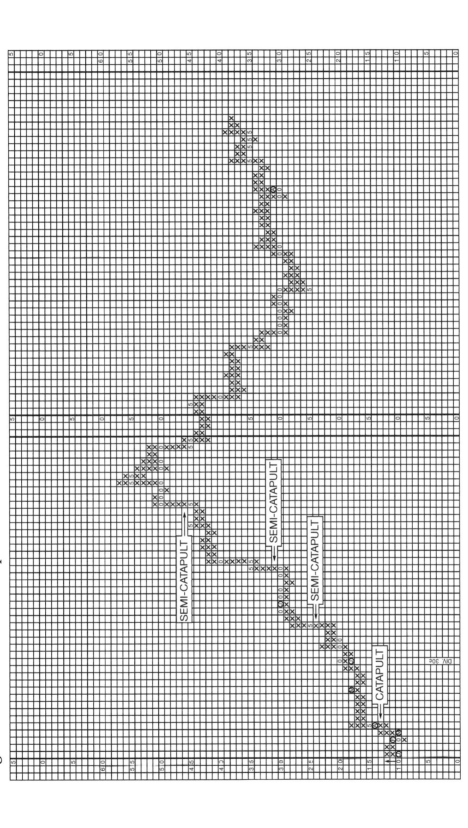

INSIDE ACCUMULATION

Here then is an example of slow, skillful, and patient inside accumulation. The indications show that sponsors had taken most of the floating supply from the market during the 1932, campaign of accumulation. In April 1933, the stock had completed its first real catapult position and our one point chart showed us that the sponsors of this issue had to take additional stock between 16, and 18, during April and part of May. Notice further signs on your point chart of a strenuous mark-up beginning with full figure 24, and again at full figure 31. These are semi-catapult points with full figure 46, duplicating the semi-catapult opportunity.

On a quick run-up from the semi-catapult at 46, the stock met heavy resistance between 49, and 57, where there are definite signs that the insiders had begun to unload their 1932, accumulations. See how clearly these facts are disclosed on our three point illustration. Note also the area of accumulation between 25, and 35, shown both on the one point, as well as on the three point chart. After you have traced and studied these moves, let us consider how the insider planned and executed a campaign of accumulating stock, around the average of 10, and distributing them at an average of 52. This is clearly disclosed for you through a coordination of the one and three point charts of Commercial Solvents, Figures 10.3 and 10.4.

MANIPULATOR'S CAMPAIGN

You have seen a typical inside campaign in ACF. It was also easy for you to recognize the manifestations of the pool manager's operations through the patterns which his activities reveal on your one and three point charts.

Insiders – pool and large scale operators – begin their operations in one of the following ways which may be used to accumulate their original positions for the campaign:

1. *They may begin by an open market operation, which is an independent position adopted either long or short, either with or without associates.*

This type of freelance operation does not have the cooperation of corporation officers, bankers, or any of the major interests holding large blocks of stock.

2. *The campaign may be conducted for the benefit of one of the major interests.*

For instance, a large stockholder desires to distribute some of his long stock without causing a break in the price, which is likely to happen if a large block of

Fig 10.3   Commercial Solvents: three point chart

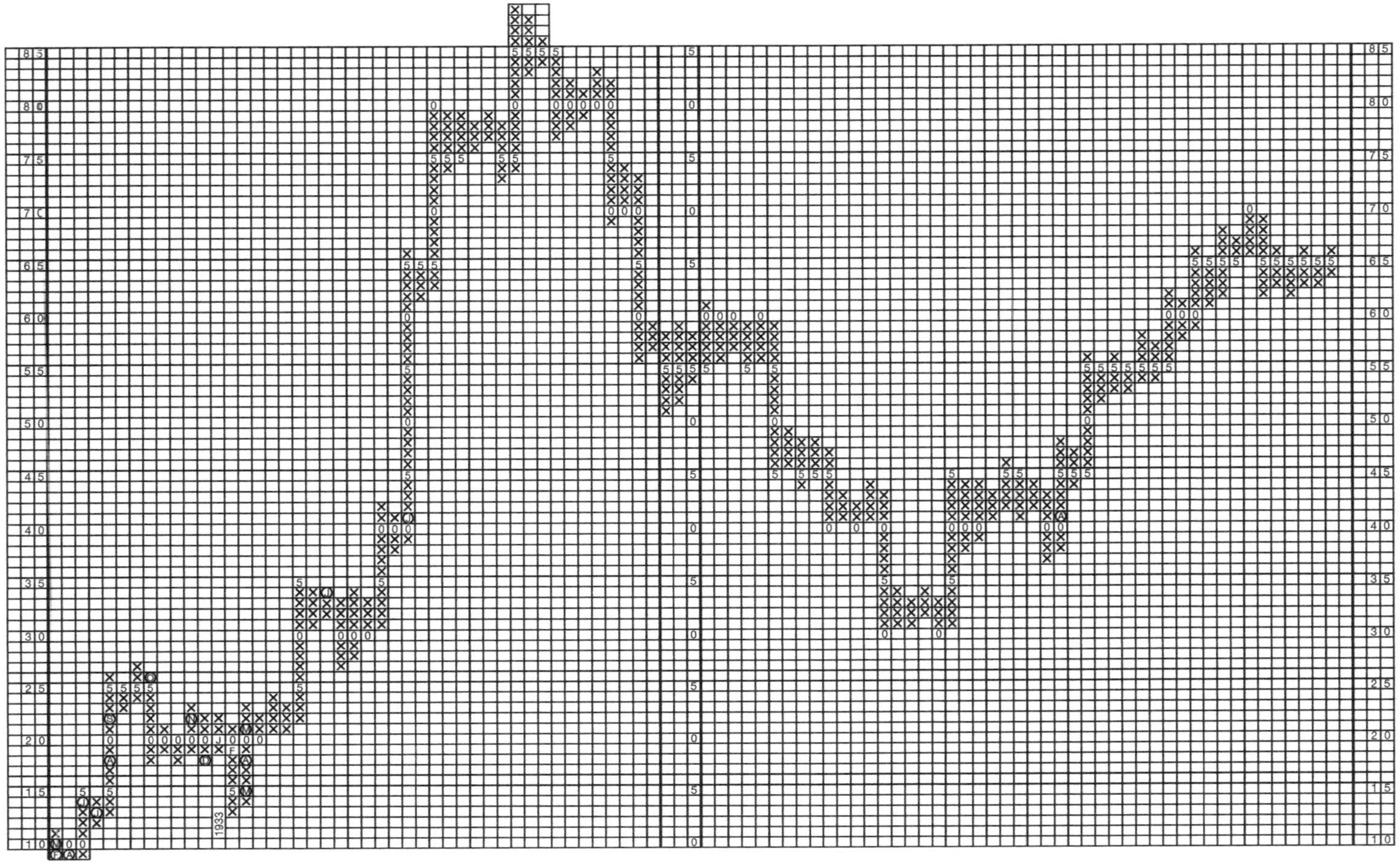

Fig 10.4   Commercial Solvents: three point chart

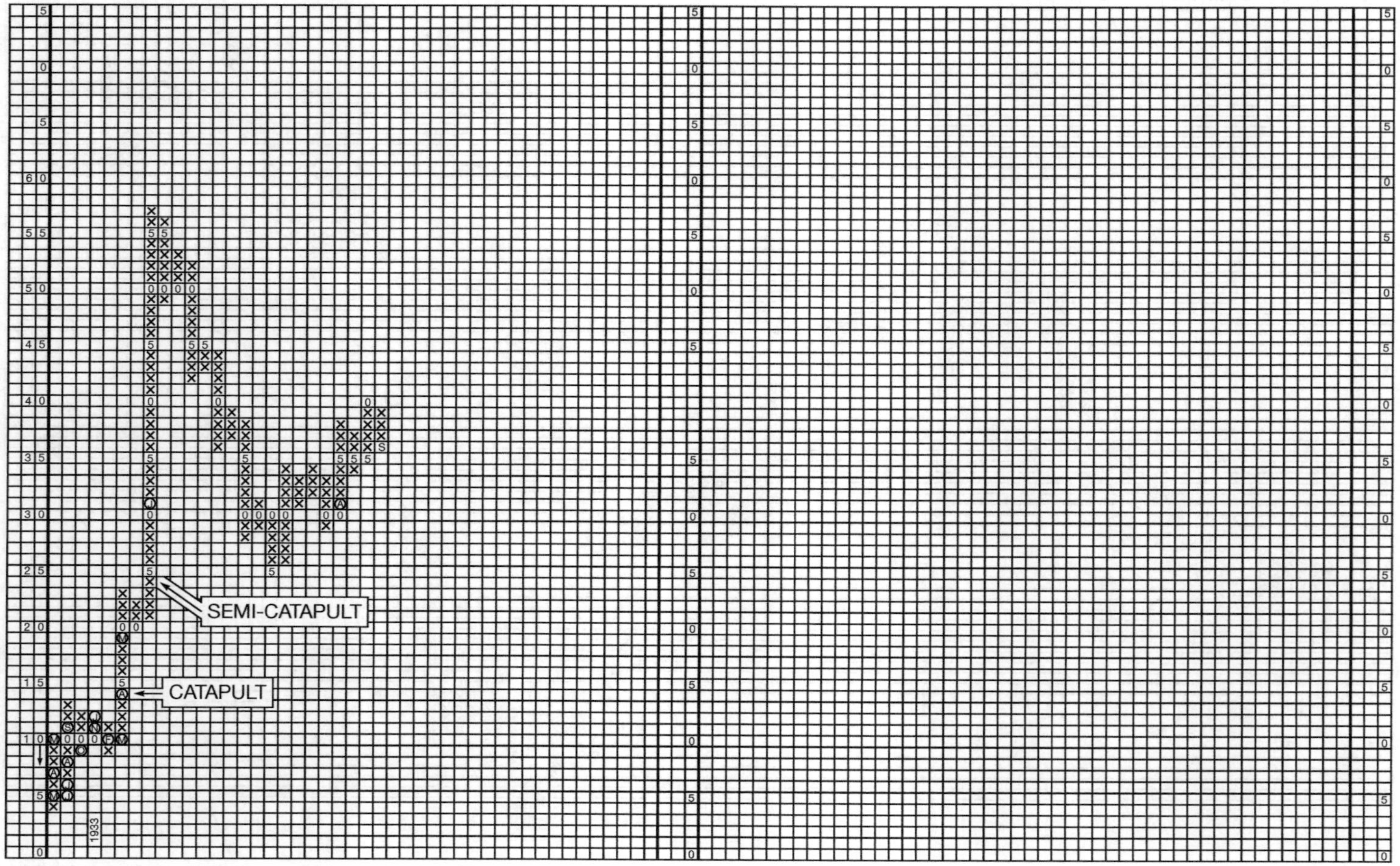

stock is thrown into the floating supply. It may also be for the purpose of acquiring a large block of stock, for a major capitalist, or the campaign may be with the view of gaining control of the corporation.

3. *A campaign may be planned solely for the purpose of speculative profits on the part of one, or a group of market operators.*

In this case the operator or pool manager may be in possession of some news which is to be revealed in the future, such as an increase in the dividend rate, an announcement regarding increased sales, the discovery of new deposits in a mining corporation, or some similar news item, not as yet known to the general public, and which, more than likely will cause a demand for the stock of the corporation.

The release of such a news item gives the pool manager a splendid opportunity to unload his holdings without regard to the number of points he may have pushed the stock up. On the other hand, if this news, which is to go out later, is to be of a bearish character, such as the reduction or passing of dividends, banking troubles, poor earnings or some other similar adverse factor, the campaign would be on the short side of the market. In such case, the extended short position established in the stock at high prices, would be used to support or stabilize it after the bad news was released, and for the purpose of again aiding a campaign on the long side after short positions were covered and re-accumulation had taken place.

4. *Occasionally an operator may obtain a call on a block of stock around current market prices, or a little higher, with further calls to be operative when the market had advanced a number of points higher.*

These contracts sometimes call for a specific number of shares, perhaps five points up, until a definite price is reached when the final and largest block of stock is released to the operator upon his call.

THE MANIPULATOR'S METHODS

There are many variations of the method by which an operator may accumulate, mark up and distribute his stock. Stocks must create their patterns on our Point and Figure Chart. None can escape this time tried Method.

THE FALSE START

In recent years, since a greater number of traders and investors are interesting themselves in scientific methods for anticipating stocks by movements, the careful operators, all of whom recognize this fact, must draw a smoke screen around their operations. Therefore, whether the campaign be on the up side or the down side, always be on the alert for a false start. Watch for periods of accumulation followed by a sharp shake-out. Get aboard on the shake-out if you are sure of the signal. Similarly, for a down side campaign if a period of distribution has formed a congestion area on your chart and a push-through falls dead after the stock has moved out onto the catapult or onto a semi-catapult, the failure of the push-up may be the indication of the false move to mislead you.

These false moves, in addition to misleading those who are watching them, tend to dislodge unwelcome company and to invite contrary positions, which in the final analysis aid the operations of the pool.

An operator conducting a bull campaign must be careful not to attract a public following, until the move has made its culmination. Therefore he aims to conceal carefully his operations, so that public interest, if any, may only build up slowly and as the move gains momentum. Tape action is created to invite public participation near the top of the move. Here near the top, the pool manager will cause his good news to be released, which will help him materially to create wide fluctuations at or near the top of his advance. This is what he needs. Good sharp run-ups with a big public following, and he will thereupon have completed his selling on balance.

POOL SWITCHES TO SHORT SIDE

After he has completely unloaded his long stock, he then prepares operations for the short side. This short interest increases the floating supply and gets into the hands of weak holders, and subsequently causes a correction of the previous upmove. This short interest which the manager has outstanding, will be used lower down, after the reaction has taken place, to support the stock, and thus create more profits for the pool. The campaign above outlined may have taken many months to complete, and may have involved the purchase and sale of tens of thousands of shares, in order to accomplish its objective.

A NEW ANGLE ON NARROW FLUCTUATIONS

We have written elsewhere in the book of the necessity of maintaining a professional attitude in your approach to stock speculation. Now, after we have explained to you a professional operation on the long side, you should begin to have a new outlook on the question of fluctuations, and the difficulty of catching the day-to-day short swings in order to consistently profit from them. The influence of group buying and selling, whether it be that of the manipulator for profit, or of the stock's sponsor trying to maintain a market for the stock, is the cause of the mysterious backing and filling, the sudden push-up, and the quick markdown in the shorter trading ranges. If you will always keep in mind the fact that every stock must have sponsorship and that many harbor group operations, you will obtain a better understanding and a clearer viewpoint from which to judge the fluctuations. This one principle should be worth hundreds of times the cost of this book to you. We cannot emphasize it too strongly. Study it. Reason it out in your mind. Realize the logic which lies behind this analysis of the cause of the narrow fluctuations, and profit thereby.

11

THE COUNT – GAUGING THE EXTENT OF FUTURE MOVES

- The theory underlying the count
- The count not an exact science
- Horizontal formation may disclose the extent of the move
- The principle of "the count"
- The one point count
- The forecast
- Anticipating the next move
- Additional charts for study
- The count by three points
- A new point for a forecast
- Accuracy of the count
- A three point test for future market action
- Cumulative implications more reliable

We concede, that though this Method is time tested and has proven of inestimable value to those who understand and follow it, it may be subject to further scientific research, since in the opinion of the authors, its scientific basis must be a foundation for other and important valuable principles which such research will uncover.

A scientific and dependable mechanical means of forecasting the future movements of the market has been the dream of many students and technicians, who have spent thousands of hours in search of their goal. Could we but evolve a method which would forecast both the direction and extent of the next probable move with accuracy, and could we rely with confidence on its implications, it would be considered the Aladdin's Lamp of modern finance.

As a result of such experiment, Mr. Thomas L. Sexsmith, with whom we were associated from 1918, to 1921, worked on the principle now known as "the count." Mr. Sexsmith, now deceased, was a writer on economics and finance, whose books and articles have become recognized as authoritative throughout the financial world.

While "the count" may be considered as a marvelous aid in many instances, and always valuable in connection with judging probable future moves, it cannot be absolutely relied upon in all cases. Its implications at times are marvelous. In some issues it will register time and time again, and can be depended upon for many moves in succession. However, for some unknown reason, it will occasionally mislead, if we rely too much upon its implications. We will do our best in this chapter to explain in full detail the theory and practice of this valuable aid to your judgment. We leave it to you to test it and decide for yourself whether or not you elect to depend upon its implications. Your authors use it and endorse it as one of the many technical aids upon which we rely for our conclusions.

THE THEORY UNDERLYING THE COUNT

We have stated that the basis upon which the Point and Figure Method rests, is strictly scientific. In Volume 1, we have illustrated how the principle of the fulcrum and of the catapult can be applied to stock price movements.

The principle of "the count" seems to have an excellent foundation in the science of ballistics. In a definition of ballistics, the *Encyclopedia Britannica* states:

> Exterior ballistics is that part of the science of ballistics in which the motion of the projectile is considered after it has received its initial impulse. The factors involved are the pressure of the powder or gas in the chamber of the gun from which the projectile secures its initial velocity, resistance of the bore before the projectile leaves

the barrel, the resistance of the air, and the influence of gravity, all must be calculated in order to determine the probable objective of the projectile.

Modern research has reduced the science of ballistics to almost an exact science. Given all the factors, our gunnery mathematicians, can calculate almost exactly, the degree of elevation, as well as other necessary factors in order for a given projectile to reach a certain objective.

THE COUNT NOT AN EXACT SCIENCE

While the scientific basis upon which the count rests seems to check fairly well with the principles of ballistics, it cannot be said that it is nearly as reliable as the science of ballistics. Just as the gunnery mathematician needs all of the factors in order to determine the objective of the projectile, so, in "the count," we need an accurate registration of all of the full figure changes of the stock under consideration. This is true whether we judge the future probable move by our one point implications or by our three point implications.

We cannot rely on newspaper quotations from which to obtain the data necessary for these calculations. It must come from the tape itself, and must show every full figure change in the congestion area. When we have all of these full figure changes from a dependable source and plot them on our one point charts, we may then proceed to determine the probable extent of the next move, whether it be in an upward or downward, direction.

HORIZONTAL FORMATION MAY DISCLOSE
THE EXTENT OF THE MOVE

"The count" is an attempt to estimate the probable move based upon the pressure generated in the congestion area. If the stock moves out of the congestion area on the up side, it is reasonable to presume that the implication of "the count" will give us the approximate point at which to expect the next congestion area, or the culmination of the move. Should the stock break out of the congestion area on the down side, we may then expect a trading range of support, at the level approximately the number of indicated squares below.

THE PRINCIPLE OF "THE COUNT"

The scientific basis of this principle depends upon the number of full figure squares which measure the extent of the congestion area and give us the count either up or down from that particular point. For example, a congestion built up around a particular price level in which the stock rallies and declines five times across that area, would indicate a probable future move five points up or down from that particular price level. *Take particular note here, that intervening blank squares are included in "the count" and are to be considered as though they were actually filled in.*

THE ONE POINT COUNT

For a clear example of the way "the count" works as a forecaster of the probable next move, turn to Figure 11.1 which represents an actual move in Baltimore & Ohio from January to August, 1933. Study carefully the following principle upon which "the count" is based.

> The number of times a figure is repeated at any horizontal point where a base or a resistance level is built up, is an indication of the probable extent of the advance or decline and is the number of points equivalent to:-
> 　　A – The number of times it registered at the average point of support or
> 　　B – The number of times it registered at the average point of resistance.

In the chart of Baltimore & Ohio, Figure 11.1, count the number of full figure 10 squares which are filled, including the blank. Count the number of 11 squares filled and the number of 13 squares filled. Notice here in this period of accumulation that full figure 10 was repeated nine times, full figure 11 was repeated nine times, and full figure 12 was repeated eleven times. This is a total of 29, an average of 10, for the three figures.

THE FORECAST

The implication was that Baltimore & Ohio would move up or down 10 points from the full figure 11, the average price of the accumulation range between 10, and 12. By this we mean if Baltimore & Ohio broke out of the congestion area on the down side, it would go down to one, while if it broke out on the up side, it meant that it would go up at least 10, points from full figure 11, or to 21. Notice now on the Baltimore & Ohio advance that the next congestion area was built up between 21, and 23, and the first objective 10, points up from full figure 11, was reached during the months of May and June. A perfect record for "the count."

No matter where you bought Baltimore & Ohio, after it left the first congestion area on the up side, you should have stayed long of this stock until it registered 21.

Fig 11.1   Baltimore & Ohio: one point chart

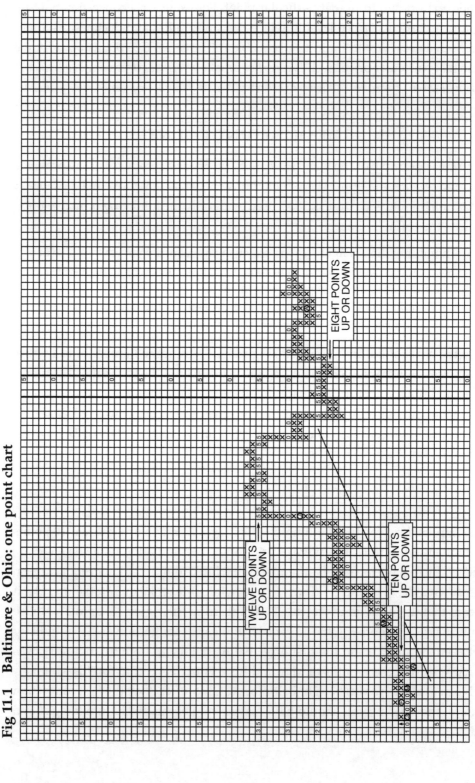

ANTICIPATING THE NEXT MOVE

Now count the full figures registered at 21, and those at 22. This is the next congestion area. There are nine 21s, and ten 22s, indicating that the next move would be either 10, points up or 10, points down from 22. The stock broke out on the up side and rallied quickly to 35, scoring another mark for "the count" system. According to this method you would have held your long position at least until it registered 32, or 33, and when the stock made 35, you would have sold out. There was little further to gain by holding your position beyond this point, because the top registered four times was 37.

Now on the upper congestion area, count the full figures 34, and 35. The average of these two is 12, and the indications were that the stock should rally 12 points from 34, or 35, or decline 12 points, therefrom. The move broke out on the down side and the implication of "the count" was that it would go down at least to 22, or 23. Here again is a one hundred per cent record for "the count" system because it did register 21, and there was ample opportunity to cover at 22.

Another congestion area was built up between 23, and 25. Count now the full figures 23, 24, and 25, and you get an average of nine. This means nine points up from 24, or 25. The stock actually made a high of 36, and a fraction during August just beyond the limitations of the chart.

Thus you have seen that "the count" worked perfectly four times in succession on Baltimore & Ohio during the year 1933, to date of publication. However, be careful when you rely on "the count." It does not always work, neither does it give the exact limits of the move. "The count" will guide you as to the approximate extent of the move, and the Point and Figure Method will indicate its direction.

ADDITIONAL CHARTS FOR STUDY

The Charts Figures 11.2, 11.3, and 11.4 show the movement of Delaware & Hudson to further illustrate "the count" system. Notice that the reaction from A, was indicated. We have added these consecutive sheets to give further illustration of the theory and application of "the count." Trace the movements, count the congestion areas and see the great number of swings which were directly forecast by the method.

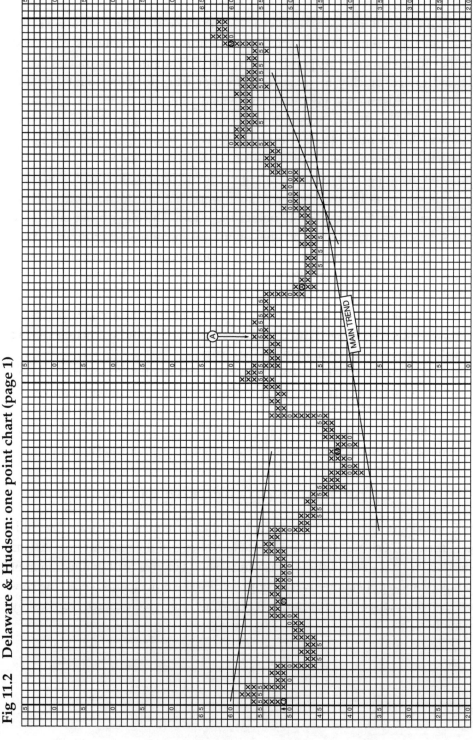

Fig 11.2   Delaware & Hudson: one point chart (page 1)

Fig 11.3   Delaware & Hudson: one point chart (page 2)

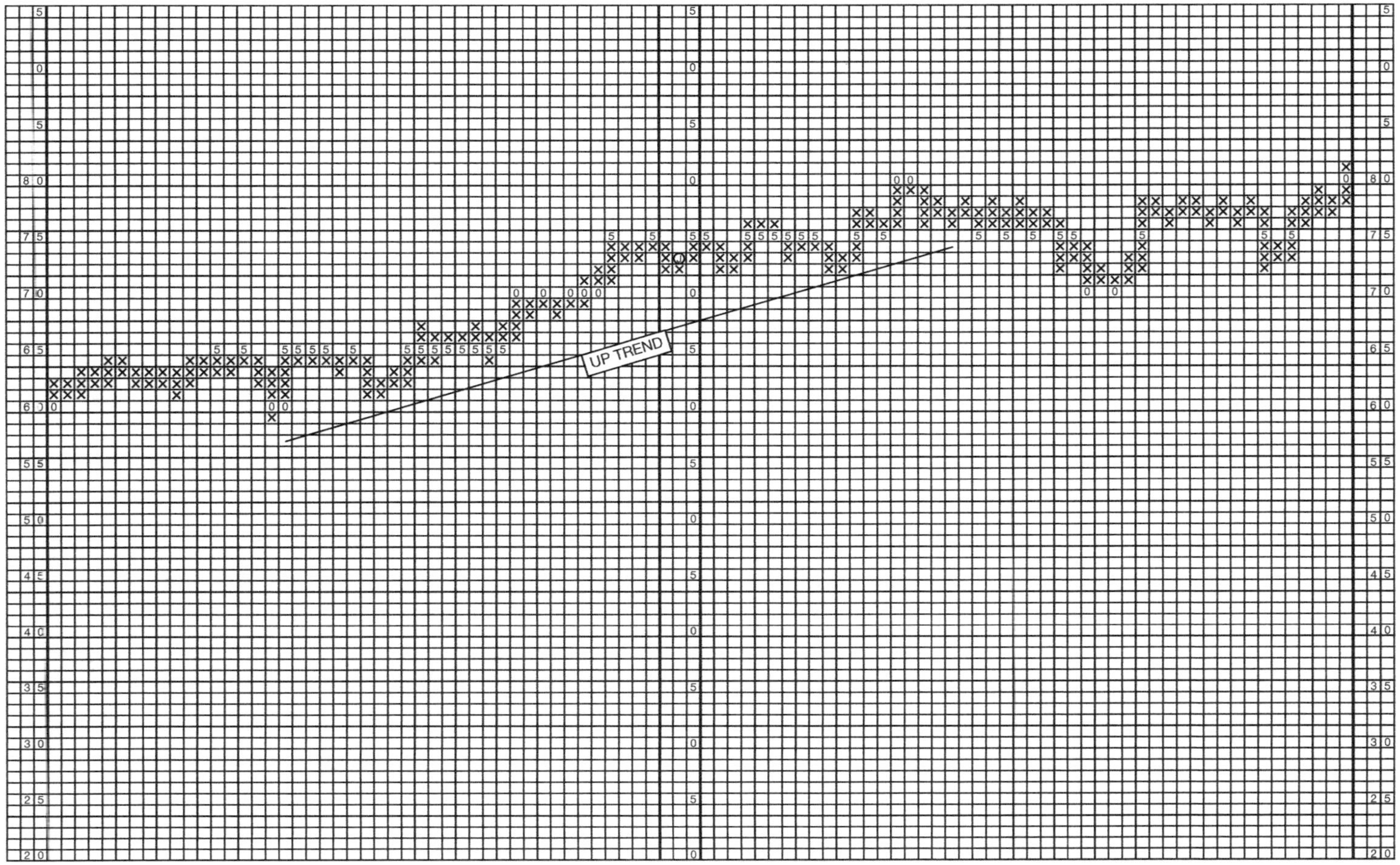

Fig 11.4   Delaware & Hudson: one point chart (page 3)

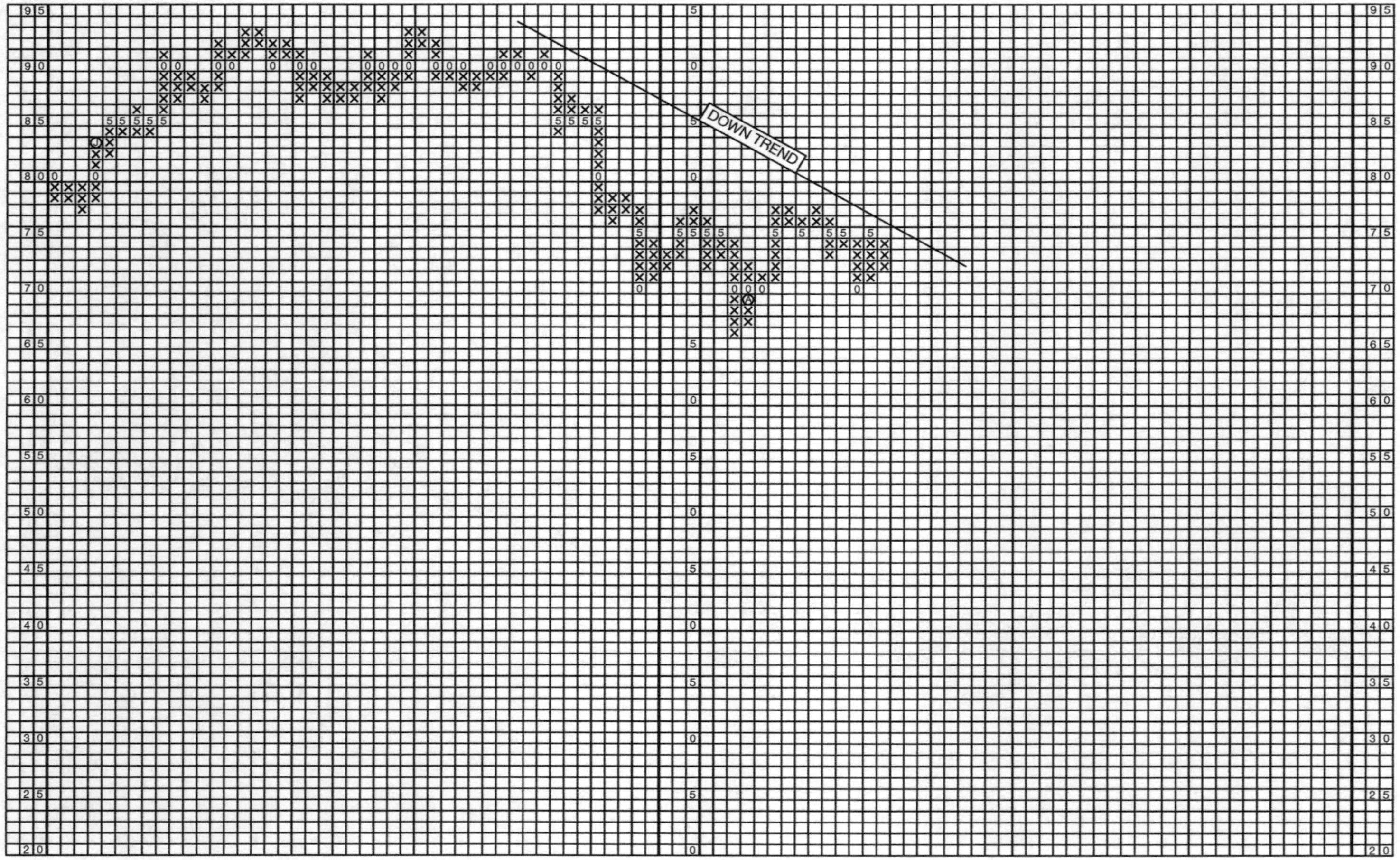

THE COUNT BY THREE POINTS

The general principles outlined for the application of "the count" system on one point patterns, also applies to three point charts. Let us examine our three point charts, for the purpose of illustrating "the count" in connection therewith. In Celanese, Figure 11.5 the first congestion area is indicated between 6, and 9. This move was a solid block of work and always constitutes a very strong signal on the three point charts. Note also that similar congestion areas appear between 30, and 33, and again between 25, and 28. From all of these points major moves could easily have been anticipated and indicate again to you, the value of your three point charts as a check on your one points. The count at the full figure 7, first congestion area on the left of our chart registers seven times. *Since this is a three point chart, we multiply seven by three* and the result is 21, which is the probable extent of the next intermediate move. By adding 21 points to the full figure 7, we get 28, as the probable objective point on the up side. Full figures 8, 9, and 10, also registered 7 squares and all indicate a probable move of 21, points. If 21 points down were counted it would take Celanese off the board. It is reasonable to expect from our chart that Celanese will rally at least 21 points; 21, plus 7, or 28, indicated long in advance as the first objective for the move in Celanese. Note after the run-up, that the first congestion area begins to build up above the full figure 29, indicated on our chart with the symbol B. The forecast made at A, is fulfilled by the congestion area formed at B.

A NEW POINT FOR A FORECAST

The minor congestion point between full figure 33, proved to be only a halting place. The period of consolidation is no indication of a change in trend, but when 34, was reached and a semi-catapult formed, we were justified in remaining bullish and again estimating the possible extent of the next rise. Here again another 21, point move was forecast. It indicated either a reaction to around 10, its previous base or a rise to the lower 50s, which was to be considered remarkable for a stock like Celanese which moved up from 2, the figure which was made in March, 1932. Note the congestion area 38, 39, indicated a probable 9 point move from 38, which was completed at the symbol D, when the stock made 47. Again at 45, we have the implication of another 9, point move to 54.

Fig 11.5 Celanese: three point chart

ACCURACY OF THE COUNT

The first sign of a real halt in the move of Celanese came in the congestion area 55, to 58, indicated with the symbol E. This was the fulfilment of the forecast made by the congestion area B, which hardly seemed possible when made but now had become an actuality. Note now that the next line of defense moves over to the area 50, 55. Here strong support was thrown in along the two lines 51, and 52. If you will count these squares indicated with the symbol F, you will note that they show a reaction or a rally due of 27 points. The count is nine times at 50, nine times at 51, and nine times at 52. The move indicated is 27 points up or down from the average of these three.

The move proved to be on the down side and was halted exactly at 23. This is again an indication of the accuracy of these forecasts. The forecast, at congestion area G, shows a move of 24 points up or down from full figure 27. At the moment of this writing Celanese has again fulfilled the promise; 52 was recently registered before the last reaction.

A THREE POINT TEST FOR FUTURE MARKET ACTION

Examine our chart, Figure 11.6, illustrating the three point moves in Standard Oil of New Jersey. This issue created a good three point base along the 23, line. The count there revealed 10 figures and spaces. This indicated a rise, or a decline of 30, points from that level. It would be quite unlikely for an issue of the type of Standard Oil of New Jersey to go off the board completely; 30 points down from full figure 23 would be an impossibility from a logical point of view. Therefore, in analyzing the move of Standard Oil of New Jersey, it is reasonable to assume from the indications there, that Standard Oil of New Jersey ultimately will go to 53.

At this writing, Standard Oil of New Jersey has not yet reached 53.

Observe, that the count at A, indicates a probable move to 53. Note also, that the count along the support area B, also reveals the objective of the move to be 53, or 54. Here you have a check, a double confirmation, an indication from two separate congestion areas both of which terminate in the zone 53, or 54.

CUMULATIVE IMPLICATIONS MORE RELIABLE

When an accumulation of implications, taken from separate congestion areas, point to the same probable objective level, more confidence can be placed on that forecast than when it is based upon but one congestion area.

Fig 11.6 Standard Oil of New Jersey: three point chart

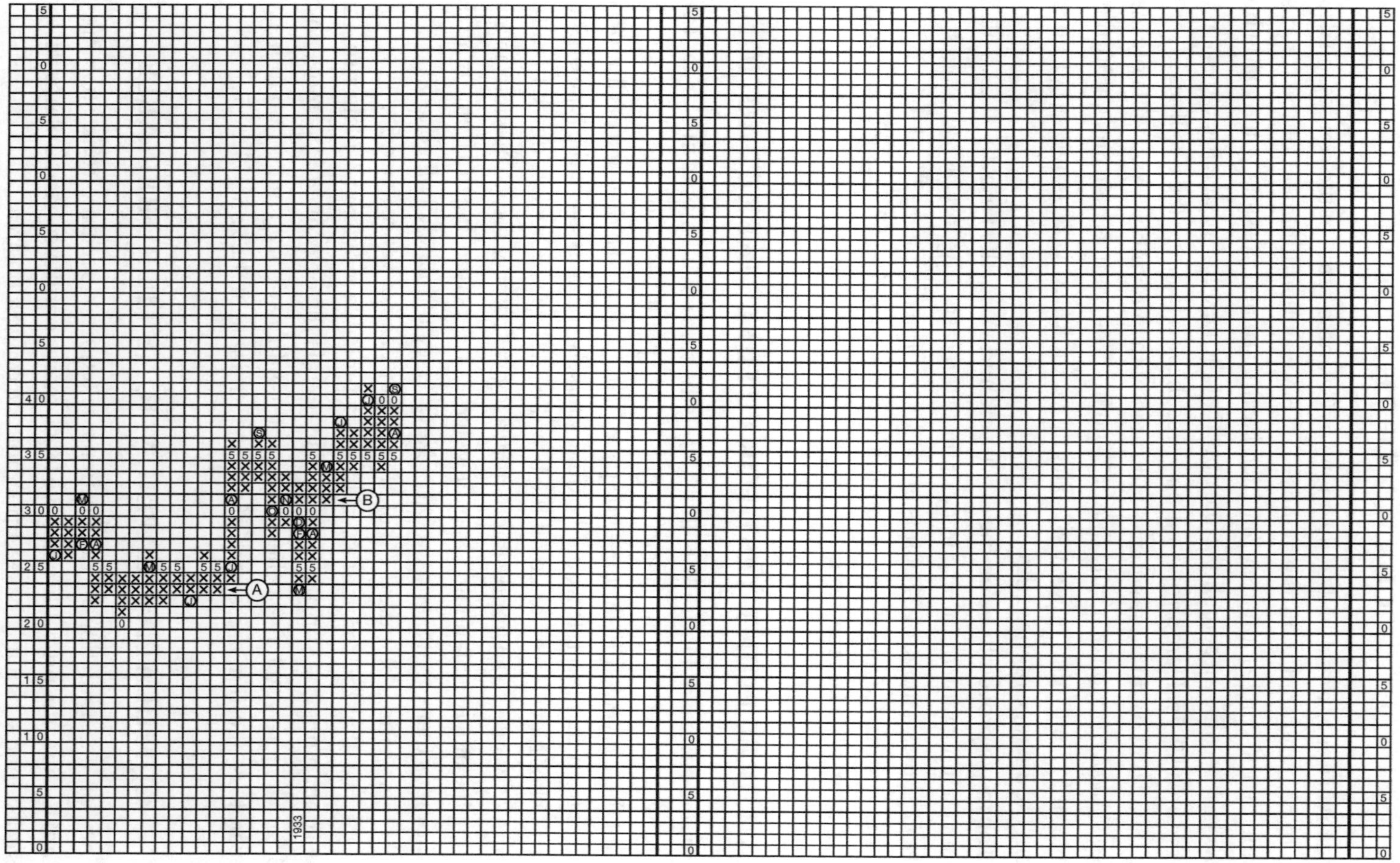

Take nothing for granted in your studies of stock price movements. Be always on the alert for the unexpected. Can the count be relied upon at all times? Our answer to this question is *no*. Will Standard Oil of New Jersey reach 53, because of the implications herein before discussed? Our answer to this question is, *it will*. It should reach 53, on a move of intermediate trend proportions in the future.

If you have been guessing on your market commitments in the past, be logical in the future. Depend upon the Point and Figure Method and its principles to guide you in your future market operations. Base your market activity upon scientific principles. It will enable you, invariably, to *buy when the insiders buy*, and *sell when they sell*.

CONCLUSION

In the preceding chapters we have endeavored to outline for you in detail, some of the more advanced theories of the Point and Figure Method used for the purpose of anticipating stock price movements. Specific and detailed charts, showing the actual movements in various stocks, and a few examples of the movements of the averages, have been carefully drawn. These charts, taken from recent market action, have been used to illustrate some of the principles underlying the Point and Figure Method.

For the purpose of further study of the basic principles, we have added some additional charts.

A clear understanding of the subject matter, keen perception, and the courage of your convictions are all necessary attributes to your judgment. These qualities are the result of constant application and study. Always keep in mind that success is not reached in a single bound. Familiarize yourself thoroughly with all of the basic principles described for you in this book, as well as Volume 1. Prepare and record carefully, and accurately, the data needed to aid you in your work. Study it constantly. Always review past performances, and compare them with the patterns as they develop on your charts. This effort and conscientious study on your part, will soon develop a clearer understanding and a better grasp of stock market technique. The principles of this time tried Method, once mastered, will materially aid your judgment, and be reflected in your stock market commitments. Until you have mastered the principles of this Method, we suggest that you trade on paper, before risking your capital. A proper and solid foundation is absolutely essential in any line of business – more so in the stock market. Remember, one of the keynotes to success is, limit your losses and let your profits run. Be sure you understand the principle of using stop orders, in connection with your commitments. Take this subject matter seriously, and apply to it the consideration and study it merits. You will have no regrets and we feel certain that you will derive pleasure, and profit from your efforts.

We invite you to consult us on any problems that may arise at any time, and which seem confusing to you. Do not hesitate to do so, since our constant aim is to assist you in the mastery of this interesting and valuable aid to stock market technique.

INDEX

Lightning Source UK Ltd.
Milton Keynes UK
UKHW030838010622
403830UK00002B/7

9 781905 641529